Law and Legislation for Social Service Workers

SECOND EDITION

David Mikelberg

emond ▪ Toronto, Canada ▪ 2018

Emond Montgomery Publications Limited
60 Shaftesbury Avenue
Toronto ON M4T 1A3
http://www.emond.ca/highered

Printed in Canada.

We acknowledge the financial support of the Government of Canada.   Canadä

Emond Montgomery Publications has no responsibility for the persistence or accuracy of URLs for external or third-party Internet websites referred to in this publication, and does not guarantee that any content on such websites is, or will remain, accurate or appropriate.

Vice president, publishing: Anthony Rezek
Director, development & production: Kelly Dickson
Developmental editor: Katherine Goodes
Production supervisor: Laura Bast
Production editor: Natalie Berchem
Copy editor: Mike Kelly

Permissions editor: Karen Hunter
Typesetter: Peggy Issenman
Text designer: Tara Agnerian
Proofreader: Dawn Hunter
Indexer: Michael Bunn
Cover image: wavebreakmedia/Shutterstock

Library and Archives Canada Cataloguing in Publication

Mikelberg, David, author
    Law and legislation for social service workers / David Mikelberg. — Second edition.

Includes bibliographical references and index.
ISBN 978-1-77255-260-7 (softcover)

    1. Social workers—Legal status, laws, etc.—Canada —Textbooks.   2. Textbooks.   I. Title.

KE450.S6M55 2017   344.7103'2   C2017-903209-7   KF390.S6M55 2017

Words to know and Index

babies
pages 4, 6–7, 8, 9, 10, 11, 14, 15, 16, 17, 19, 21, 22, 23

back yards
pages 5, 6, 9, 10, 11, 14, 16, 19

ducks

birds
pages 5, 7, 8, 14, 15

chipmunks and squirrels
pages 5, 6, 7, 9, 10, 14, 18, 20, 23

foxes
pages 4, 5, 7, 9, 18

homes (shelter)
pages 6, 10–11, 13, 17, 18, 16, 19, 22, 23

pets
pages 7, 12–13, 18, 19, 22, 23

raccoons
pages 5, 6, 9, 11, 16

rats and mice
pages 5, 7, 12, 17, 18

skunks
pages 5, 6, 9, 11, 17

Other index words
carnivores pages 9, 18–19
coyotes pages 5, 18, 19
endangered animals
 pages 4, 22
food pages 5, 8, 9, 10, 14, 15, 16, 17, 18, 20, 21
helping animals pages 22–23
herbivores page 9
mothers pages 4, 10, 17, 21
omnivores pages 9, 18
opossums pages 6, 9, 11
parks pages 5, 6, 8, 10, 17, 18, 19
people pages 4, 5, 6, 10, 11, 12, 13, 14, 15, 16, 17, 18, 19, 20, 22, 23
predators pages 10, 18, 19

Many homeless animals live in animal shelters. They are fed, walked, and receive help if they need it. People come to these shelters to adopt pets.

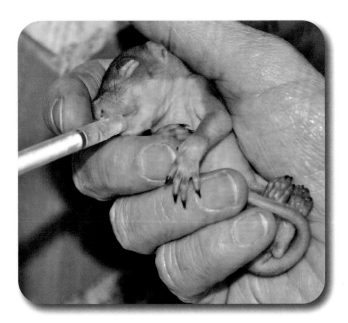

*The squirrel pup on the left and the **owlet**, or baby owl, on the right, are being helped by volunteers at a city wildlife center. Wildlife centers take care of animals that have been injured or have lost their parents. Baby animals that are injured or whose parents are dead cannot survive without help.*

Brief Contents

Detailed Contents

5 Mental Health Law

6 Child Protection Law, Notes, Reports, and Records

7 Family Law and Adoption

8 Education Law

9 Income Assistance

10 Criminal and Civil Law

11   Alternative Dispute Resolution and Restorative Justice

12   Youth Criminal Law

13   Correctional Services for Adults

14   Immigration and Refugee Law

15 Privacy and Access to Information and Accessing Legal Services

Preface

Social service workers are engaged in many areas that involve the law. These service delivery areas can include human rights, consent and capacity issues, mental health, child protection, family law, education, income assistance, and civil and criminal matters.

It is essential for social service workers to be aware of the various laws and cases that apply to their areas of expertise and to have a basic understanding of the law as it applies to their work. As they are not lawyers, social service workers are not qualified to provide legal advice; however, they can provide legal information. The nature of social service work makes it important for social service workers to become familiar with and to understand their professional obligations, responsibilities, and liabilities.

In this edition of *Law and Legislation for Social Service Workers*, we have revised and restructured the original edition. The second edition has streamlined chapters to more closely reflect the areas of work in which social service workers provide expertise and follows the topics discussed in many social work and the law courses. As a result, this book will serve as an important resource for social service workers.

A highlight of the second edition of *Law and Legislation for Social Service Workers* is Chapter 6, Child Protection Law, Notes, Reports, and Records. This chapter discusses the issues of child protection in Ontario in light of the new *Child, Youth and Family Services Act, 2017*, which will be in force in 2018. Additionally, Chapter 6 covers issues that relate to the recent amendments to the current *Child and Family Services Act*, which were due to come into force in fall 2017. This second edition provides social service workers who specialize in this area with current information and legislation, allowing workers to stay up to date and informed.

Chapter 12, Youth Criminal Law, provides current information to individuals working with young persons who find themselves in conflict with the law. Information relating to the *Youth Criminal Justice Act* and current cases provide social service workers with key information related to this area of social service expertise.

The second edition of *Law and Legislation for Social Service Workers* also contains chapters dealing specifically with other essential areas, including up-to-date legislation and cases relating to mental health, consent and capacity, and income assistance, along with chapters on the legal system; human rights; the *Canadian Charter of Rights and Freedoms*; family law; education law; criminal, civil, and restorative justice; social service work liability; access to records; and how to access legal services. Each chapter contains key terms, suggested resources, and discussion questions. As well, an accompanying resource for instructors includes test bank questions and PowerPoint presentations relating to the material in each chapter.

An essential part of social service work is to stay current with relevant legislation and cases. The second edition of *Law and Legislation for Social Service Workers* provides this important information.

Acknowledgments

Thank you to all those who contributed to this edition. The contributions made by the consultants and reviewers to this edition were essential and are much appreciated. Thank you to Pamela Serff, St. Lawrence College; Jane Jones, Algonquin College; and Leslie Huys, Medix College of Healthcare.

About the Author

David Mikelberg is a youth criminal justice lawyer and teaches in the Police Foundation, Justice Studies, and Family and Community Social Services departments at Humber College and the University of Guelph-Humber. David's current practice and previous experience at the Toronto youth legal agency Justice for Children and Youth focus on matters involving criminal, child welfare, education, social assistance, mental health, and other social justice issues. As well, David has an extensive background in public legal education and community development, producing various materials that provide legal information.

Social Work and the Law

1

LEARNING OUTCOMES

After reading this chapter, you should be able to:

■ Explain why social service workers need to know about the law.

■ Explain what it means to give legal advice, and why social service workers should never do so.

■ List some of the situations in which a social service worker might work with a lawyer.

■ Describe the role of the Ontario College of Social Workers and Social Service Workers.

■ Identify the consequences that social service workers can experience in the event of serious errors.

■ Understand the complaint and discipline process under the Ontario College of Social Workers and Social Service Workers.

■ Understand the concepts of criminal and civil liability.

Introduction

Many people give little thought to the law until some event—a divorce, a criminal charge for an offence, or a dispute with an employer—happens to bring them into contact with the legal system. However, the reality is that almost every aspect of our daily lives is regulated, at least to some degree, by laws. For example, if you live in Ontario and drive to work, you are expected to comply with the *Highway Traffic Act*.[1] Your relationship with your employer is regulated by a number of statutes, including the *Employment Standards Act, 2000* and the *Occupational Health and Safety Act*.[2] Your professional status as a social service worker is regulated by the *Social Work and Social Service Work Act, 1998*.[3]

This book is designed to raise your awareness of the legal context of social service work. This is important for a number of reasons:

- It enhances your understanding of the limits of your practice—which activities fall within the scope of your duties and which do not.
- It helps you avoid actions or omissions that might expose you to professional **sanctions**, criminal charges, or civil **liability** (lawsuits).
- It helps you understand your legal rights and the legal rights of your clients.
- It helps you understand which benefits and services are available to your clients, as well as the circumstances in which benefits or services may be denied.

Social service work encompasses a broad and diverse range of services, and social service workers may be employed in a variety of public and private sector settings. These can include the following:

- youth programs
- women's shelters and programs
- children's aid societies
- anger management programs
- addictions counselling
- programs for disabled persons
- immigrant services
- housing and community development
- rehabilitation programs

Each of the service delivery areas in which social service workers are active is subject to legal regulation. In some cases, such as health and long-term care, multiple statutes

sanctions
officially imposed consequences that follow misconduct or the failure to meet compulsory standards of performance; can include fines, suspension of licence, or loss of privileges

liability
the legal responsibility to fulfill an obligation

---

1   *Highway Traffic Act*, RSO 1990, c H.8.

2   *Employment Standards Act, 2000*, SO 2000, c 41; *Occupational Health and Safety Act*, RSO 1990, c O.1.

3   *Social Work and Social Service Work Act, 1998*, SO 1998, c 31.

and regulations are applicable to a social service worker's daily activities. This text provides an overview of the more important legal issues in particular service areas.

It is important to keep up to date with changes in the law. Statutes are frequently amended, repealed, proposed, or enacted by consent of the legislature. If you need to be certain of the exact state of the law on a particular issue, you should check the current official version of the applicable statute and regulations.

Working with the Law and Lawyers

Legal Advice

Social service workers need to have a basic understanding of the law as it applies to their work. With experience, they may become very familiar with particular laws and how they apply to clients' situations. They may find that they can quite accurately identify the legal implications of a client's situation, or predict how the law will apply to something that a client is proposing to do.

However, social service workers are not lawyers. They are not qualified to provide legal advice, and they must not give clients the impression that they can act as a substitute for a lawyer.

Generally, it takes years of legal training and experience to acquire the knowledge needed to provide reliable legal advice. In addition, even if, over time, you acquire detailed knowledge of the law relating to a particular issue, there are other reasons why you must not advise a client on matters of law:

- You may be sued for misrepresentation and **malpractice**. If your advice has resulted in financial loss or other harm, you may be held liable for damages and required to pay compensation to the client. Moreover, you will likely face disciplinary action by the governing body that regulates your profession, with potentially serious consequences for your professional standing.

- Communications between a lawyer and a client are protected by a rule of confidentiality known as solicitor–client privilege. There is no similar rule to protect the confidentiality of communications between a social service worker and a client in the event of litigation. As a result, if your advice to a client leads to or is implicated in a criminal charge or a lawsuit, any written or oral communication between you and your client may be subject to disclosure to the prosecutor or litigants.

It is very important that social service workers restrict their professional practice to the field in which they are trained. This is required by the standards of the profession and by the expectations of employers and clients. When legal services are required, your professional duty compels you to refer your client to a lawyer.

Legal Information

While social service workers should never give legal advice, they are often asked to provide **legal information**. The difference between advice and information generally relates to the level of specificity.

malpractice
failure of a professional to perform in compliance with one's professional duty

legal information
general information about the law without specific reference to an individual's particular circumstance

For example, if a client asks you how to obtain legal immigrant status in Canada, you may list the various categories under which an immigrant may apply, and provide a government brochure explaining the different categories and the application process. However, you should not express an opinion on whether the client's application would be successful, since that would constitute legal advice.

Social service workers must ensure that the legal information they provide is accurate. If brochures or information sheets are not available from government sources, one strategy is for service agencies to produce their own lawyer-approved handouts for clients. For example, the agency's service personnel, including social service workers, could identify the legal matters that arise frequently for their clients, and work with a lawyer to develop a handout that summarizes the relevant law. The summary would be either prepared or approved by the lawyer and presented in a reader-friendly format. The handout would include a recommendation that the reader obtain legal advice on how the law would apply in his or her particular situation.

Working with a Client's Lawyer

When a client has retained a lawyer to handle a legal matter, sometimes it is useful for the lawyer and the social service worker to communicate directly. However, the respective obligations of the social service worker and the lawyer to protect the confidentiality of client information pose a challenge regarding communications between them. To address this problem, the client can be asked to sign waivers that release both professionals from their obligations to maintain confidentiality in their communications with each other with respect to certain client information.

Sharing information allows for a multidisciplinary approach to the client's needs. Consider the example of a prison inmate who has applied to the parole board for early release. He is working with a social service worker to develop a plan for addictions counselling after his release, while a lawyer is representing him in his application to the board. If the two professionals share information directly, the lawyer will get complete and accurate information about the counselling and will be better able to present a persuasive case to the parole board. However, the inmate must first give his express consent to the sharing of information—preferably in writing. Consent is always required before a social service worker discloses personal information about a client to the client's lawyer, or to anyone else.

Social service workers may also work with lawyers when acting as a client's support person during a legal proceeding. For example, a social service worker may accompany a victim of spousal abuse to court to offer moral support. In this situation, the social service worker will best serve her client by taking care to establish a good working relationship with the client's lawyer. Here too, boundaries must be respected. When you, as a social service worker, accompany a client to court, hearings, or other formal meetings, you should take care not to answer questions on behalf of the client, express an opinion about the legal advice given, or attempt to influence the client's instructions to the lawyer. You must act only in your professional capacity and limit your role to providing support to the client.

Working with Your Employer's Lawyer

There are many situations in which a social service agency may need to consult a lawyer, including the following:

- The agency wants to incorporate or seeks charitable status.
- The agency needs advice about service issues.
- The agency needs to defend itself in a lawsuit or wants to sue another party.
- The agency needs advice on the legal implications of a proposed activity.

As an employee of the agency, you may be asked to work with the agency's lawyer on these and other legal matters.

One of the more common situations in which social service workers deal with agency lawyers is in the context of preparing documents that create or limit legal rights—for example, consent forms, releases, or other contracts. These and any other legal documents should be reviewed by a lawyer.

Ideally, a lawyer should also be consulted any time a social service agency proposes to undertake a new activity that may have legal implications, such as offering access to a sports or fitness program or arranging for transportation for participants.

Sometimes, in the course of your work, you may find yourself in need of a lawyer's advice about a service issue. When this happens, speak with your supervisor and request that the question be put to the agency's lawyer. It is important, however, to distinguish your own legal interests from the agency's interests. If your question relates to the employer and not to you personally—for example, you notice that young clients and their friends are using the agency's parking lot for skateboarding and you're worried about the agency's liability for any injuries—it is appropriate to raise your concern with the employer's lawyer. However, if the question relates to you personally—for example, you have a violent client with whom you don't want to be alone, and the employer is not listening to your concerns—you may need to talk to your own lawyer.

Working with Your Own Lawyer

As suggested above, situations may arise in which you need to consult a lawyer on your own behalf in a matter related to your professional practice. For example, you may question the legal basis for a decision made by your employer that affects you directly, or a client may make a formal complaint accusing you of professional misconduct. Whatever the circumstances, you must remember that your duty to the client comes first. That duty requires you to act in the best interests of the client, even when it is against your own interests to do so, and to maintain the confidentiality of the client's information. These duties can be onerous, and you should consult with your own lawyer as to a course of action.

The Regulation of Social Service Professionals: The Ontario College of Social Workers and Social Service Workers

The social service professions in Ontario—social workers and social service workers—became self-regulating in 1998, when the Ontario government enacted the *Social Work and Social Service Work Act, 1998*. Other professions, including medicine, nursing, law, psychiatry, psychology, and engineering, have been self-regulated for many years.

The regulating body is the Ontario College of Social Workers and Social Service Workers (OCSWSSW). It is governed by a 21-member council equally representing social workers, social service workers, and the public. The college carries out a number of responsibilities or functions on behalf of the membership and the public. These include setting the criteria for membership, establishing a code of ethics, defining standards of practice, and maintaining professional standards through sanctions for non-compliance.

Code of Ethics

code of ethics
a system of moral principles designed to guide the conduct of a person or profession

A **code of ethics** reflects the core values of a profession, defines the profession's commitment to the clients whom it serves, and provides a principled framework to guide individual practice. Table 1.1 outlines the college's code of ethics.

TABLE 1.1   Code of Ethics

Maintain the best interests of the client.
Respect the intrinsic worth of the persons she or he serves.
Carry out her or his professional duties and obligations with integrity and objectivity.
Have and maintain competence in the social service work to a client.
Do not exploit the relationship with a client for personal benefit, gain, or gratification.
Protect the confidentiality of all professionally acquired information, and disclose such information only when required by law.
Do not allow outside interests to affect the social work relationship with the client.
Do not provide social work services in a manner that discredits the profession or diminishes the public's trust.
Advocate for workplace conditions and policies according to the profession's standards.
Promote excellence in the profession.
Advocate for change in the best interests of the client, society, environment, and global community.

Source: Adapted from Ontario College of Social Workers and Social Service Workers, "Code of Ethics," *Code of Ethics and Standards of Practice Handbook*, Second Edition – 2008 (Toronto: Author, 2008), p. ii, online: <http://www.ocswssw.org/wp-content/uploads/2017/03/Code-of-Ethics-and-Standards-of-Practice-March-2017.pdf>.

Standards of Practice

Professional standards are benchmarks against which a professional is expected to measure his or her performance; these standards serve as a guide to the development of good practices. For clients and the public, professional standards facilitate the assessment of the quality of the services received. Table 1.2 outlines the subjects in the OCSWSSW's current *Standards of Practice Handbook*.

professional standards
benchmarks against which a professional is expected to measure performance

TABLE 1.2   Standards of Practice Handbook Subject Areas

Relationship with clients
Competence and integrity
Responsibility to clients
Social work and social service work record
Confidentiality
Fees
Advertising
Sexual misconduct

Source: Adapted from Ontario College of Social Workers and Social Service Workers, "Code of Ethics," *Code of Ethics and Standards of Practice Handbook*, Second Edition – 2008 (Toronto: Author, 2008), p. iii, online: <http://www.ocswssw.org/wp-content/uploads/2017/03/Code-of-Ethics-and-Standards-of-Practice-March-2017.pdf>.

It is clearly important for a social service worker to be thoroughly familiar with the code of ethics and the standards of practice applied by the profession. Doing your job competently and with integrity is the best protection against both professional and legal penalties. For social service workers in today's world, doing your job competently includes understanding how the law applies to you and your work.

Professional Misconduct and Incompetence

As outlined earlier, the professions of social work and social service work are regulated by the Ontario College of Social Workers and Social Service Workers. One of the key goals of the college is to maintain standards of practice that promote high-quality service to clients, and thereby build public confidence in the work of social service. To this end, the college has authority to call its members to account for failure to meet the established standards of the profession.

Liability Issues

Social service workers seldom harm others out of malice or recklessness. However, mistakes happen. Social service workers often carry large caseloads. Overwork, inexperience, lack of support, and other factors can contribute to situations in which a social service worker fails to take correct action on behalf of a client, or makes an error in judgment.

There are three main kinds of consequences that social service workers can experience in the event of serious errors:

- sanctions for professional misconduct
- criminal charges
- lawsuits under the **civil law** of torts

civil law
all non-criminal law;
differs from judge-
made common law

Reasonable everyday errors or missteps made in the course of performing assigned duties are unlikely to land a social service worker in legal trouble. Problems tend to arise, instead, where an error is unreasonable given the circumstances—for example, where a social service worker's efforts have fallen markedly below the recognized standards of the profession. Taking actions that are outside the acceptable scope of your professional duties, such as giving legal advice, can also cause problems. Finally, any action motivated by malice, personal gain, or other inappropriate objectives is automatically outside the scope of a social service worker's duties, and can lead to legal or professional consequences.

Complaints and Discipline

An instance of professional incompetence or misconduct typically comes to the attention of the college when someone—often a client or a family member of a client—makes a written complaint about the social service professional to the college.

A complaint is defined as an expression of concern about the conduct or actions of a member relating to professional misconduct, incompetence or incapacity on the part of a member of the college.

Professional misconduct is defined as conduct that violates the *Social Work and Social Service Work Act*, the regulations under that Act, or the by-laws of the college.

Incompetence generally means being unable to do one's job properly through lack of experience, skill, effort, or application.

Incapacity is different from incompetence and means not being able to do one's job because of a physical or mental condition or disorder.

When a complaint is made, the college provides the social service worker with a copy or written summary of the complaint. The social service worker has at least 35 days to prepare a written response. The response is delivered to the complainant, who is allowed to provide additional information for clarification. If necessary, the college makes additional inquiries (for example, speaks to other witnesses) to obtain any other information that may be needed.

Complaints Committee

Once the information has been gathered, the complaint is reviewed by a three-member panel of the Complaints Committee. The panel does not hear oral submissions; it only reviews documents. The panel is generally required to provide a decision and written reasons within 120 days, where possible, but sometimes the process takes longer.

The panel of the Complaints Committee can take a range of actions, which include the following:

- doing nothing
- requiring the social service worker to appear before the committee to be "cautioned" (given a formal warning)
- taking "any action permitted by the legislation or by-laws" (such as referring the matter to a mediator for an attempt at resolution)
- referring the matter to the Discipline Committee to make a determination regarding professional misconduct or incompetence of the member
- referring the matter to the Fitness to Practice Committee to make a determination regarding incapacity of the member

The panel of the Complaints Committee does not have authority to make an order of damages. Complainants who are seeking monetary compensation must pursue a civil lawsuit (discussed later under the heading "Tort Liability").

Discipline Committee

When a complaint is referred to the Discipline Committee, the college can temporarily suspend the social service worker's membership, pending resolution of the complaint.

The Discipline Committee deals with complaints through a formal hearing process with oral submissions and witness testimony. The hearings are usually open to the public. Because an adverse discipline decision remains on the member's record and can have a significant impact on his or her future career, it is a good idea for anyone facing discipline to hire a lawyer. For example, if the college proposes to suspend the individual's membership pending the resolution of the complaint, the member has 14 days in which to prepare written submissions about why the membership should not be suspended. A lawyer's advice would be very useful for the purpose of drafting these submissions.

If the Discipline Committee finds the member guilty of professional misconduct or incompetence, it may make any of the following orders (as provided in section 26 of the *Social Work and Social Service Work Act, 1998*):

1. Revocation of any certificate of registration held by the member under this Act.
2. Suspension of any certificate of registration held by the member under this Act for a specified period, not exceeding 24 months.
3. Imposition of specified terms, conditions, or limitations on any certificate of registration held by the member under this Act.
4. Direction that the imposition of any of the above be postponed for a specified period and not be imposed if specified terms are met within that period.

Additional orders are available if the member is found guilty of professional misconduct (but not incompetence), as follows:

1. Reprimand, admonishment, or counselling, and if considered warranted, recording of such on member's record.
2. Fine to a maximum of $5,000.
3. Publication of the case, in detail or in summary, with or without the name of the member, in the official publication of the college and in any other manner or medium considered appropriate in the particular case.
4. Costs of the discipline hearing to be paid by the member.

The college maintains a register of members, with a record of any revocation or suspension of an individual's membership. In some cases, the college can order that the fact that a member was found guilty of disgraceful or dishonourable conduct, or professional misconduct, be entered on his or her permanent record.

Criminal Offences

The *Criminal Code* covers a wide range of criminal acts, and it's conceivable that a social service worker could commit a variety of crimes in the course of his or her work.[4]

The risk of assault is present whenever a client is difficult to manage physically, or "hard to handle." This category includes a wide variety of clients and service contexts.

Social service workers who work with physically hard-to-handle clients should receive thorough training in the use of restraints (physical restraints and/or submission holds) and other measures involving the application of force. The use of restraints is permitted in certain settings (for example, hospitals that treat mental illness) within very strict guidelines.

As a general rule, unless you have been made aware of a specific employment policy permitting the use of force in your work, and unless you have undergone appropriate training in support of that policy, as a social service worker, you should avoid the use of force completely. In fact, unless physical care is included in your job description (as it may be if you work in a daycare centre or a long-term care facility), you should try to avoid any physical contact with clients, particularly those who are known to be hard to handle.

To prevent unwarranted suspicion or accusations, social service workers should be diligent in avoiding any behaviour that might be deemed inappropriate, including suggestive or ambiguous comments and, particularly, physical contact with clients.

The best policy on the question of physical contact is to exercise extreme caution, particularly in high-risk situations. Unless it is part of the job, limit physical contact with clients to, at most, a brief and formal handshake, preferably initiated by the client.

negligence
implies a lack of action in circumstances where action is warranted

While assault generally implies some degree of action, the concept of **negligence**, which also exists in tort law, implies a lack of action in circumstances where action (or caution) is warranted.

---

4 *Criminal Code*, RSC 1985, c C-46.

Civil Lawsuits

Tort Liability

Torts fall into two basic categories: **intentional torts** and unintentional torts. An intentional tort, as the name suggests, is harm caused intentionally to one person by another. The events that form the basis for an intentional tort lawsuit are often similar to those that give rise to offences under criminal law—the key difference being that in the latter case, a criminal charge is laid and prosecuted by the Crown.

Unintentional torts are based on the civil concept of negligence. There are a number of elements that must be proved by the plaintiff in a negligence case—namely, duty of care, standard of care, causation, and remoteness.

intentional torts
a category of tort that involves causing harm on purpose rather than through negligence

Vicarious Liability

It is important to realize that unprofessional practice that results in harm to a client can have legal consequences not only for the social service worker but also for his employer.

Generally, under the doctrine of **agency**, an employer may be held responsible for mistakes of its employees made in the course of carrying out their duties. Agency applies to actions of an employee taken in the line of duty—that is, actions taken on the employer's time that are within the employee's job description. In addition, in limited circumstances, employers can be held accountable, under the doctrine of **vicarious liability**, for actions that fall outside the scope of the employee's work. For example, vicarious liability could arise where the employer ignores complaints from clients alleging inappropriate sexual advances or touching by a social service worker, and eventually a client sues the social service worker for sexual battery under the law of torts. Knowing about (and ignoring) the social service worker's inappropriate behaviour while promoting his or her access to vulnerable clients will likely make the employer liable to compensate the victims, even though the social service worker's actions fall outside the scope of duties in the employee's job description.

agency
applies to actions of an employee taken in the line of duty—that is, actions taken on the employer's time that are within the employee's job description

vicarious liability
when employers are held accountable for actions that fall outside the scope of the employee's work

Where a social service worker's actions result in liability for the employer, the consequences may be worse than just costing the employer money. Many social service providers operate on a non-profit basis. The cost of a lawsuit may force the service provider to go out of business. Proven harm to a client may also cause the agency to lose a licence that it requires to do business (for example, a daycare licence under the *Day Nurseries Act*,[5] or status as a non-profit housing provider for the purpose of government funding).

Social service workers must realize that failing to perform their job to expected professional standards, and within the requirements of the law, not only harms existing clients but may also result in reduced access to services for others in the community. In addition, successful lawsuits erode the public trust in social service providers.

---

5 *Day Nurseries Act*, RSO 1990, c D.2.

KEY TERMS

agency, 11
civil law, 8
code of ethics, 6
intentional torts, 11
legal information, 3
liability, 2
malpractice, 3
negligence, 10
professional standards, 7
sanctions, 2
vicarious liability, 11

SUGGESTED SOURCES

The Ontario College of Social Workers and Social Service
Workers, <http://www.ocswssw.org>

REVIEW QUESTIONS

1. Why should a social service worker never provide legal advice? Give three reasons.

2. Explain the difference between legal information and legal advice, and give an example of each.

3. A code of ethics reflects the core values of a profession. Describe five different values that are reflected in the Code of Ethics of the Ontario College of Social Workers and Social Service Workers.

4. Professional standards are benchmarks against which a professional is expected to measure his or her performance. Name three areas that serve as a guide to the development of good practices.

5. Name three kinds of consequences that can arise when social service workers commit serious professional errors.

6. If a complaint against a registered social service worker is referred to the Discipline Committee of the college and the committee finds the member guilty of incompetence or professional misconduct, what consequences can follow?

The Canadian Legal System

2

LEARNING OUTCOMES

After reading this chapter, you should be able to:

■ Describe Canada's federal system of government and how the law-making authority of governments is established.

■ Describe, in general terms, the scope of federal and provincial or territorial legislative responsibility.

■ Explain the differences between statutes, regulations, and policies, and their respective functions.

■ Describe the origins of and differences between common law and statute law.

■ Explain how the common law evolves and is applied.

■ Understand the role of the *Canadian Charter of Rights and Freedoms.*

■ Explain the nature and function of administrative tribunals.

■ Describe the basic structure of the Canadian court system.

Introduction

Laws and policies are relevant to social service work. They can be found in the case law, in federal and provincial or territorial statutes and regulations, in municipal by-laws, in the written and unwritten policies of all three levels of government, and in the by-laws and policies of private and quasi-private organizations, such as charities and not-for-profit corporations.

As a social service worker, it's important for you to have a general understanding of all of these sources of law and policy, and how they fit together within the Canadian legal system. You also need to understand the structure of the justice system that applies the law, and the system of administrative tribunals that assists in the administration of myriad government policies.

Sources of Law

This section provides an overview of four sources of the law in Canada:

- common law (case law) created by judges
- statute law (legislation) created by federal and provincial or territorial legislatures
- the Constitution
- by-laws created by municipal councils

Laws applicable to social services can be found in all four sources.

Common Law

common law
a body of legal principles
established through
the decisions made
in court cases

The **common law** is a body of legal principles, established through court decisions (cases), that govern legal issues or subject areas that are not fully addressed by statutes. Many of these principles have been applied so frequently that they have become widely accepted and well-settled legal rules. Judges try to develop rules that can be applied over and over again in order to create certainty and predictability in the application of the law.

To achieve predictability, our common law system requires courts to make decisions in accordance with precedent. Precedent requires courts to decide like cases alike. Common law rules created in legal decisions bind the decision-makers in future decisions, at least where those decisions turn on the same or similar facts. The decisions of higher-level courts (provincial or territorial courts of appeal or the Supreme Court of Canada) must be respected and followed in lower courts unless the facts of the new case differ substantially.

Common law rules are sometimes the precursors of legislative provisions; that is, a legislature might create a statute that incorporates rules derived from the case law. The federal *Criminal Code*, for example, has generally supplanted the common law with respect to criminal law. It is the statute, created by the elected legislature, that primarily governs.[1]

---

1 *Criminal Code*, RSC 1985, c C-46.

Statutory provisions, in turn, can be interpreted by common law rules. For example, a provision in the *Criminal Code* (s 215) that requires parents to provide "necessaries of life" for a child has been interpreted by the courts to include the provision of medical treatment. Even though medical treatment is not mentioned in the statutory provision, the next time a case involving a parent withholding necessary medical care for a child comes up, the court will likely find that, according to the common law, medical care is a necessary of life for the purposes of the legislative provision.

Statute Law and Regulations

Statutes

Statutes (also called "acts" or "legislation") are written "codes" of law. Statutes typically deal with a particular subject matter, which is often identified in the title of the statute (for example, the *Child and Family Services Act* or the *Mental Health Act*).[2] Many statutes are accompanied by regulations, which are supplementary rules that fill in the details of how the provisions of the statute are to be implemented.

Statutes are created by a legislature, either the federal Parliament in Ottawa or the legislature of a province or territory. The legislature is the elected arm of government, accountable to the electorate (citizens entitled to vote). In creating statutes, legislatures may refer to the case law and enact provisions that embody, or codify, well-known and settled common law rules. Sometimes, however, legislatures may choose to override a principle set out in the case law by clearly stating a different rule in the statute, provided that the statutory rule does not violate constitutional principles (as discussed below).

Many statutes affect how social service workers do their job. These statutes will be discussed throughout this text. For an overview, consider the statutes listed in Table 2.1 and the questions they may answer.

As Table 2.1 illustrates, legislatures have been quite active in codifying rules in statutes for different areas of the law. But it must be remembered that statutes are not the only source of law. Where a statute is silent on a particular issue, the common law will still apply. Also, courts may make decisions about the proper interpretation of statutory provisions, and this body of case law becomes part of the law under that statute.

statutes
laws that are passed by either the federal Parliament or a provincial/territorial legislature

TABLE 2.1   Examples of Statutes Applicable in the Social Services Context (to be replaced by the *Child, Youth and Family Services Act*)

Area of Law	Statute	Example of Application
Child protection	*Child and Family Services Act*	Everyone has a duty to report suspicion of child abuse.
Family law	*Family Law Act*[3]	Parents have an obligation to support their children to the extent that they are able.
	Children's Law Reform Act[4]	Determination of custody and access is based on the best interests of the child.

---

2   *Child and Family Services Act*, RSO 1990, c C.11; *Mental Health Act*, RSO 1990, c M.7.

3   *Family Law Act*, RSO 1990, c F.3.

4   *Children's Law Reform Act*, RSO 1990, c C.12.

Area of Law	Statute	Example of Application
Income maintenance	*Ontario Works Act, 1997*[5]	Generally, a recipient of benefits under the Act must demonstrate continued efforts to find employment.
Employment	*Employment Standards Act, 2000*[6]	Generally, an employee is entitled to return to his or her job after taking unpaid parental leave.
Immigration	*Immigration and Refugee Protection Act*[7]	Fear of persecution is a ground for claiming refugee status, but famine is not.
Housing	*Residential Tenancies Act, 2006*[8]	Tenants are entitled to a hearing before they may be evicted.
Human rights	*Human Rights Code*[9] *Canadian Human Rights Act*[10]	Ontario employers are responsible for ensuring that employees are not sexually harassed in the workplace. Federally regulated employers may not discriminate against candidates for employment on the basis of religion.

Regulations

regulations
rules made by authority provided in a statute, which help guide the application of the statute

Many statutes authorize the creation of **regulations**, subordinate forms of legislation that clarify how the statute is to be implemented. Regulations cannot exist on their own without a parent statute. For a regulation to lawfully exist, the statute must include a provision that designates regulation-making authority. Under that authority, regulations are prepared by legal and other administrative staff in the responsible department or ministry. Unlike statutes, regulations do not have to be passed by the legislature.

Regulations tend to be very practical and can include lists, schedules, diagrams, forms, and charts. The information contained in regulations is important in understanding the requirements for compliance with the statute; for example, regulations under the *Child and Family Services Act* establish the housing standards to be met (e.g., room sizes, number of children to a room) for children in care.

Regulations are published separately from the statute and may be revised when changes are made to the statute. If you need to consult a statute in the course of your work, you must also consult the regulations made under that statute.

---

5 *Ontario Works Act, 1997*, SO 1997, c 25.

6 *Employment Standards Act, 2000*, SO 2000, c 41.

7 *Immigration and Refugee Protection Act*, SC 2001, c 27.

8 *Residential Tenancies Act, 2006*, SO 2006, c 17.

9 *Human Rights Code*, RSO 1990, c H.19.

10 *Canadian Human Rights Act*, RSC 1985, c H-6.

Canada's Constitution

The Division of Powers

The **Constitution** is the supreme law of the land. It is the basic framework under which all other laws are created, and it establishes the basic principles to which all other laws must conform. Canada's *Constitution Act, 1867*, creates a federal system of government, according to which law-making powers are divided between the national (or federal) government and the provincial or territorial governments according to subject matter.[11] The federal government has jurisdiction over matters of national and international interest that affect Canadians from coast to coast. It also has law-making jurisdiction with respect to the territories. The provincial and territorial governments have jurisdiction over matters of provincial and local importance, including the creation of municipalities with local governing authority.

The division of powers is set out in the *Constitution Act, 1867*. Federal powers include the authority to regulate defence, currency, and criminal law. The basic rule is that matters that require a national standard are within the jurisdiction of the federal government. The federal government also has a residual power to make laws for the peace, order, and good government of Canada in all matters that do not come within a provincial or territorial head of power. This means that any matters not specifically delegated to the provinces or territories are matters over which the federal government has jurisdiction. An example is the law applicable to immigrants and refugees. The decision as to who may enter and take up residence in Canada is a matter of national and international significance, and requires a uniform set of legal rules and standards to be applied across the country. Therefore, this responsibility falls within federal jurisdiction.

Provincial and territorial powers include authority to make laws governing property, civil rights, and other matters of local concern (such as public works and education).

This division of powers means that the provinces and territories have legislative responsibility over many more aspects of daily life than the federal government. As a result, there are more provincial and territorial statutes, and accompanying regulations, than federal statutes and regulations.

Statutes created by both levels of government may be applicable in a particular area of the law. For example, with respect to children's rights, the federal *Youth Criminal Justice Act* will govern rights in the context of criminal offences,[12] while Ontario's *Child and Family Services Act* will govern a child's civil rights.

Occasionally, one level of government passes a law that appears to intrude on the jurisdiction of the other. Censorship is a good example. Controlling the sale of sexually explicit literature and images can be viewed as either a provincial or territorial concern (trade and commerce within a province) or a federal concern (the distribution of obscene matter as a criminal offence).

Where someone alleges that a law is outside the jurisdiction of the government that passed it, courts are often called upon to settle the issue. If a law does not fit squarely into one camp or the other, the federal government takes jurisdiction under the principle of paramountcy.

Constitution
the statute that establishes the political structure of a nation and sets out its fundamental law

---

11 *Constitution Act, 1867* (UK), 30 & 31 Vict, c 3, reprinted in RSC 1985, Appendix II, No 5.

12 *Youth Criminal Justice Act*, SC 2002, c 1.

The Canadian Charter of Rights and Freedoms

The *Canadian Charter of Rights and Freedoms* is part of the Constitution of Canada, enacted by the *Constitution Act, 1982*.[13] The Charter expresses the fundamental values and principles of our society, centred on Canada's perception of itself as a free and democratic country. Essentially, the Charter provides a mechanism for balancing the rights and freedoms of individuals against the broader need to protect society, including its more vulnerable members.

The enactment of the Charter has had a profound impact on Canadian law. It entrenches specific rights and freedoms, including equality, freedom of religion, and freedom of expression, and it provides that government legislation and actions cannot infringe on those rights and freedoms unless the infringement can be reasonably justified in a free and democratic society.

Therefore, the Charter has two important effects:

- If any law or government policy contravenes the provisions of the Charter, a court or an administrative tribunal may declare that law or policy to be unconstitutional and of no force and effect.
- Any action of an agent or a representative of any level of government that contravenes any right or freedom protected in the Charter can be challenged.

Reasonable Limits on Rights and Freedoms

Section 1 of the Charter is a very important provision. It provides that all rights and freedoms are subject to "such reasonable limits prescribed by law as can be demonstrably justified in a free and democratic society." Each time a court is asked to determine whether a law violates the Charter, it must consider whether the law imposes a reasonable limit as described in section 1. A law will be struck down only when both of the following conditions are present:

- The law infringes on a Charter right or freedom.
- The law cannot be justified as a reasonable limit in the particular circumstances.

For example, consistent with the duty of society to protect children from sexual exploitation, the government has enacted laws prohibiting the production and distribution of child pornography. In cases where these laws are challenged as a violation of the right to freedom of expression under the Charter, the courts have generally concluded that the law does infringe on the Charter right but that the infringement is reasonable and justified.

---

13 *Canadian Charter of Rights and Freedoms*, Part I of the *Constitution Act, 1982*, being Schedule B to the Canada Act 1982 (UK), 1982, c 11; *Constitution Act, 1982*, being Schedule B to the *Canada Act 1982* (UK), 1982, c 11.

Scope of Application

The precise scope of the Charter's application has been a matter of debate and litigation. Although it is clear that the Charter applies to the content and effects of statute law and to the nature and effects of government action, it has sometimes been difficult to define what is meant by "government" action. A multitude of organizations and regulated industries in Canada have some connection to government; many cases have been argued that turn on whether an action of a quasi-governmental organization is a government action.

Unregulated private activity within a province or territory is not intended to be subject to the Charter. For example, if an apartment building owner discriminates against potential renters by refusing to rent to people with children, this is not likely a Charter violation. The Charter would apply only if the discriminatory act resulted from the application of law or government policy. To protect equality rights in situations outside the scope of the Charter, the federal and provincial or territorial governments have enacted human rights legislation.

It is important for social service workers to be aware of Charter rights and to be alert to circumstances where they may be infringed. Whether such infringement is justified is a matter for the courts to decide.

Some examples of Charter rights (see Table 2.2) are freedom of religion (s 2[a]); freedom of expression (s 2[b]); the right not to be unreasonably searched (s 8); the right to a lawyer (s 10[b]); the right to life, liberty, and the security of the person and to fundamental justice (s 7); and equality rights (s 15).

The case of a teacher in Alberta who was communicating anti-Semitic statements to his students about the Holocaust illustrates the balance between an individual's rights under the Charter (s 2[b], freedom of expression) and the *Criminal Code* (s 319[2], prohibiting hate propaganda). The teacher stated that the law infringed on his right to freedom of expression. The Supreme Court of Canada (SCC) held that the *Criminal Code* law infringement was reasonably justified in a free and democratic society.[14]

Carter v Canada (Attorney General) also illustrates the balance between society's laws and an individual's Charter rights. Section 241(b) of the *Criminal Code* prohibits persons from aiding or abetting another person to commit suicide, and section 14 of the *Criminal Code* prohibits persons from consenting to death being inflicted upon them. Together these provisions prevent assisted dying in Canada. The SCC ruled that the *Criminal Code* provisions did infringe on the individual's Charter right to life, liberty, and the security of the person and to fundamental justice (s 7) and that the infringement was not reasonably justified in a free and democratic society. It should be noted that the SCC outlined certain conditions that must be present in striking down the law. In this case the court gave the government 12 months to create new laws on physician-assisted dying in certain circumstances.[15]

---

14 *R v Keegstra*, [1990] 3 SCR 697.

15 *Carter v Canada (Attorney General)*, 2015 SCC 5, [2015] 1 SCR 331.

TABLE 2.2   Some of the Rights under the Charter of Rights and Freedoms

Section 1	The *Canadian Charter of Rights and Freedoms* guarantees the rights and freedoms set out in it subject only to such reasonable limits prescribed by law as can be demonstrably justified in a free and democratic society.
Section 2	(a) freedom of conscience and religion (b) freedom of thought, belief, opinion and expression, including freedom of the press and other media of communication (c) freedom of peaceful assembly (d) freedom of association
Section 6	(1) Every citizen of Canada has the right to enter, remain in and leave Canada.
Section 7	Everyone has the right to life, liberty and security of the person and the right not to be deprived thereof except in accordance with the principles of fundamental justice.
Section 8	Everyone has the right to be secure against unreasonable search or seizure.
Section 9	Everyone has the right not to be arbitrarily detained or imprisoned.
Section 10	(b) to retain and instruct counsel without delay and to be informed of that right
Section 11	(d) to be presumed innocent until proven guilty according to law in a fair and public hearing by an independent and impartial tribunal
Section 12	Everyone has the right not to be subjected to any cruel and unusual treatment or punishment.
Section 15	(1) Every individual is equal before and under the law and has the right to the equal protection and equal benefit of the law without discrimination and, in particular, without discrimination based on race, national or ethnic origin, colour, religion, sex, age or mental or physical disability.

Municipal By-Laws

by-laws
rules created by a municipality, county, or other level of government smaller than a province or territory

The fourth source of law under the Canadian legal system is municipal **by-laws**, which are passed by municipal councils. Municipal councils are the government bodies responsible for municipalities (cities, towns, or regions). Provincial and territorial governments create municipalities by statute and provide specific designated powers to municipal councils. Municipal councils exercise these powers by making municipal by-laws. Municipalities are responsible for many basic local services, including sewage and water supply, police, public health, public transit, garbage collection and disposal, libraries, and arenas.

Policy

Government policy is not law; however, it is a very important source of guidance for many social service workers. While legislation often sets basic rules for interactions between individuals and their government, sometimes those laws, and even the regulations made under them, cannot capture all of the details of how a sphere of activity is managed by government. Especially where legislation leaves room for discretion in administrative decision-making, how the law will be applied in practice often evolves as a matter of government policy.

Policies can be formal or informal, written or unwritten. They can also have a wide range of objectives—for example, promoting fairness to users of a program or service, or setting priorities for the allocation of government resources.

As discussed above, government policy should be guided by the Charter. In addition, it must not have objectives or operate in a way that runs counter to the spirit of any applicable legislation. If policies are found to operate in a way not contemplated by the legislation, courts may choose not to support their enforcement.

As a social service worker, it is your responsibility to be familiar not only with the legislation that applies to your work but with the government policies, practices, and guidelines that support that legislation. For example, if you work in the mental health field in Ontario, you should be familiar with the policies of the Ministry of Health and Long-Term Care. If your work involves assisting Ontario clients with obtaining income support, you should familiarize yourself with the policies of the Ministry of Community and Social Services.

Policies are often developed to respond to local needs and circumstances. As a result, the policies of the Ministry of Municipal Affairs and Housing (for example) in one region of the province or territory might be quite different from those just a few counties away. It is important for you to become familiar with how the government does business in your jurisdiction.

Government policy documents are often made available to the public on the website of the relevant ministry, or copies can be picked up at local government offices.

Governments are not the only organizations that create policies. Most private corporations, associations, and charitable organizations have policies (sometimes called by-laws) of their own. If you work for a private organization, such as a nursing home, you will be expected to know and comply with its policies. Also, when you do business with an outside organization in the course of your work, you or your client may be required to comply with that organization's policies.

Occasionally, you may find yourself in the position of having to advocate for clients who feel they have been wronged by an organizational policy. For example, if you work in a program that provides income assistance, and you have a client whose financial troubles have led to the loss of electricity in his apartment, you may need to help the client challenge the hydro company's policy governing the cancellation of service. In such situations, it is important to remember that an organization's policies are *only* policies; they are not laws. Where they conflict with the law (for example, a law that prohibits shutting off the supply of electricity during extreme weather), the law overrides.

Administrative Law

Administrative law is the body of law that governs how government administrators and employees exercise the decision-making powers granted to them under statute. Generally, these decisions involve conferring some kind of benefit or right on citizens; as a result, administrative decisions may have important consequences for the individuals concerned.

Depending on the provisions of the particular statute, administrative decisions may be made quickly and routinely (as in the case of registration of a driver's licence), or they may be quasi-judicial, involving a hearing and an impartial decision-maker. Often decisions will start out as routine, but if a person who is denied a right or benefit

administrative law
the body of law that governs how government administrators and employees exercise the decision-making powers granted to them under statute

chooses to challenge the decision, it will be reviewed by a more senior official, and eventually by an independent board or tribunal.

Administrative decisions may also be reviewed by a court; however, it is a principle of administrative law that deference should be given to the government official or tribunal that made the decision, owing to their expertise in the particular regulatory regime. The rights of appeal and judicial review differ depending on the governing statute, so it is important to refer to that statute for the particulars.

The decisions of administrators are made within a defined scope of authority; laws and/or policies place limits on the range of decisions that an administrator can make. Within this range, an administrator's decisions must be guided by administrative discretion. The social service workers employed in government departments and agencies must make choices every day in responding to particular circumstances. This exercise of administrative discretion is called discretionary power. The principles of administrative law require that discretionary power be exercised in a fair and reasonable manner.

Many decision-making functions have aspects of procedural fairness built into the policies that guide them. For example, where the decision affects whether an individual will receive benefits (such as social assistance) or services (such as Wheel-Trans), it is common for the agency's policies to require that clients who are denied access to benefits or services be given written reasons for the denial. This requirement makes it easier for a client to challenge the decision. A challenge of an administrative decision may proceed through several stages of review, from the level of the agency to a tribunal and ultimately to a court. The review process is described below.

Administrative Tribunals

Administrative tribunals are created by statutes. Their purpose is to provide a mechanism for resolving disputes over administrative decisions relating to the rights, entitlements, or duties described in the particular statute. A person who disagrees with the decision of an administrator may apply for a review by the appropriate administrative tribunal.

For example, an applicant for Ontario Works benefits whose application is refused by the local Ontario Works office may challenge the decision by submitting a written request to the office for an internal review. The decision will be reviewed by an officer other than the original decision-maker. If the decision is confirmed, the applicant may apply to the Social Benefits Tribunal for a further, independent review. The Social Benefits Tribunal was created by the *Ontario Works Act, 1997* and the *Ontario Disability Support Program Act, 1997*, and has authority to review administrative decisions made pursuant to those statutes.[16] Other examples of administrative tribunals that are often relevant to social service workers and their clients are the *Human Rights Code* and the Ontario Human Rights Tribunal, and the *Residential Tenancies Act, 2006* and Landlord Tenant Board.

An advantage of an administrative tribunal is that hearing procedures are generally much less formal than trial procedures, and matters can be resolved more quickly.

---

16   *Ontario Works Act, 1997*, SO 1997, c 25; *Ontario Disability Support Program Act, 1997*, SO 1997, c 25, Schedule B.

However, tribunals vary widely with respect to the style and level of formality of their proceedings. If you are called upon to assist a client with a submission to an administrative tribunal, it's a good idea to obtain a copy of the tribunal's procedures so that you can talk to the client about what will happen at the hearing and how he or she can prepare. (But remember that your role is to provide information, not legal advice.)

Judicial Review and Appeal to Court

A party may apply to the Ontario Divisional Court for **judicial review** of a tribunal's decision where he or she has reason to question the decision on procedural grounds. Judicial review does not involve consideration of the legal merits of the decision—that is, whether the tribunal arrived at a correct legal result. Instead, the issue before the court is whether the tribunal acted within its jurisdiction, or statutory authority, with respect to the decision-making process. If the court finds that the tribunal did not act within its jurisdiction (for example, if it failed to follow specified rules of procedural fairness), the court may order a rehearing.

judicial review
a legal challenge to a tribunal decision on procedural grounds

Unlike judicial review, an appeal does involve examination of the legal merits of the decision. On appeal, the tribunal's decision may be overturned if the court finds that it was based on an erroneous interpretation or application of the law—in other words, that the decision was "wrong."

Court System and Hierarchy

In broad terms, the hierarchy of Canadian courts consists of three main levels:

- trial courts
- appeal courts
- the Supreme Court of Canada

This simplified picture is deceptive, since there are separate federal and provincial or territorial court systems that include courts to deal with specific areas of the law. For example, there are federal trial and appeal courts, and special courts (such as the Tax Court of Canada), as well as a military court system. For the purposes of this book, it is the provincial court systems that are most relevant, and particularly the Ontario system. This will be the focus of the discussion here and in the chapters that follow.

Trial Courts

Provincial courts where a dispute is first heard are called trial courts, and these include specialty courts like the Small Claims Court, Family Court, and Youth Court.

In Ontario, and some other provinces, there are two levels of trial courts. Generally, lower provincial courts deal with civil disputes and lesser offences, and more serious offences are tried in a superior court. Also, in some limited situations, a decision of a lower court can be appealed to a superior court; for example, decisions of a judge in the Small Claims Court may be appealed to a judge of the Ontario Superior Court of Justice.

Appeal Courts

The provincial court of appeal is the highest level of the provincial court system. Decisions made by trial courts can be appealed to the court of appeal. The appeal court will consider whether the trial court made any significant legal errors such that the case was decided wrongly. The appeal court may reverse the trial decision, uphold it, or order a new trial.

Supreme Court of Canada

The Supreme Court of Canada is the court of final appeal and the highest court in the country. It decides only a limited number of cases every year, and there is no automatic right to appeal except in certain criminal matters. Otherwise, only parties with cases of national importance and general public interest are granted leave (permission) to appeal to the Supreme Court of Canada.

For information on federal statutes and regulations, visit the website of the Department of Justice at <http://www.justice.gc.ca>. Information on Ontario statutes and regulations is available at <https://www.ontario.ca/laws>. Information on federal and provincial statutes and on case law is available from the Canadian Legal Information Institute at <https://www.canlii.org>. Figure 2.1 illustrates Canada's court system.

FIGURE 2.1 Canada's Court System

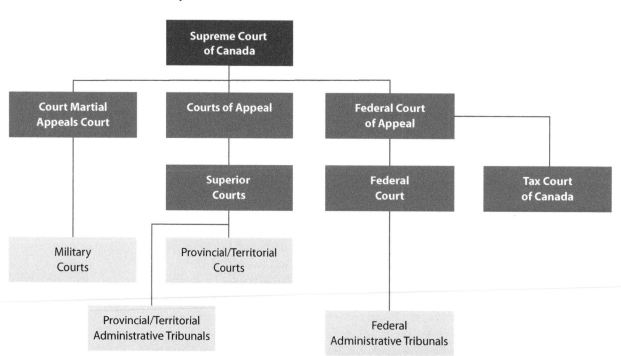

Source: Adapted from Canada, Department of Justice, "The judicial structure," online: <http://www.justice.gc.ca/eng/csj-sjc/just/07.html>.

KEY TERMS

administrative law, 21

by-laws, 20

common law, 14

Constitution, 17

judicial review, 23

regulations, 16

statutes, 15

SUGGESTED SOURCES

Department of Justice, <http://www.justice.gc.ca>

Ontario statutes and regulations, <https://www.ontario.ca/laws>

Case law is available from the Canadian Legal Information Institute, <http://www.canlii.org>

REVIEW QUESTIONS

1. Name four sources of law.

2. What is precedent, and why is it important?

3. What is the difference between a statute and a regulation?

4. Explain how the Charter protects the rights and freedoms of individuals.

5. Describe a law that infringes upon a Charter right that has been ruled as being reasonably justified in a free and democratic society.

Human Rights Law, Employment, and Housing

3

LEARNING OUTCOMES

After reading this chapter, you should be able to:

- Identify the federal and Ontario statutes that define and protect human rights.

- Describe the scope of application of the federal and Ontario human rights statutes.

- List the grounds on which it is illegal to discriminate under these statutes.

- Explain how a person can seek redress for a violation of human rights.

- Suggest the steps that a person might take to assert his or her rights on termination of employment.

- Describe some of the legal rights and obligations of employers and employees within the employment context.

- Explain some of the practices that might be considered discrimination within the employment context.

- Describe some of the legal rights and obligations of landlords and tenants and how human rights legislation protects access to housing.

Human Rights Legislation

While the Charter guarantees certain rights by prohibiting governments from making laws or authorizing actions that infringe those rights, human rights legislation provides protection against infringement of other specified rights through the actions of other persons, including individuals, corporations, and administrators of government offices and agencies. In particular, human rights statutes codify the right to be free from discrimination or harassment on specified grounds, such as race, sex, or disability, with respect to access to, or receipt of, goods and services, employment, and housing. For example, refusing to serve a customer in a restaurant because of his race, deciding not to hire someone because of her sex, or refusing to rent an apartment to someone because of his disability would be in violation of human rights law.

Service providers should be aware of their obligation not to discriminate against clients on the basis of any of the prohibited grounds. Social service workers may also be called upon to assist clients who have experienced discrimination or harassment in employment, housing, or the provision of goods and services, contrary to human rights legislation.

The federal human rights statute is the *Canadian Human Rights Act*.[1] At the provincial or territorial level, each province and territory has its own human rights statute, which is applicable to matters under provincial or territorial jurisdiction. Ontario's statute is called the *Human Rights Code* (referred to here as "the Ontario Code").[2] The scope of application of each statute is described below.

Jurisdiction

The Federal Statute

The *Canadian Human Rights Act* prohibits discrimination and harassment in matters that fall under the jurisdiction of the federal government, as prescribed by the division of powers set out in the *Constitution Act, 1867*.[3] Many aspects of the day-to-day lives of social service clients—housing, employment, education, family services, and health care—are governed primarily by the provinces and territories. Matters that fall into the federal regulatory sphere, and are subject to the protection provided by the *Canadian Human Rights Act*, include the following:

- immigration
- employment in the federal public service
- telecommunications
- federal taxation
- the federal pension system

---

1   *Canadian Human Rights Act*, RSC 1985, c H-6.

2   *Human Rights Code*, RSO 1990, c H.19.

3   *Constitution Act, 1867* (UK), 30 & 31 Vict, c 3 reprinted in RSC 1985, Appendix II, No 5.

- the design and administration of federal aid programs (excluding programs targeted to specific disadvantaged groups)
- the approval of plans in federal spheres of activity that are designed to assist people with disabilities

Ontario's Statute

The Ontario *Human Rights Code* applies to the following matters under the jurisdiction of the province (including those delegated to municipalities):

- property, including housing, real estate, and the regulation of residential tenancies
- civil rights, including contract and tort rights, most aspects of family law, and a wide range of commercial and economic rights
- the incorporation of provincial companies
- the regulation of employment
- public hospitals and health care
- education

Prohibited Grounds

Both the federal and provincial statutes list prohibited grounds of discrimination. Although there are some differences, generally they include the following:

- race
- national or ethnic origin
- colour
- religion
- age
- sex
- sexual orientation
- marital status
- family status (including pregnancy and child-bearing)
- physical or mental disability (including dependence on alcohol or drugs)
- pardoned criminal convictions

Discrimination

The Supreme Court of Canada has stated the following:

> The essence of discrimination is in the arbitrariness of its negative impact, that is, the arbitrariness of the barriers imposed, whether intentionally or unwittingly. ... It is the link between that group membership and the arbitrariness of the disadvantaging criterion or conduct, either on its face or in its impact, that triggers the possibility of a remedy.[4]

Discrimination can be divided into four categories: direct discrimination, adverse-effect discrimination, systemic discrimination, and harassment (see Table 3.1). As well, human rights law in Canada specifies certain areas where discrimination is not permitted and certain prohibited grounds of discrimination.

Direct Discrimination

direct discrimination
discrimination that is blatant and obvious

Direct discrimination occurs when a rule, practice, preference, or restriction makes a distinction that on its face discriminates on a prohibited ground.[5] An example of direct discrimination is not allowing Asian men to be employed at a company regardless of whether the rule was intended to discriminate or not. No harm needs to be established.[6]

Adverse-Effect Discrimination

adverse-effect discrimination
discrimination that is indirect and often unintentional

Adverse-effect discrimination is a rule, practice, preference, or restriction that is not discriminatory on its face but still may be discriminatory because of its effect.[7] The Supreme Court of Canada has ruled in cases where adverse-effect discrimination occurs that the court will not hold a respondent liable for discrimination if he or she has made reasonable efforts to accommodate the complainant. The court described the duty as follows:

> ... to take reasonable steps to accommodate the complainant, short of undue hardship:
> ... to take such steps as may be reasonable to accommodate without undue interference in the operation of the employer's business and without undue expense to the employer.[8]

Systemic Discrimination

systemic discrimination
discrimination that permeates or is incorporated into policies and practices

Systemic discrimination is unintentional and has its roots in long-standing stereotypes that create a discriminatory effect.[9] Affirmative action programs are often used to combat systemic discrimination.

---

4   *McGill University Health Centre (Montreal General Hospital) v Syndicat des employés de l'Hôpital général de Montréal*, 2007 SCC 4, [2007] 1 SCR 161 at paras 48, 49.

5   RW Zinn, *The Law of Human Rights in Canada* (Aurora, ON: Canada Law Book, 2008) at 1-3.

6   *Ibid* at 1-5.

7   *Ibid* at 1-6.

8   *Ontario Human Rights Commission v Simpson-Sears*, [1985] 2 SCR 536 at para 23.

9   *CN v Canada (Canadian Human Rights Commission)*, [1987] 1 SCR 1114.

Harassment

Both the federal and the Ontario statutes prohibit **harassment**. Harassment differs from discrimination in that the harasser need not be in a position of power—that is, in a position to subject the victim to "unequal treatment." Generally, harassment means behaving in such a manner as to trouble or annoy the victim, or to make him or her uncomfortable. If such behaviour causes the victim to fear for his or her safety, it may constitute criminal harassment under section 264 of the *Criminal Code*.[10]

Harassment is defined in the Ontario *Human Rights Code*, much more broadly than in the *Criminal Code*, as "engaging in a course of vexatious comment or conduct that is known or ought reasonably to be known to be unwelcome" (s 10(1)). This definition suggests repeated behaviour rather than a single event.

Both human rights statutes prohibit harassment in the context of employment and housing, but only the federal Act prohibits harassment in the provision of goods and services. Harassment is prohibited on the same grounds as discrimination (as enumerated in the particular statute). In the employment setting, an employer may be held responsible for the harassment of an employee if the employer is aware of it and fails to take reasonable steps to make it stop.

harassment
engaging in a course of vexatious comment or conduct that is known or ought reasonably to be known to be unwelcome

TABLE 3.1 Types, Areas, and Prohibited Grounds for Discrimination

Types of Discrimination	Areas of Discrimination	Prohibited Grounds
• Direct	• Employment	• Race
• Adverse-effect	• Housing (accommodation)	• Colour
• Systemic	• Services	• Ancestry
• Harassment	• Contracts	• Creed (religion)
		• Place of origin
		• Ethnic origin
		• Citizenship
		• Sex (including pregnancy, gender identity)
		• Sexual orientation
		• Age
		• Marital status
		• Family status
		• Disability
		• Receipt of public assistance

---

10 *Criminal Code*, RSC 1985, c C-46.

Sexual Harassment

Sexual harassment is singled out in both the federal and Ontario human rights statutes because it is such a prevalent and serious issue. While the majority of sexual harassment complaints involve women complaining about harassment by men, men may also be sexually harassed by women, and both men and women may be harassed by others of the same sex.

Sexual harassment is defined broadly by the courts to include a wide range of behaviour. Examples are threats, stalking, sexual touching, and assault (any of which could be considered a criminal offence). Other examples include the following:

- sexual jokes, comments, or insults within earshot of a person
- sexually explicit images displayed in the workplace (e.g., calendars, posters, figurines, computer screen savers)
- staring or inappropriate compliments
- unwanted hugging or similar touching
- requiring an employee to wear a revealing uniform

If a client tells you that she has been sexually harassed, you should encourage her to record the details of the incident(s) in writing, including the date and time, the precise conduct or remarks that she found offensive, and the names of any witnesses. If the client decides to proceed with a formal complaint of sexual harassment, you may be called upon to provide emotional support. It is fairly common in sexual harassment cases for the complainant to be questioned about the incident, including, for example, her reaction to the alleged harasser's actions. Those who are asked to investigate the claim will want to determine whether the complainant said or did anything to encourage the alleged harasser, and she may find it upsetting to face suggestions that she may have welcomed the advances. Victims often feel shame and blame themselves. Your role may include helping the person to sort through these feelings.

Enforcing Human Rights

People who believe that their human rights have been denied or violated can make a complaint to either the Canadian Human Rights Commission (CHRC), in the event of a violation of the federal Act, or to the Ontario Human Rights Commission (OHRC), in the event of a violation of the Ontario code. For violations of the Ontario code, possible remedies include an order requiring payment of monetary losses suffered by the complainant, compensation for mental anguish of up to $10,000, and additional fines of up to $25,000.

A complaint should be made as soon as possible after the event. The procedure is outlined below.

1. The complainant contacts the appropriate commission and obtains a complaint form.
2. The complainant files the complaint with the commission, which then informs the person or party against whom the complaint is made.
3. The person or party who is the subject of the complaint must prepare and file a written response.

4. Various means of resolution are explored, such as mediation (described in Chapter 11).

5. If the issue remains unresolved, the commission may choose to investigate the complaint.

6. If there is an investigation, it typically involves reviewing the complaint and the response, and, if necessary, interviewing the parties or other individuals.

7. The investigator prepares a report and communicates the commission's findings to the parties, who may respond.

8. The case may be resolved at this point by arriving at a settlement, through negotiation or mediation, based on the investigator's report.

9. If the case is not resolved, it is reviewed by the commission, which then decides what action to take. For example, the commission may

    a. refer the parties to a conciliator, and/or approve a settlement arrived at by the parties;

    b. refer the parties to the Canadian Human Rights Tribunal or the Ontario Human Rights Tribunal for adjudication; or

    c. dismiss the complaint.

10. If the case goes before a tribunal, the tribunal will schedule and conduct a hearing and issue a decision.

11. The tribunal may declare that the complaint was without merit, or it may offer a remedy in favour of the complainant. Remedies can include

    a. an order that the discriminatory practice stop, including a change to policy;

    b. compensation to the victim for lost wages and/or other losses that resulted from the discriminatory practice;

    c. compensation to the victim for additional costs of obtaining alternative goods, services, facilities, or accommodation, and for any expenses incurred by the victim as a result of the discriminatory practice; and

    d. compensation for pain or suffering that the victim experienced as a result of the discriminatory practice.

12. In certain cases, decisions of the Ontario tribunal can be appealed to the Divisional Court.

Hearings before a human rights tribunal are quite formal, and parties are generally represented by a lawyer. A support person, such as a social service worker, may also attend. Parties may be called to give oral testimony, and there may be other witnesses, including expert witnesses, called by either side.

If a party makes a complaint to the CHRC or the OHRC, regardless of the outcome—whether it is settled at mediation, dismissed by commission staff, settled after conciliation, dismissed by the tribunal, or decided in favour of the complainant— the person who is the subject of the complaint may not make reprisals against the complainant. **Reprisals** include any action or statement that is intended to punish, threaten, intimidate, or discriminate against the complainant.

reprisals
actions or statements intended to punish, threaten, intimidate, or discriminate against a complainant

Areas Covered Under Human Rights Laws

Generally, human rights laws prohibit discrimination in employment, housing (accommodation), services, and contracts.

Regarding human rights laws related to services and contracts, note the following:

- All individuals are entitled to equal access to and treatment in services and facilities.[11]
- In Ontario, every individual has a right to contract on equal terms without discrimination on any prohibited grounds.[12]

The remainder of this chapter details human rights laws related to employment and housing.

The Law Related to Employment

In Canada today, most of the working population earn a livelihood by working for an employer. To facilitate access to employment, and provide for safe and reasonable working conditions, the federal and provincial/territorial governments have enacted a number of statutes that require employers to respect certain employee rights and comply with certain employment standards. These statutes have been passed against a backdrop of common law principles that have evolved over time.

Employment legislation is designed, in part, to address the imbalance of power that often exists between employers and employees. Employees need to work in order to support themselves, and especially in times of high unemployment, employers may exploit this need by dictating terms of employment that favour their own interests over those of their employees. Before employment laws were passed, employees were reluctant to complain about poor working conditions or inadequate pay, because the employer could simply fire them and find others to fill their jobs.

Social service workers are often called upon to work with clients who have lost their job, are having trouble finding employment, or are prevented from working for reasons of poor health or disability. Other clients may be employed but facing difficulties in the workplace. There are many federal and provincial or territorial statutes that may apply in such circumstances, including employment insurance, employment standards, human rights, and workplace health and safety legislation. It is important that social service workers acquire a broad understanding of employment law and the applicable statutes so that they can recognize issues and pursue remedies and resources for their clients.

prohibited grounds
grounds upon which discrimination is forbidden, which typically include race, nationality, religion, sex, disability, family status, criminal record, and age

The federal and provincial or territorial governments have enacted human rights legislation that prohibits discrimination and harassment in an employment setting, on specified grounds. Each jurisdiction has a slightly different list of **prohibited grounds,** but these typically include race, nationality, religion, sex, disability, family status, criminal record, and age.

---

11   *Supra* note 5 at 2-16.

12   *Ibid* at 2-25.

Both direct and indirect discrimination are prohibited. For example, an employer who advertised a job opportunity restricted to "white Canadian" applicants would be discriminating directly on the prohibited grounds of race and nationality. An employer who required "excellent skills in writing and speaking English" for the job of gardener could be considered to be discriminating indirectly on the prohibited grounds of national or ethnic origin and/or race.

Human rights legislation makes an exception for **bona fide job qualifications**—specific skills or training that a prospective employee needs in order to perform the job. For example, while it would usually not be reasonable to require a gardener to have "excellent skills in writing and speaking English," this would be a reasonable requirement for a high school English teacher. Likewise, a bona fide job qualification for a truck driver would be a valid driver's licence, even though this requirement would exclude an applicant who is legally blind, and thus would violate the prohibition against discrimination based on disability. Human rights legislation recognizes that in some circumstances, discrimination is legitimate. However, the onus is on the employer to prove the reasonableness of the job requirements and performance standards.

bona fide job qualifications
specific skills or training that an employee must have to be able to perform a job

Social service workers need to be able to recognize employer conduct that is contrary to human rights legislation, so that they can provide information and support to clients, and a referral to a lawyer if necessary. The Ontario Human Rights Commission is a good source of information, and individuals who believe that their rights have been violated may make a formal complaint to the commission.

Every province and territory in Canada has legislation to regulate the quality of the work environment. Some statutes, including Ontario's *Employment Standards Act, 2000* (ESA), impose minimum standards governing the terms of employment—for example, pay and time off.[13] The ESA also provides for an administrative review procedure to allow an employee to seek a remedy where an employer fails to comply with a legislated standard. The ESA imposes minimum standards for the treatment of employees, with respect to such matters as wages, overtime, vacations, parental leave, and notice of termination (or pay in lieu of).

As a social service worker in Ontario, you may encounter a client who has been denied a legislated employment right under the ESA. In such a situation, the employee should first seek a remedy from the employer by bringing the matter to the employer's attention and requesting compliance with the ESA.

If a written request to the employer does not result in resolution of the problem, the employee may choose to file a complaint with the Ministry of Labour. However, before doing so, he or she should seek advice from a lawyer. Generally, filing a complaint under the ESA precludes filing a lawsuit on the same issue. In some cases, such as wrongful dismissal, the remedy available from a court is substantially greater than that offered by the ESA, so the pros and cons of the two ways of proceeding should be carefully weighed. Also, if the workplace is unionized, the provisions of the collective agreement govern, and the process for dealing with a dispute is grievance arbitration pursuant to the collective agreement.

---

13 *Employment Standards Act, 2000*, SO 2000, c 41.

If the employee decides to proceed with a formal complaint, he or she should fill out the ministry's claim form, either online at the ministry website or in person at a Service Ontario Information Centre. (These information centres are found in more than 60 communities across Ontario.) Once the claim is filed, the ministry first tries to negotiate a resolution. If this fails and the ministry believes that the complaint has validity, an investigation may be launched.

Provincial and territorial governments have also enacted workers' compensation legislation to provide for the payment of compensation where an employee suffers a loss of income as a result of a work-related injury or illness. In Ontario, the governing statute is the *Workplace Safety and Insurance Act, 1997* (WSIA).[14] Generally, the WSIA provides that an employee with a valid claim against an insured employer is entitled to compensation, and the employer is protected from legal action and potential liability for damages. The *Occupational Health and Safety Act* is a fairly general statute that is given specific operation to particular workplaces and hazards.[15] The Act prescribes a cooperative approach to safety by prescribing roles for employers, supervisors, and workers themselves.

To compensate employees for work-related injuries and illnesses, and to minimize recourse to expensive lawsuits in such cases, Ontario instituted an insurance scheme, established and governed by the WSIA and mandatory for most workplaces where a risk to worker health or safety exists.

The Law Related to Housing

Adequate housing is fundamental to a person's health, security, and well-being. For most people, it is their largest single household expense. Those who can afford to purchase a home are generally less likely to seek assistance from a social service agency in meeting their housing needs than those who rent. It is useful for social service workers to have a general knowledge of the legislation governing landlord–tenant relations. However, because the law in this area changes frequently, to be certain that a particular rule still applies, you will need to refer to the current legislation and any pending amendments.

In an unregulated rental market, tenants are generally at a disadvantage in negotiating with landlords over rent, repairs, and other issues. To protect them, governments have enacted legislation regulating many aspects of the rental housing system. It has been a challenge for policy-makers to arrive at a regime that achieves a fair balance between the rights of tenants and those of landlords, and landlord–tenant legislation has a history of frequent amendment. Ontario is no exception.

rent control
legislated restrictions on rent increases on rental properties under certain circumstances

The *Residential Tenancies Act, 2006*[16] (RTA) provides that a landlord may increase the rent only once per year where there is no change in tenant. The Act also provides for minimum rights for all tenants, including the right to quiet enjoyment of the property and the right to have it maintained, and procedures for eviction. **Rent control** refers to the government's regulation of maximum annual rent increases for rental

---

14   *Workplace Safety and Insurance Act, 1997*, SO 1997, c 16, Schedule A.

15   *Occupational Health and Safety Act*, RSO 1990, c O.1.

16   *Residential Tenancies Act, 2006*, SO 2006, c 17.

properties. A landlord can apply to increase the rent above the permitted rate where the increase can be justified on the basis of additional costs, such as renovation of the unit or an unusual increase in fuel or electricity costs. The landlord must submit the application to the Landlord and Tenant Board (LTB) and inform the tenant of the requested increase. The tenant is entitled to contest the increase at a hearing of the tribunal. A landlord is also required to give a tenant notice of any increase in rent at least 90 days before the proposed increase will take effect. If a landlord does not comply with the increase and notice requirements, and attempts to raise a tenant's rent above the guideline, the tenant can file an application with the LTB to have the rent reduced, or to have the increase limited to the maximum permitted by the guideline.

Quiet enjoyment refers to the right to occupy and use the rented premises free from unexpected intrusions by the landlord. In general, a landlord cannot enter the rented premises except at the tenant's request (for example, to make a repair) unless the landlord gives the tenant notice of entry, usually at least 24 hours in advance. This restriction may be suspended or altered in case of emergency, or where the tenant is planning to move out and is required to provide access for the purpose of showing the premises to prospective new tenants.

quiet enjoyment
the right to occupy and use rented premises free from unexpected intrusions by the landlord

The RTA governs maintenance of the property and the landlord's duty to keep the premises in good repair. Tenants are expected to facilitate maintenance by advising the landlord of problems and by giving the landlord reasonable access to the premises so that repairs may be made.

Because shelter is an essential need, the RTA limits the ability of landlords to evict tenants. Tenants are generally entitled to at least one month's notice of eviction, even if the tenant is not paying the rent or is otherwise in breach of the tenancy agreement. A tenant who comes home to find that the locks have been changed is almost always entitled to re-entry. If the landlord refuses, the tenant should call the police.

In certain circumstances, the RTA permits a landlord to evict a tenant with less than one month's notice. Examples of such conduct can include the following:

- conducting an illegal trade, business, or occupation on the premises, such as selling drugs
- wilfully or negligently causing damage to the premises, such as kicking holes in the wall
- interfering with the "reasonable enjoyment" of other tenants, such as hosting loud, late-night parties
- seriously impairing the safety of another person on the premises, such as allowing a vicious dog to roam the building
- allowing occupation of the unit by more people than are permitted by local by-laws

If the offending behaviour stops, the tenant may be allowed to stay.

Tenants are also required to provide notice of termination; the notice period varies according to the terms of the tenancy agreement. Generally, where a tenant has a 12-month lease, he or she must give notice at least 60 days in advance. If the tenant wants to move out before the expiry of the term, he or she still owes payment of rent for

sublet
to lease a property from the
first tenant to a new tenant,
who is called the subtenant

the remaining months of the lease. In this situation, the tenant may consider finding a new tenant to move in and **sublet**. Provided that the rent continues to be paid, the landlord may not unreasonably refuse to allow a subtenant to occupy the unit.

The Landlord and Tenant Board was created to resolve problems that arise between landlords and tenants. Both landlords and tenants have the right to apply to the LTB for relief, depending upon the circumstances. The most common relief sought by landlords is an eviction order. Tenants typically come before the board requesting an order that the landlord make repairs. Either party can apply to the LTB for an order with respect to rent. Proceedings at the LTB are relatively brief, and are designed to be simple enough to allow parties to represent themselves, without the presence of a lawyer. In order to assist clients who expect to appear before the LTB, a social service worker should become familiar with the board's procedures.

Non-Profit Housing

Finding affordable housing is often difficult for low-income people, particularly in cities, where the demand for modestly priced rental accommodation typically exceeds the supply. To address this problem, government subsidies are available to non-profit housing providers.

All three levels of government—federal, provincial/territorial, and municipal—contribute funds for non-profit housing, as do many community organizations and charitable donors. **Non-profit housing** providers encourage the building of affordable housing units and offer these units to people who cannot afford to pay market rents. In non-profit housing, sometimes called social housing or supportive housing, rent is typically paid by tenants on a geared-to-income scale. Most housing advocates agree that to be considered "affordable," housing costs should not exceed 30 percent of family or household income.

The administration of non-profit housing in Ontario is currently governed by the *Social Housing Reform Act, 2000* (SHRA) and regulations.[17] Relations between the tenants and the non-profit housing provider (the landlord) are governed by the RTA, except with respect to the amount of rent paid. The *Social Housing Reform Act, 2000* and regulations govern eligibility for public housing and provide that local service managers may make rules that apply to the projects and providers under their control. The Act requires a coordinated access system to fairly manage applications for non-profit housing. Potential tenants may also apply for a subsidy that allows them to pay rent-geared-to-income.

Currently, the supply of non-profit housing in Ontario falls far short of the demand. In 2015, the Ontario Non-Profit Housing Association reported that 171,360 Ontario households were waiting, on average, nearly four years for affordable housing.[18] While new units are under construction or in the planning stages, these will not come close to meeting existing and projected needs.

non-profit housing
providers encourage the
building of affordable
housing units and offer
these units to people
who cannot afford to
pay market rents

---

17 *Social Housing Reform Act, 2000*, SO 2000, c 27.

18 Laurie Monsebraaten, "Ontario's Affordable Housing Wait List Grows," *Toronto Star* (25 May 2016), online: <https://www.thestar.com/news/gta/2016/05/25/ontarios-affordable-housing-wait-list-grows.html>.

Access to Housing: Human Rights Issues

Since everyone needs shelter, human rights abuses in the context of access to housing have a particularly serious impact. As discussed earlier, federal and provincial or territorial human rights legislation prohibits discrimination on specified grounds. In Ontario, the prohibited grounds include sex, age, race, family status, and disability. Receipt of public assistance is an additional prohibited ground of discrimination specific to housing; landlords may not discriminate against tenants and prospective tenants because they are receiving public assistance.

Examples of discrimination that may be prohibited by Ontario's *Human Rights Code* include the following:

- refusing to rent to an unmarried couple
- asking for a higher amount of rent from a gay or lesbian couple
- refusing to rent to a disabled person because he or she was unable to fill out the application form
- refusing to rent to families with young children
- asking for a deposit greater than the last month's rent because the prospective tenant is receiving public assistance

An exception is made permitting restricted access to a housing program aimed specifically at helping people of a particular disadvantaged group, such as mentally ill single men or teenaged parents. This kind of "reverse discrimination" is permitted because such programs are designed to relieve hardship for people who may otherwise face obstacles in finding the housing they need.

While many human rights abuses can arise in the housing context, three issues are of particular interest, being the subject of important court decisions. These involve refusal of housing on the basis of rent-to-income ratios, on the basis of youth, and on the basis of an "adults only" rental policy. Each of these forms of discrimination is discussed below.

RENT-TO-INCOME RATIOS

In the past, it was not uncommon for private landlords in Ontario to require prospective tenants to provide information about their income so that the landlord could assess the risk that a particular applicant might be unable to pay the rent. The landlord applied what is known as a rent-to-income ratio to decide whether the applicant could afford the apartment. Typically, the rule was that rent could not exceed 30 percent of income.

In the 1990s, this practice was challenged before an Ontario human rights board of inquiry. In *Kearney v Bramalea Ltd*, a landlord refused to rent apartments to three low-income applicants on the basis that the rent amounted to more than 30 percent of their income.[19] The complainants were represented by a lawyer who took the case

---

19   *Kearney v Bramalea Ltd*, [2001] OJ No 297 (Div Ct).

on a pro bono basis. The issue in the case was of wider public interest because the use of rent-to-income ratios can leave people homeless and forced to live in shelters even though they are able and willing to pay rent. Often the people who are put in this position are those with modest incomes and heavy financial responsibilities, such as young single parents and recent immigrants.

The board of inquiry found that the use of rent-to-income ratios is a discriminatory practice, and that the evidence (including a 1999 research report prepared for the Ontario Human Rights Commission) showed that low-income tenants are no more likely to default on the rent than other tenants.

The board of inquiry also found that while it is acceptable for a landlord to request references from previous landlords and to conduct a credit check, it is not acceptable to refuse to rent to an applicant who has no references and no credit history (as opposed to bad references and/or a bad credit history). Again, young people, newly separated single parents, and new immigrants often cannot provide such information, and denying them access to housing on this basis constitutes indirect discrimination.

YOUNG PEOPLE

Landlords are often hesitant to rent apartments to young people in their teens and early twenties, because of a common perception that they will likely default on the rent or be otherwise irresponsible. However, the law is clear that anybody aged 18 and over may rent an apartment, and teens aged 16 and 17 who have legally withdrawn from parental care and control can rent and can sign the lease in their own right. A landlord is not entitled to require that a parent sign the lease or accept responsibility under the lease on behalf of a young person.

"ADULTS ONLY" BUILDINGS

A landlord may legally designate a building exclusively for people aged 65 and over. However, apart from this "seniors exception," it is discriminatory and illegal to designate a rental apartment as "adults only," or to refuse to rent to someone on the basis that he or she has children. It is also discriminatory to refuse to rent a unit on the basis of the number of intended occupants unless to do otherwise would violate a local overcrowding by-law.

Responding to Housing-Related Human Rights Issues

If the social service worker uncovers evidence of discrimination, as a first step it may be appropriate for the client to go back to the landlord and try to resolve the problem informally. If the client is able to arrange a personal interview with the landlord, the social service worker might offer to accompany the client. Sometimes it is enough to make the landlord aware of the client's legal rights.

If informal attempts to resolve the problem don't help, the social service worker can refer the client to an advocacy agency for tenants.

Despite the protections provided by human rights law, social service workers have many clients who encounter persistent obstacles in their search for accommodation. Helping these "hard-to-house" clients often involves advocacy, as well as practical assistance such as providing information about housing options and referrals to appropriate agencies.

When seeking housing for clients, social service workers must strike a balance between the ideal and the practical. While it is not possible to take every difficult landlord to court, discrimination in housing will continue to flourish unless somebody speaks up. Clients who are motivated to stand up for their rights should be directed to legal aid and provided with appropriate support by social service workers.

Ultimately, a tenant who has grounds for a formal complaint may bring the case to the attention of the Ontario Human Rights Commission. A social service worker may provide assistance with a referral to a lawyer, if required, and may also provide support during the hearing process.

KEY TERMS

adverse-effect discrimination, 30
bona fide job qualifications, 35
direct discrimination, 30
harassment, 31
non-profit housing, 38
prohibited grounds, 34
quiet enjoyment, 37
rent control, 36
reprisals, 33
sexual harassment, 32
sublet, 38
systemic discrimination, 30

SUGGESTED SOURCES

Canadian Human Rights Commission,
    <http://www.chrc-ccdp.gc.ca>
Ontario Human Rights Commission,
    <http://www.ohrc.on.ca>
Ministry of Labour, <https://www.labour.gov.on.ca>
Landlord and Tenant Board,
    <http://www.sjto.gov.on.ca/ltb>

REVIEW QUESTIONS

1. Why are the laws governing human rights of interest to social service workers?

2. Explain what is meant by indirect or adverse-effect discrimination.

3. What is the "bona fide job qualification" in the employment context?

4. What is rent control, and why is it important?

5. How can a social service worker assist a client who says she is having trouble finding housing because the landlords she has approached are discriminating against her?

Consent and Capacity and Issues Related to Health Care and the Elderly

4

LEARNING OUTCOMES

After reading this chapter, you should be able to:

- Outline the types of consent and when consent is deemed to be valid.

- Describe the role of substitute decision makers and power of attorney in representing an incapable patient.

- Understand some of the laws that are related to consent and capacity, including the *Health Care Consent Act* and the *Substitute Decisions Act*.

- Explain the concepts of assisted dying and euthanasia.

- Understand some of the issues related to health care and the elderly.

Introduction

The Supreme Court of Canada has stated that

> ... every patient has a right to bodily integrity. This encompasses the right to determine what medical procedures will be accepted and the extent to which they will be accepted. Everyone has the right to decide what is to be done with one's own body.[1]

Relevant Laws

The relevant legislation related to consent and capacity issues in Ontario include the following:

- *Health Care Consent Act, 1996* (HCCA)[2]
- *Substitute Decisions Act, 1992* (SDA)[3]
- *Personal Health Information Protection Act, 2004* (PHIPA)[4]

The *Health Care Consent Act* and the *Substitute Decisions Act* fill in the details of consent to treatment issues and what happens when a patient is deemed unable to consent to or guide his or her own care. The Consent and Capacity Board may appoint a representative to act as a substitute decision maker for patients who are incapable of consenting to treatment.

Types of Consent

express consent
consent that can be obtained in writing or orally

implied consent
consent that can be given by a person's actions or inactions

Consent can be obtained by express form and by implied form. **Express consent** can be obtained in writing or orally. An example of express consent would be signing a written consent form for a specific surgical procedure. **Implied consent** is given by a person's actions or inactions—for example, rolling up your sleeve and putting out your arm for a blood sample.[5]

When Consent Is Deemed to Be Valid

Under the *Health Care Consent Act* (HCCA), before a treatment is administered and before a person is admitted to hospital for treatment or to a care facility for care, a health practitioner must determine whether the patient is capable of giving or refusing consent to the treatment or admission.

A person is capable if he or she is able to understand the information required for making a treatment or admission decision and able to understand the consequences

---

1 *Ciarlariello v Schacter*, [1993] 2 SCR 119 at 135.

2 *Health Care Consent Act, 1996*, SO 1996, c 2, Schedule A.

3 *Substitute Decisions Act, 1992*, SO 1992, c 30.

4 *Personal Health Information Protection Act, 2004*, SO 2004, c 3, Schedule A.

5 Edward Etchells, Gilbert Sharpe, Phil Walsh, John R Williams & Peter A Singer, "BioEthics for Clinicians: 1. Consent" (1996) 155:2 CMAJ 177.

of the decision (s 4(1) of the HCCA). Patients should be presumed to be capable unless there is evidence to the contrary. This evidence will vary from case to case. In some cases, a person may appear unable to understand a treatment that is being proposed—for example, by refusing to listen to information or asking questions that suggest a lack of comprehension. In other cases, a person may express wishes that are clearly irrational, such as refusing a treatment that has a high success rate, few risks, and few side effects.

Capacity must be specific to a particular treatment and to a specific time frame. A person can consent to a particular treatment at one time but not to the same procedure at another time. As well, consent must be obtained prior to the treatment. Once consent is given it can be withdrawn.[6]

Consent must be informed with the benefits and risks of the treatment outlined by the practitioner. All material risks must be outlined.[7]

Consent must be voluntary. There can be no coercion or undue influence.

Any treatment provided without consent may result in criminal charges of assault or civil action. No intent of harm is necessary.

The courts have ruled that in an emergency situation where the patient is not capable of consenting, it is the surgeon's duty to act in order to save the life of the patient. It is important that the procedure was in fact an emergency and that waiting for consent was not an option.[8]

When determining whether consent is valid, the issue of age is relevant. When providing medical treatment to a minor, health care providers are guided by provincial or territorial legislation and case law. Ontario uses a capacity-based model and looks to whether the minor is capable of understanding and appreciating the nature and consequences of the treatment. Practitioners will look to the maturity level of the minor and focus on the intellectual and emotional level of the minor to understand the risk and benefits of the procedure. The views of the mature minor will be considered but not necessarily followed in all instances.[9] Child welfare legislation as it relates to children in need of protection can at times conflict with the wishes of the mature minor. The courts will consider factors such as the seriousness of the treatment and procedure, the age of the minor, the level of maturity of the minor, and other issues when deciding on the issue of consent.[10]

Social service workers often find themselves in situations where they are working with both the child and the family. Social service workers must determine the child's capacity to consent to a procedure. In situations where the child does not have the legal capacity to consent, it is common to obtain the child's agreement, verbally or in writing. In this way, although not legally binding, the child's views are heard, respected, and documented.

capacity
the ability to understand the information required for making a decision regarding treatment or admission to a facility, and to understand the consequences of the decision

---

6   Lorne E Rozovsky, *The Canadian Law of Consent to Treatment*, 3rd ed (Toronto: Butterworths, 2003).

7   *Reibl v Hughes*, [1980] 2 SCR 880.

8   *Marshall v Curry*, 1933 CanLII 324 (NSSC).

9   Lucinda Ferguson, *The End of Age: Beyond Age Restrictions for Minors' Medical Treatment Decisions* (Ottawa: Law Commissions of Canada, 2004).

10   *AC v Manitoba (Director of Child and Family Services)*, 2009 SCC 30, [2009] 2 SCR 181.

Advance Directives

Advance directives are directives regarding a person's wishes for care should that person at some point be incapable of consenting. An advance directive can include the person's wishes as they relate to whether specific treatments should or should not be administered. Advance directives become operable only when a person is deemed incapable of granting consent.

If the health practitioner believes the patient to be incapable, and there is no advance directive, the practitioner must obtain consent for the treatment from someone who is authorized to provide it on the patient's behalf. Section 20 of the HCCA lists the people able to consent on behalf of an incapable patient:

- a guardian of the person, if the guardian has authority to consent to treatment
- an attorney for personal care, if the power of attorney confers authority to consent to treatment
- a representative appointed by the Consent and Capacity Board under section 33 of the HCCA, if the representative has authority to give consent to treatment
- the person's spouse or partner (but not if separated)
- an adult child (aged 18 or over) or parent of the person, or a children's aid society or other person who is lawfully entitled to give consent to treatment in the place of the parent (but not a parent who has only a right of access)
- a parent who has only a right of access
- a brother or sister
- any other relative

When seeking consent to treat a patient, the health professional must work his or her way down this list, in the sequence shown, to determine who is authorized to act on the patient's behalf. This process is facilitated if the patient, or a person accompanying the patient (such as a social service worker), can identify the person who has authority to give consent and can provide the necessary contact information.

A person who consents on behalf of an incapable person must do so in accordance with that person's best interests, and after receiving full information about the treatment.

A social service worker with a client who suffers from a mental disorder (or other serious illness) should address the subject of treatment decisions at a time when the client is mentally capable. This is important because a person who is incapable cannot execute a valid power of attorney. Once a person is incapable of consenting to treatment, it is also too late to appoint an attorney. Therefore, it is essential to plan ahead and anticipate the client's future needs.

Where a health professional has reasonable grounds to believe that a patient, when capable, expressed a wish to refuse a certain treatment, the health practitioner cannot give the treatment later if the person becomes incapable (s 26 of the HCCA). For example, if there is a notation in a chronically ill patient's medical records that the patient, when capable (and over the age of 16), mentioned that he or she did not want to receive a particular treatment, that wish must be respected.

If a patient disagrees with the health practitioner's finding that he or she is incapable of giving consent, the patient can apply for a review of that finding. This application is made to the Consent and Capacity Board.

Application to the Consent and Capacity Board

The Consent and Capacity Board is an independent tribunal created under the HCCA. It conducts hearings of issues arising under the *Mental Health Act*, the *Health Care Consent Act*, the *Substitute Decisions Act*, and the *Personal Health Information Protection Act*.[11] Board members include psychiatrists, lawyers, and laypeople appointed by the lieutenant governor in council. To avoid bias, members who are employees of a hospital may not participate in decisions relating to that hospital. Decisions may be made by a single member or by panels of three or five members.

The HCCA and the board's rules of practice contemplate (but do not require) that parties appearing before the board will be represented by a lawyer. The board has the power under section 81 of the HCCA to arrange for legal representation for a party, or to serve notice of the hearing on the children's lawyer in the case of a patient under the age of 16. The social service worker should strongly encourage the client to retain a lawyer or, if this is difficult, to ask the board for help in arranging for legal representation.

If the review is urgent, the social service worker may need to assist the client in preparing application documents before a lawyer's services can be secured. If at all possible, a lawyer should review the application before it is delivered to the board. However, if this is impossible, the board will assist the patient in correcting any deficiencies in the application.

Once the board has received a patient's application for a review, it must hold a hearing within seven days and issue its decision within one day of the hearing. If the patient has applied for a review of a finding of incapacity, treatment cannot proceed until the board has completed its review, except in the case of an emergency.

A patient who disagrees with the results of a review can appeal the result to Ontario's Superior Court of Justice. The patient will need expert legal assistance to do this. A social service worker can help by providing contact information for a legal aid office or lawyer referral service.

A patient who has been found incapable by a health practitioner and is willing to accept that finding can request that the board appoint someone to be his or her representative for the purpose of consenting to or refusing treatment. Alternatively, a person can apply to be the representative of the patient. In practice, there is not much difference, because at this stage it is likely that another person will already be involved, at least informally, in the patient's care. The board's involvement in appointing a substitute decision maker helps to ensure that the patient's wishes and best interests are taken into account in the choice of a representative.

---

11 *Mental Health Act*, RSO 1990, c M.7.

Substitute Decision Making

When a person suffering from a serious physical or mental illness seems unable to manage his or her care competently, or to make reasonable care decisions, health care providers are required to obtain consent for that patient's treatment or admission to care from another person who has the power to speak on his or her behalf. The general term used for this representative is **substitute decision maker**.

substitute decision maker
a person who makes decisions about legal, financial, or health matters on behalf of a person who is incapable of making these decisions

Substitute decision makers can step forward or be chosen in a variety of ways, including informal selection of a relative at the health care facility, appointment by a government tribunal (the Consent and Capacity Board) under the HCCA, appointment by power of attorney, and appointment of a guardian under the SDA.

Power of Attorney

In the context of substitute decision making, **attorney** means a representative formally appointed by a person to make decisions on his or her behalf. The attorney need not be, and usually is not, a lawyer. Usually, a friend or relative is appointed.

attorney
a representative who is formally appointed by a person to make decisions on his or her behalf

There are two kinds of attorneys. One, an attorney for property, makes decisions regarding property, such as bank accounts, real estate, and investments. The other, an attorney for personal care, makes decisions regarding personal care, such as health-care and treatment decisions. One person may be appointed for both purposes, a different person may be appointed for each, and sometimes two people share the decision-making.

The main advantage of appointing an attorney, rather than choosing a different form of representation, is that the individual's preferences are more fully taken into account:

- The person chooses the representative.
- The person can communicate in advance his or her actual wishes to the representative.

Appointment of an attorney requires advance planning; however, people in the early stages of an illness that may lead to incapacity can often benefit greatly by choosing a trusted person to act as attorney, formalizing the relationship while they still can.

The first step in appointing an attorney is to obtain the consent of the person chosen to act as substitute decision maker. Then the person making the appointment ("the grantor") must prepare a legal document, usually with a lawyer's help, and sign it in the presence of two witnesses. The legal document—the power of attorney—will describe the extent of the powers granted to the attorney to act on the grantor's behalf. The grantor can give the attorney some powers and specifically exclude others. The grantor can also include a provision that requires a second person to confirm that he or she is incapable before the attorney takes over decision-making authority, or another provision naming a second person (an "alternate") in case the attorney cannot act for the grantor at some future time. Again, the grantor must first obtain the alternate's consent. Once the power of attorney has been signed, the grantor can communicate his or her specific wishes to the attorney, either in writing or orally. The grantor and the attorney should each keep a copy of the power of attorney. The original should be kept by the lawyer or in some other secure place.

Social service workers can explain the advantages of a power of attorney to their clients and can assist clients in finding a lawyer to complete the necessary documents. Social service workers who work with mentally ill clients should ask for and keep on file the contact information of the client's attorney(s) for property and/or personal care. A social service worker may occasionally be asked to serve as a client's attorney for personal care. However, section 46(3)(b) of the *Substitute Decisions Act* prohibits this in most circumstances.

The *Substitute Decisions Act* provides a process for appointing powers of attorney over personal care and property and for court-ordered guardianship.

Guardians

The law that governs substitute decision making, including power of attorney, is codified in the SDA. It covers such issues as the following:

- how legal incapacity is determined
- how to confer, continue, or revoke a power of attorney
- how an attorney can resign from the role
- how an attorney's actions can be challenged, or how to remove the person from the role
- how a guardian of property and/or a guardian of the person can be chosen for a person who has no attorney in place to carry out these roles

The SDA stipulates that where a person who has no attorney is found incapable of managing his or her property, or of making decisions with respect to his or her own care and treatment, the public guardian and trustee (PGT) becomes his or her guardian of property or guardian of the person, as the case may be.

The Office of the Public Guardian and Trustee is part of the Family Justice Services Division of Ontario's Ministry of the Attorney General. The PGT has various responsibilities, including protecting mentally incapable people. Section 62 of the SDA allows the PGT to apply for an order designating itself as temporary guardian of the person where a person's inability to handle his or her personal care threatens to cause "serious adverse effects." A guardianship ordered under this section lasts a maximum of 90 days.

Guardianship by the PGT is often used as a stop-gap measure to address a crisis, until a family member or trusted friend can be appointed. The PGT cannot offer truly personalized and responsive representation to every Ontarian who needs it.

Section 55 of the SDA provides that a court can appoint a person to be an incapable person's attorney for personal care. The court will not make such an appointment if it believes that there is an alternative method to handle personal-care decision-making that is "less restrictive of the person's decision-making rights." A typical less-restrictive method would be for a caregiver to obtain consent to care or treatment from a family member under section 20 of the HCCA (as discussed above), without having a formal guardian appointed.

An order appointing a guardian of the person includes, as part of its application, a finding that the person is incapable of consent or refusal of treatment and of managing his or her own care.

Section 59 of the SDA sets out the powers of a guardian of a person who has full rights of guardianship. These include the right, on behalf of the incapable person, to make decisions in relation to the following matters:

- living arrangements
- litigation
- disclosure of medical records
- decisions under the HCCA, including consent to treatment, personal care, and moving into a care facility
- health care, nutrition, and hygiene
- employment, education, training, clothing, and recreation
- any social services provided to the person

A guardian can be given partial guardianship for certain things and not others, if the court determines that the person is incapable only with respect to certain aspects of his or her own care.

Social service workers are generally ineligible to be appointed as a guardian of the person for a client, according to section 57 of the SDA. This is similar to the restriction against choosing a social service worker to act as power of attorney for personal care.

Besides caring for clients with a mental illness, social service workers may find themselves in the position of supporting clients who have family members in need of guardianship. In cases like these, the social service worker can (1) provide basic information about the substitute decision making options available (power of attorney; applying for guardianship under the SDA), (2) refer the client to the Ministry of the Attorney General as a source of information about these issues, and (3) assist the client in finding a lawyer. Specific advice on decisions relating to guardianship and power of attorney should be provided by a lawyer.

Issues Related to Health Care and the Elderly

With the baby boomer generation moving into its senior years, and a low provincial birthrate, Ontario's population is steadily aging. This trend has important implications for health care and social services in Ontario. The elderly population has widely varying needs, depending upon particular circumstances, including general health, disabilities, financial situation, housing, and support network (family and friends). In recognition of this diversity of needs, Ontario has developed a complex framework of community health support and residential care options available to seniors. A Community Care Access Centre (CCAC) is the first point of contact for many seniors to assess the services available and formulate a plan for care.

Care in the Community

Seniors and disabled adults who are in good general health and who can manage most daily activities without assistance usually prefer to remain in their own home. For these individuals, four different kinds of in-home care are available through a CCAC: visiting health professional services, personal care and support, homemaking, and community support services (collectively referred to as "home and community support services"). Which of these services are appropriate for a particular client is determined by a CCAC assessment. Each type of in-home care is described briefly below.

The agencies that deliver home and community support services often employ social service workers.

Visiting Health Professional Services

Professionals such as nurses, physiotherapists, occupational therapists, and social service workers may provide health care and support in a client's home. Services include assessing needs, planning, providing care, and teaching clients how to manage their health condition. Services may be provided temporarily (for example, during recovery from surgery) or on an ongoing basis.

Personal Care and Support

Personal care and support workers may offer assistance with everyday activities such as eating, bathing, dressing, and using the toilet. They may also assist with escorting clients to health care appointments.

Homemaking

Homemaking services may assist with routine household activities and chores such as shopping, preparing meals, laundry, cleaning, and banking.

Community Support Services

Community support services are many and varied. They include meal delivery, transportation, caregiver relief, adult day programs, social and recreational services, and safety and security checks. Providers may be either non-profit organizations or for-profit businesses. A few of the many community support services available are described below.

- *Safety and security checks.* Security checks may involve regular check-in phone calls or visits by a volunteer to ensure that the client is not in distress. Some for-profit businesses also offer emergency response system technologies, which include in-home monitoring devices and transmitters worn by the client.

- *Transportation.* Many communities provide assisted transportation through various organizations such as Wheel-Trans (in Toronto), service clubs, and religious organizations.

- *Meal services.* Meal services may deliver a meal per day for a few days or every day of the week, depending on need and availability. There are also organizations that provide transportation to a dining facility, where a meal is served to many clients.
- *Caregiver respite and counselling.* Caregiver respite provides a break to the regular caregiver (often a family member) by providing either a replacement person for a brief period, or an activity outside the home to occupy the client. Caregiver counselling attends to the social and emotional needs of caregivers. Caregiver services are important to encourage family members to take on what can be a crushing responsibility, and to reduce the risk of elder abuse by caregivers who become unable to cope.

Residential Care

Many seniors eventually move from their own home into some form of accommodation where support services are offered. The kinds of specialized housing available to seniors vary enormously (see Table 4.1). The choices include government-sponsored housing, private housing paid for by the residents, and resident-ownership housing. There are also different levels of care. At one end of the spectrum, there is apartment-style housing where residents occupy self-contained units and handle much of their own care, while living in a community of seniors with benefits such as recreational activities. At the opposite end of the spectrum are long-term care facilities, which accommodate residents in private or shared rooms or wards, and provide different levels of nursing and personal care, depending on individual needs. These facilities often provide recreational activities and special events for residents as well.

Retirement Homes

Retirement homes or "communities" provide rental accommodation for seniors. They are owned by private landlords with no government funding of accommodation or on-site services. Prospective residents apply directly to the landlord without prior consultation with or referral from a CCAC.

Because they don't receive provincial funding, retirement homes are not regulated by the Ministry of Health and Long-Term Care, though some municipalities have passed by-laws establishing standards of care for these residences. Some aspects of their operations, such as food-service standards and occupational health and safety, may also be subject to inspection and regulation by the province or municipality. In addition, membership in the Ontario Retirement Communities Association (ORCA) requires ongoing compliance with ORCA standards for retirement home operations and services.

Landlord–tenant issues are governed by the *Residential Tenancies Act, 2006.*[12]

---

12 *Residential Tenancies Act, 2006*, SO 2006, c 17.

TABLE 4.1 Residential Care for Ontario Seniors

Type of Residence	Ownership	CCAC Referral/ Assessment	Level of Care	Governing Statute
Retirement home	Private for profit	No	Low to moderate	*Residential Tenancies Act, 2006*
Life lease housing	Owned by non-profit corporation	No	Low or none	*Condominium Act, 1998*
Supportive housing	Private for profit or non-profit	Yes	Low to moderate	*Residential Tenancies Act, 2006* *Home Care and Community Services Act, 1994*
Nursing homes	Private for profit or non-profit	Yes	Moderate to heavy	*Long-Term Care Homes Act, 2007*
Home for the aged and rest homes	Non-profit	Yes	Moderate to heavy	*Long-Term Care Homes Act, 2007*
Charitable institutions	Non-profit	Yes	Moderate to heavy	*Long-Term Care Homes Act, 2007*

Life Lease Housing

Life lease housing is similar, in many respects, to a condominium. The residential units are apartments, with fees similar to condo fees. The complex is owned by a non-profit corporation; no government funding is provided. Residents purchase from the non-profit corporation the exclusive right to occupy a particular suite and to use the common facilities. When the resident moves out, he or she receives market value for the apartment.

Many of these projects offer light support services, such as housekeeping, hair care, and personal care, for which residents pay a user fee.

These facilities fall within the *Condominium Act, 1998*.[13] They are not subject to ministry inspection or regulation.

Supportive Housing

Supportive-housing facilities provide rental accommodation and limited on-site or in-home support services. Residents must be assessed and referred by a CCAC.

These facilities are generally owned and operated by municipal governments or other non-profit organizations, such as religious or cultural groups, service clubs, and seniors' organizations. While they may receive some government funding, they are not fully regulated by the ministry. The form of accommodation, on-site services, costs, and the availability of government subsidies vary, and the particulars are set out in a contract between the service provider and the tenant.

Supportive housing is sometimes located on the same property as a long-term care (LTC) home, to give residents access to additional services, such as personal care,

---

13 *Condominium Act, 1998*, SO 1998, c 19.

daily visits, meals, and assisted transportation. Residents may also apply for visiting health professional services through the local CCAC.

Providers and residents of supportive housing facilities are subject to the *Residential Tenancies Act, 2006* and the *Home Care and Community Services Act, 1994.*[14] Where the service portion is funded by the ministry, inspection and regulation are governed by the *Long-Term Care Act, 1994.*[15]

Long-Term Care Homes

People seeking admission to long-term care (LTC) must apply through a local CCAC. Following assessment and confirmation of eligibility, the CCAC will make a referral on behalf of the applicant to one or more facilities of his or her choice. Often the applicant's name is placed on a waiting list until the requested accommodation becomes available.

All LTC homes receive government funding through the ministry. Because of the vulnerability of individuals who require long-term care, and the complexity of the services provided to them, these residential care facilities are the most closely regulated by the government. Classified by service provider, there are three kinds of LTC homes, each governed by a different provincial statute:

- Nursing homes can be non-profit or for-profit, and are usually owned by private corporations.
- Homes for the aged are required to be established by each municipality, are run by the municipality, and are always non-profit.
- Charitable institutions are usually owned by charitable organizations and are always non-profit.

The ministry is responsible for regulating all LTC homes. Regulation includes the following:

- defining eligibility (who can access each level of care)
- managing wait lists
- setting standards for all aspects of residence operations and delivery of care
- ensuring the promotion and protection of residents' rights
- conducting inspections, including the imposition of sanctions for unmet standards

The *Long-Term Care Homes Act, 2007*[16] was proclaimed in 2010 and replaced the *Nursing Homes Act*, the *Homes for the Aged and Rest Homes Act*, and the *Charitable Institutions Act*. It sets standards to protect the rights of residents and ensure that their health care needs are met.

---

14 *Home Care and Community Services Act, 1994*, SO 1994, c. 26

15 *Long-Term Care Act, 1994*, SO 1994, c 26.

16 *Long-Term Care Homes Act, 2007*, SO 2007, c 8

In regulating LTC homes, the ministry refers to the statutes cited above and the regulations made under those statutes, and to general health policy guidelines. A detailed description of the legislation and regulations is well beyond the scope of this book; however, social service workers who work in an LTC home will need to be familiar with the applicable standards.

The *Long-Term Care Homes Act, 2007* governs all three kinds of LTC homes (nursing homes, homes for the aged, and charitable institutions).

Some LTC homes are accredited by the Accreditation Canada. Accreditation Canada accredits facilities that meet and maintain its standards for care. The government encourages LTC homes to become accredited by providing extra funding for accredited homes.

INSPECTIONS

All LTC homes are inspected by ministry-appointed inspectors at least annually, to determine whether they are in compliance with relevant legislation and standards. Inspectors issue a finding of "unmet" when they determine that a standard is not being met, and a "citation" when the LTC is found not to be in compliance with legislation. Inspection findings must be posted in a public area on the premises for viewing by residents and family.

LTC homes subject to a citation must respond with a plan of corrective action, which is filed with the ministry. The ministry then monitors whether the plan is being carried out. If no plan is filed or the changes are not made within a specified period of time, the ministry can impose sanctions. Available sanctions vary depending on the circumstances and the type of home, but in general, they can include suspending the home's right to accept new patients. In certain serious cases, the ministry can take over the operation of the home.

The ministry also plays a role in investigating complaints by residents or their family members. Every LTC home operator must have an internal complaints review process posted in the home where it can be easily seen by residents and visitors.

The *Long-Term Care Home Act* includes a Residents' Bill of Rights, which ensures that residents of homes are fully respected and promoted (see Table 4.2).

TABLE 4.2   Residents' Bill of Rights

Every licensee of a long-term care home shall ensure that the following rights of residents are fully respected and promoted:
1. Every resident has the right to be treated with courtesy and respect and in a way that fully recognizes the resident's individuality and respects the resident's dignity.
2. Every resident has the right to be protected from abuse.
3. Every resident has the right not to be neglected by the licensee or staff.
4. Every resident has the right to be properly sheltered, fed, clothed, groomed and cared for in a manner consistent with his or her needs.
5. Every resident has the right to live in a safe and clean environment.
6. Every resident has the right to exercise the rights of a citizen.
7. Every resident has the right to be told who is responsible for and who is providing the resident's direct care.

Every licensee of a long-term care home shall ensure that the following rights of residents are fully respected and promoted:
8. Every resident has the right to be afforded privacy in treatment and in caring for his or her personal needs.
9. Every resident has the right to have his or her participation in decision-making respected.
10. Every resident has the right to keep and display personal possessions, pictures and furnishings in his or her room subject to safety requirements and the rights of other residents.
11. Every resident has the right to, i) participate fully in the development, implementation, review and revision of his or her plan of care, ii) give or refuse consent to any treatment, care or services for which his or her consent is required by law and to be informed of the consequences of giving or refusing consent, iii) participate fully in making any decision concerning any aspect of his or her care, including any decision concerning his or her admission, discharge or transfer to or from a long-term care home or a secure unit and to obtain an independent opinion with regard to any of those matters, and iv) have his or her personal health information within the meaning of the *Personal Health Information Protection Act, 2004* kept confidential in accordance with that Act, and to have access to his or her records of personal health information, including his or her plan of care, in accordance with that Act.
12. Every resident has the right to receive care and assistance towards independence based on a restorative care philosophy to maximize independence to the greatest extent possible.
13. Every resident has the right not to be restrained, except in the limited circumstances provided for under this Act and subject to the requirements provided for under this Act.
14. Every resident has the right to communicate in confidence, receive visitors of his or her choice and consult in private with any person without interference.
15. Every resident who is dying or who is very ill has the right to have family and friends present 24 hours per day.
16. Every resident has the right to designate a person to receive information concerning any transfer or any hospitalization of the resident and to have that person receive that information immediately.
17. Every resident has the right to raise concerns or recommend changes in policies and services on behalf of himself or herself or others to the following persons and organizations without interference and without fear of coercion, discrimination or reprisal, whether directed at the resident or anyone else, i) the Residents' Council, ii) the Family Council, iii) the licensee, and, if the licensee is a corporation, the directors and officers of the corporation, and, in the case of a home approved under Part VIII, a member of the committee of management for the home under section 132 or of the board of management for the home under section 125 or 129, iv) staff members, v) government officials, vi) any other person inside or outside the long-term care home.
18. Every resident has the right to form friendships and relationships and to participate in the life of the long-term care home.
19. Every resident has the right to have his or her lifestyle and choices respected.
20. Every resident has the right to participate in the Residents' Council.
21. Every resident has the right to meet privately with his or her spouse or another person in a room that assures privacy.

Every licensee of a long-term care home shall ensure that the following rights of residents are fully respected and promoted:
22.   Every resident has the right to share a room with another resident according to their mutual wishes, if appropriate accommodation is available.
23.   Every resident has the right to pursue social, cultural, religious, spiritual and other interests, to develop his or her potential and to be given reasonable assistance by the licensee to pursue these interests and to develop his or her potential.
24.   Every resident has the right to be informed in writing of any law, rule or policy affecting services provided to the resident and of the procedures for initiating complaints.
25.   Every resident has the right to manage his or her own financial affairs unless the resident lacks the legal capacity to do so.
26.   Every resident has the right to be given access to protected outdoor areas in order to enjoy outdoor activity unless the physical setting makes this impossible.
27.   Every resident has the right to have any friend, family member, or other person of importance to the resident attend any meeting with the licensee or the staff of the home.

Source: *Long-Term Care Home Act, 2007*, SO 2007, c 8, s 3(1).

End-of-Life Decisions

Mentally competent people in Canada can refuse treatment. Health care professionals must respect competent adults voluntarily making decisions to refuse or to continue life-sustaining treatment. The courts have held that a person can refuse treatment and that the physician would not be assisting suicide if the removal of treatment resulted in a natural death.[17] Doctors must also act according to the patient's wishes if under an advance directive. Do not resuscitate (DNR) orders are common directives that direct medical staff not to resuscitate a person if the patient's heartbeat and breathing have stopped. In cases where the patient is not able to provide consent and there is not an advance directive, the medical practitioner will look to a substitute decision maker for consent to withdraw or withhold life support. The practitioner must feel that the decision being made is in the best interests of the patient, and can appeal before the Consent and Capacity Board or the courts.

Euthanasia

Euthanasia is a "deliberate act undertaken by one person with the intention of ending the life of another person to relieve that person's suffering where that act is the cause of death."[18] Euthanasia is a *Criminal Code* offence (s 14). Consent or mercy does not provide a defence to the charge of murder. The case involving Robert Latimer dealt with the euthanasia issue. Latimer's daughter suffered from cerebral palsy. In order to relieve his daughter's physical and mental suffering, Latimer asphyxiated his

euthanasia
a deliberate act undertaken with the intention of ending the life of another person to relieve the suffering of that person

---

17   *Nancy B v Hotel-Dieu de Quebec*, 1992 CanLII 8511 (QCCS).

18   Senate of Canada, Special Senate Committee on Euthanasia and Assisted Suicide, *Of Life and Death—Final Report* (June 1995), at chap VIII, online: <https://sencanada.ca/content/sen/committee/351/euth/rep/lad-e.htm#viii>.

daughter. In 2001 the Supreme Court of Canada unanimously upheld the conviction of second-degree murder stating that his motive to put his daughter out of her pain was not relevant.[19] Although the Latimer case resulted in a murder conviction, most Canadian mercy-killing cases are resolved through a plea bargain with the Crown accepting a lesser charge and reduced sentence.

Assisted Dying

The law pertaining to physician-assisted dying has recently changed in Canada. Section 241(b) of the *Criminal Code* stated that everyone who aids or abets a person in committing suicide commits an indictable offence, and section 14 said that no person may consent to death being inflicted on them. Together, these provisions prohibited the provision of assistance-in-dying in Canada. In 2015 the Supreme Court of Canada looked at whether the prohibition against physician-assisted dying violated the section 7 Charter rights of competent adults who are suffering intolerably as a result of a grievous and irremediable medical condition. The SCC allowed the appeal and ruled that section 241(b) and section 14 of the *Criminal Code* unjustifiably infringe section 7 of the Charter, and are of no force or effect to the extent that "they prohibit physician-assisted death for a competent adult person who (1) clearly consents to the termination of life; and (2) has a grievous and irremediable medical condition (including an illness, disease, or disability) that causes enduring suffering that is intolerable to the individual in the circumstances of his or her condition."[20] The declaration of invalidity was suspended for 12 months.[21]

In June 2016 the federal government in Canada enacted a new law creating the framework for medically assisted dying. Under the new law, medically assisted dying is legal if certain conditions and safeguards are in place. Some of these provisions include the following:

- Persons are at least 18 years of age and capable of making decisions with respect to their health.
- They have a grievous and irremediable medical condition.
- They have made a voluntary request for medical assistance in dying that, in particular, was not made as a result of external pressure.
- They give informed consent to receive medical assistance in dying after having been informed of the means that are available to relieve their suffering, including palliative care.[22]

---

19   *R v Latimer*, 2001 SCC 1, [2001] 1 SCR 3.

20   *Carter v Canada (Attorney General)*, 2015 SCC 5, [2015] 1 SCR 331 at para 127.

21   *Ibid* at para 128.

22   *Criminal Code*, RSC 1985, c C-46, at s 241.2(1).

The *Criminal Code* section continues to describe that persons have a grievous and irremediable medical condition only if they meet all of the following criteria:

- They have a serious and incurable illness, disease, or disability.
- They are in an advanced state of irreversible decline in capability.
- The illness, disease, or disability or that state of decline causes them enduring physical or psychological suffering that is intolerable to them and that cannot be relieved under conditions that they consider acceptable.
- Their natural death has become reasonably foreseeable, taking into account all of their medical circumstances, without a prognosis necessarily having been made as to the specific length of time that they have remaining.[23]

Additional safeguards include written requests involving two independent witnesses along with a second medical practitioner's approval and a mandatory reflection period of at least 10 days.

The new law is more restrictive than the *Carter* decision as it includes two provisions that are much narrower in scope. To qualify for assisted dying, an individual must be in "an advanced state of irreversible decline and their natural death must be reasonably foreseeable."[24] Some have argued that this would lead physicians to allow only those persons who are "imminently" dying to qualify.

---

23 *Ibid* at s 241.2(2).

24 *Ibid.*

KEY TERMS

advance directives, 46

attorney, 48

capacity, 45

euthanasia, 57

express consent, 44

implied consent, 44

substitute decision maker, 48

SUGGESTED SOURCES

Community Care Access Centre,
<http://healthcareathome.ca>

Office of the Public Guardian and Trustee,
<http://www.attorneygeneral.jus.gov.on.ca/
english/family/pgt>

Consent and Capacity Board, <http://www
.ccboard.on.ca>

Accreditation Canada, <https://accreditation.ca>

REVIEW QUESTIONS

1. If a health practitioner believes that a patient is incapable of consenting to or refusing a treatment, who should the health practitioner approach to seek consent? What is the legal basis (statute? section number?) for your answer?

2. List some of the criteria for consent deemed to be valid.

3. What is a power of attorney for personal care? Why might a client consider executing one?

4. Outline the new law related to assisted dying in Canada and compare it to the Supreme Court of Canada case in *Carter v Canada (Attorney General)*.

5. What are the four different kinds of in-home care that are available through Community Care Access Centres for seniors and disabled adults who are in good health and who can manage most daily activities?

Mental Health Law

5

LEARNING OUTCOMES

After reading this chapter, you should be able to:

- List the statutes that define the mental health system in Ontario.

- Describe the circumstances under which a person can be admitted into hospital voluntarily for a mental health crisis.

- Understand the mechanisms by which a person can be detained in hospital involuntarily for a mental health crisis.

- Explain the rights of a mentally ill hospital patient.

- Explain the nature and function of community treatment orders.

- Outline the four criminal justice categories and designations related to mental health disorders.

Introduction

According to the Canadian Mental Health Association, one in five Canadians will be affected by a mental illness at some time in their lives.[1] Mental illness is disproportionately common in certain populations that are heavy users of social services: youth, homeless people, and the poor.

All social service workers will, at some point in their career, be called upon to support clients who are struggling with mental illness. For this reason, it is essential that social service workers be familiar not only with the facts about mental illness but also with the legal framework for mental health service delivery in Ontario.

The focus of this chapter is on supporting mentally ill clients in their efforts to navigate the health care delivery system, and not on working within mental health settings (hospitals, long-term care facilities, etc.).

How Common Is Mental Illness?

The Canadian Mental Health Association provides some striking statistics about the prevalence of mental illness:

- Approximately 8 percent of adult Canadians suffer from a depressive disorder.
- Almost 20 percent of children and youth are affected by a mental illness or disorder.
- Two-thirds of the clients of homeless shelters have some form of mental illness.
- Of the ten leading causes of disability worldwide, five are mental disorders: major depression, schizophrenia, bipolar disorder, alcohol use disorder, and obsessive compulsive disorder.[2]

Relevant Law

Three statutes form the legal framework for mental health service delivery in Ontario:

- *Mental Health Act* (MHA)[3]
- *Health Care Consent Act, 1996* (HCCA)[4]
- *Substitute Decisions Act, 1992* (SDA)[5]

---

1 "Fast Facts about Mental Illness," Canadian Mental Health Association, online: <http://www.cmha.ca/media/fast-facts-about-mental-illness>.

2 *Ibid.*

3 *Mental Health Act*, RSO 1990, c M.7.

4 *Health Care Consent Act, 1996*, SO 1996, c 2, Schedule A.

5 *Substitute Decisions Act, 1992*, SO 1992, c 30.

The focus of Ontario's mental health legislation is on hospital-based treatment. The MHA explains, among other things, how a person is identified as an appropriate candidate for hospital care; how a decision to detain a person without his or her consent is made; how the use of restraints and other intrusive measures is to be managed; how hospital placements are extended, reviewed, and terminated; and what happens if a person does not cope well with release. The HCCA and SDA fill in the details of consent-to-treatment issues, and what happens when a patient is deemed unable to consent to or guide his or her own care.

Substitute Decision Making

When persons suffering from serious physical or mental illness seem unable to manage their care competently, or to make reasonable care decisions, health care providers are required to obtain consent for their treatment or admission to care from another person who has the power to speak on their behalf. The general term used for this representative is substitute decision maker.

Substitute decision makers can step forward or be chosen in a variety of ways, including informal selection of a relative at the health care facility, appointment by a government tribunal (the Consent and Capacity Board) under the HCCA, appointment by **power of attorney**, and appointment of a guardian under the SDA. More detailed information on consent and capacity is found in Chapter 4 of this text.

substitute decision maker
a person who makes decisions about legal, financial, or health matters on behalf of a person who is incapable of making these decisions

power of attorney
the legal act that appoints someone as another person's attorney for property or attorney for personal care

Mental Health Act

The *Mental Health Act* explains how to identify those in need of hospitalization for psychiatric care; how a decision to detain a person without his or her consent is made; how the use of restraints and other intrusive measures is to be managed; how hospital placements are extended, reviewed, and terminated; and what happens if a person does not cope well following discharge.

Health Care Consent Act, 1996

The *Health Care Consent Act, 1996* fills in the details of consent-to-treatment issues and what happens when a patient is deemed unable to consent to or guide his or her own care. The Consent and Capacity Board may appoint a representative to act as a substitute decision maker for patients who are incapable of consenting to treatment.

Substitute Decisions Act, 1992

The *Substitute Decisions Act, 1992* provides a process for appointing powers of attorney over personal care and property and for court-ordered guardianship.

Admission to a Mental Health Facility

A person may be considered for admission to a hospital or other mental health facility via a number of different routes. Many patients make their way to hospital on their own after deciding that they cannot cope with a mental health crisis. Other patients are escorted to hospital—voluntarily or not—by relatives, friends, or helping professionals such as counsellors, therapists, social workers, or social service workers. Some people arrive at hospital after being apprehended by the police.

Under the MHA, a hospital is not required to admit a person simply because the person arrives in the emergency room. In general, because of the limited number of beds available for mentally ill patients, hospitals admit only those patients who are suffering a serious crisis and/or who may be at risk of harming themselves or others.

Voluntary or Informal Admission

Under section 12 of the MHA, doctors have the discretion to admit patients whom they believe to be "in need of the observation, care and treatment provided in a psychiatric facility." Doctors may admit patients who do not necessarily meet the criteria for involuntary admission, described in the next section. Typically, these voluntary or "informal" patients are admitted for a brief period only, to allow for observation for signs of the need for a further stay, or to see how the patient responds to an adjustment in medication. Voluntary or informal patients cannot be detained or restrained, and may leave the hospital at any time if they wish to do so.

In some cases, children may be admitted as informal patients for a longer stay than would apply to an adult. The MHA contains provisions allowing children between the ages of 12 and 16 to challenge their admission.

Involuntary Admission

Any person who is examined by a doctor may be deemed in need of an assessment to determine whether involuntary admission to a mental health facility is appropriate. In practical terms, this means that any time a patient with mental health concerns goes to the doctor or to a hospital emergency room, there is at least a possibility that the patient may be admitted involuntarily to a hospital or other mental health facility, and prevented from leaving.

Because of the shortage of hospital beds and the MHA's formalized process for evaluating hospital candidates, in most cases where a doctor concludes that hospitalization is warranted, it really is. However, social service workers must be frank with clients about the possibility that seeking treatment during a mental health crisis could lead to a hospital stay.

Considerations Before Going to Hospital

A social service worker working with a mentally ill client can help prepare for a trip to the hospital. This may involve planning for the possibility of involuntary admission. The kind of assistance provided can range from arranging for someone to collect the mail or look after the cat to exploring the issue of appointing a substitute decision maker in the event that the client is found to be incapable of consenting to treatment.

If there is time available, the social service worker can suggest that the client retain a lawyer to prepare a power of attorney for personal care. In more urgent circumstances, the client might get in touch with the person that the client would like to have as a representative and communicate his or her general wishes; then, if the need arose, that person could be declared a guardian under the SDA or a representative under the HCCA.

A social service worker who has a good understanding of the law related to substitute decision makers will be able to support the client in ensuring that the client's wishes are respected.

The "Form 1" Process

Upon examining a patient, a doctor may apply for a psychiatric assessment under section 15 of the MHA in the following circumstances.

The doctor reasonably believes that the patient has been or is currently

- threatening or attempting to cause bodily harm to himself or herself,
- behaving violently toward another person,
- causing another person to fear bodily harm, or
- showing a lack of competence to care for himself or herself;

and the doctor is also of the opinion that the person is apparently suffering from a mental disorder that likely will result in

- serious bodily harm or serious physical impairment to the patient, or
- serious bodily harm to another person.

Where a patient has previously received treatment for a chronic or recurring mental disorder that poses a risk when not treated, and for which treatment has shown clinical improvement in the past, the test for a psychiatric assessment is less stringent. Behaviour typical of the illness may be considered when considering the risk to the patient and others, even if the patient is not currently behaving in such a manner.

In 2000, the Ontario government passed amendments (known as "Brian's Law") that expanded the criteria for a psychiatric (form 1) assessment. Brian's Law (named after an Ottawa man, Brian Smith, whose killing by a mentally ill person in 1995 led to a critical review of the existing legislation) changed some provisions in the MHA and the HCCA, and made it easier to commit a psychiatric patient. Before Brian's Law, it was necessary for a physician to find that a person was an "imminent" threat to himself or herself or others before he or she was eligible for an assessment. This wording proved to be confusing and, as critics pointed out, excluded certain people who clearly ought to be assessed (such as Smith's killer). Brian's Law removed the word "imminent" from MHA section 15.

It also listed additional criteria for ordering a form 1 assessment, making it easier for a person with a chronic mental disorder who poses a risk to be admitted involuntarily for assessment and to receive treatment before a crisis occurs.

Another important change made by Brian's Law was the introduction of a community treatment option pursuant to a "community treatment order," discussed in a later section of this chapter.

When an application for a psychiatric assessment is made, the patient is said to be "placed on a form 1" (referring to the application form). A patient who is subject to a form 1 application has the right to consult a lawyer.

When a patient is placed on a form 1, he or she will be detained in hospital for up to 72 hours. During that period, the patient will be observed by a psychiatrist, who will decide whether he or she is well enough to be released during or at the end of the 72-hour period, or whether he or she should be detained as an involuntary patient—often called "committed to hospital" or "placed on a form 3."

Rights Arising on Form 3 Admission

If, as a result of a form 1 assessment, a person is found to be in need of admission to a mental health facility, he becomes an involuntary patient—"placed on a form 3." As soon as possible after a patient is placed on a form 3, he or she must be visited by a rights adviser. The rights adviser will advise the patient of his or her right to apply for a review of the decision to place him or her on a form 3.

rights adviser
a person who is available to speak with patients about their legal rights

A **rights adviser** is a helping professional who has completed a government training course to qualify for this special designation. The rights adviser is not involved in the patient's clinical care. A rights adviser may, but need not, be a lawyer; a social service worker can apply to be designated in this role.

A form 3 placement lasts up to two weeks; patients can be released earlier if they improve. When a form 3 expires, a doctor who believes that the patient should remain admitted will apply for a form 4 extension.

When the initial form 3 is issued, and each time a physician applies to extend a patient's admission via a form 4, the patient has a right to challenge the decision before the Consent and Capacity Board. The board must hear the application within seven days. The rights adviser must visit each time a new form is ordered, to assist the patient in applying for a review if the patient so chooses, and in finding a lawyer to represent him or her. The procedures for applying to the board for a review and the hearing process are discussed in more detail below under the heading "Treatment and Release."

A patient who is in hospital on a form 3 or form 4 may not leave unless he or she is discharged; the patient may be physically restrained, if necessary, to prevent him or her from leaving. The MHA and the HCCA contain rules for the use of restraints and the administration of intrusive treatments such as sterilization, shock therapy, and surgery. Social service workers who regularly work with hospitalized mental health patients should familiarize themselves with these rules. Further discussion here is beyond the scope of this book.

About Brian's Law

After Brian Smith, an Ottawa sportscaster, was shot and killed in the parking lot of his workplace by a mentally ill attacker, his wife, Alana Kainz, vowed to make sure that no one else would suffer the same fate. She was the driving force behind Brian's Law, amendments to the MHA and the HCCA, passed in 2000, that make it easier to commit dangerous patients to hospital and ensure that they receive treatment, either in hospital or in the community under a community treatment order.

Many family members of the mentally ill welcomed the change. Previously, their hands were largely tied with respect to getting their loved ones into treatment. A common characteristic of mental illnesses involving delusional thinking, such as schizophrenia, is the inability to recognize the illness in oneself; refusal of treatment can be considered a symptom of the illness. According to the Ontario Ministry of Health and Long-Term Care, "the legislative changes remove barriers to families, police and social workers by ensuring that people posing a risk to themselves or others get the care and treatment they need."[6]

Not everyone agrees that Brian's Law is a good idea. Psychiatric patient advocacy groups, poverty groups, and even the Canadian Mental Health Association have raised concerns that the law swings the pendulum back too far, reminiscent of human rights abuses in the days of insane asylums.

Critics of the law argue that community treatment orders criminalize the mentally ill, and that forcing patients to take medication violates their human rights and dignity. Some argue that more emphasis should be placed on community and social supports and housing, rather than quick-fix pharmaceuticals.

Admission to a Care Facility

The HCCA defines certain non-hospital facilities as "care facilities." These facilities include homes for the aged, rest homes, and nursing homes. In most cases, people decide on their own, or in collaboration with family members, to move into care facilities. However, if a person is not in agreement about moving, family members or an "evaluator" (a social service worker employed by the facility) may seek to have the person moved without his or her consent.

In the event that a person is incapable of giving consent to move into a care facility, the situation is analogous to consent to treatment (discussed in Chapter 4), and it is addressed by the HCCA in a similar way. The same procedures for appointing a substitute decision maker apply.

The Psychiatric Patient Advocate Office (PPAO) provides advocacy services to individual patients, addresses facility-based or provincial systemic issues affecting patients' rights, and provides public and health care professional education through speaking engagements, published reports, and media releases.

---

6   "Mental Health: Bill 68 (Mental Health Legislative Reform), 2000," Ontario Ministry of Health and Long-Term Care, online: <http://www.health.gov.on.ca/en/public/publications/mental/treatment_order.aspx>.

Treatment and Release

Once admitted to hospital, a patient's treatment raises a number of legal issues, most of which revolve around the concept of consent. The HCCA is intended to achieve the following objectives regarding consent to treatment, admission to care facilities, and personal assistance services:

- Provide rules that apply consistently in all settings.
- Facilitate decision-making for persons lacking the capacity to make their own decisions.
- Enhance the autonomy of the patient.
- Allow those found incapable to have the finding reviewed by a tribunal.
- Ensure a significant role for supportive family members.
- Permit intervention by the public guardian and trustee (PGT) only as a last resort on behalf of incapable persons.

Community Treatment Orders

As discussed above, the legislative amendments known as Brian's Law introduced community treatment orders (CTOs), in addition to a lower assessment threshold. The purpose of a CTO is to address the revolving-door situation where a patient is admitted to hospital, stabilized, and released, only to stop treatment and again require hospitalization. CTOs are designed to allow patients to be treated in the community even though they meet the criteria for being involuntarily admitted to a mental health facility. A patient can be put on a CTO to avoid a new hospital admission, or in order to be released from hospital despite meeting the criteria for a form 3 or 4 placement. Treatment and monitoring that are part of a typical CTO include medication, therapy, and regular medical appointments.

A patient who is mentally ill can enter into a CTO only if the criteria set out in section 33.1(4) of the MHA are met. In general terms, these criteria are as follows (see Table 5.1):

- The patient has a prior history of hospitalization.
- A community treatment plan for the person has been completed and approved.
- The patient has been examined by a physician within the 72-hour period immediately preceding his or her entry into the CTO plan.
- The patient is considered to be capable of complying with the CTO.
- The patient and, if applicable, his or her substitute decision maker have consulted a rights adviser.
- The patient or his or her substitute decision maker consent to the CTO.

TABLE 5.1   Community Treatment Orders

Prior history of hospitalization
CTO plan completed and approved
Examination by physician within 72-hour period immediately preceding entry
Patient considered capable of complying with plan
Patient (and substitute decision maker) consultation with rights adviser
Patient (and substitute decision maker) consent to plan

In preparation for seeking a CTO, the health care professionals, helping professionals, relatives, and other supporters of a mentally ill person must collaborate in developing a plan of care for the ill person, and the plan must be approved before the CTO is ordered. A social service worker may be one of the professionals named in a client's plan of care and may be in a position to contribute to the plan.

Once in place, a CTO lasts six months, but it can be renewed. To ensure that the rights of the patient are respected, the patient is entitled to challenge the making of the CTO (or CTO renewal) before the Consent and Capacity Board, much as the patient might challenge a form 3 or a finding that he or she is incapable, as discussed above.

A patient who fails to comply with a CTO may be admitted to hospital as an involuntary patient, if warranted, pursuant to a form 1 application.

In support of the use of CTOs, the Ontario government has cited research in other jurisdictions suggesting that CTOs can reduce hospitalization, increase treatment compliance, decrease the victimization of mentally ill persons in the community, and decrease violence against members of the general public. However, a CTO will be ineffective if the treatment resources needed to support it do not exist in the community or are underfunded.

Social service workers may be employed by agencies that provide treatment services under CTOs. In those roles, social service workers can serve their clients not only directly but also by advocating for the proper funding of these services and the development of new, high-quality treatment resources designed to meet the needs of individual communities.

Appropriate conflict and crisis management training should be a part of any position that involves working with a client who is on a CTO. The social service worker should have the contact information for caregivers named in the client's plan of care, so that appropriate referrals can be made and any issues adequately communicated and followed up. The MHA provides for sharing of records between those caregivers under certain circumstances; thus, privacy rules may differ, in this context, from the usual norms of client–service provider confidentiality.

Medication Versus Psychosocial Therapy

In a March 2002 article in the *New York Times*,[7] Courtenay Harding, then a senior director at Boston University's Center for Psychiatric Rehabilitation, criticized the current North American focus on medication as the primary treatment for mental illness. Harding was also very critical of the "self-fulfilling prophecy of a downward course" that seems to characterize the modern approach to mental illness.

---

7 Courtenay M Harding, "Beautiful Minds Can Be Reclaimed," *New York Times* (10 March 2002), online: <http://www.nytimes.com/2002/03/10/opinion/beautiful-minds-can-be-reclaimed.html>.

Harding cited a Vermont study from the 1950s involving mentally ill patients, including chronic schizophrenics, who participated in a psychosocial rehabilitation-focused program that challenged the notion of mental illness as incurable. The study noted that these patients were often well enough to leave the hospital, while others who were treated by medication alone were not. Thirty years later, when a follow-up study was done, 62 to 68 percent of the patients were enjoying better mental health than they had when originally diagnosed, and 45 percent showed no signs of mental illness at all.

These numbers seem to challenge the current pessimistic view of schizophrenia as essentially incurable, and bring into question an approach that relies heavily on medication alone. In fact, a 1980 World Health Organization study[8] noted that people in developing countries recover more quickly and fully from mental illness than their peers in developed countries with sophisticated health care systems.

Harding urged a radical change in the medical system's approach to mental illness—away from medication, institutionalization, and pessimism, and toward a rehabilitative approach:

> Although there are many pathways to recovery, several factors stand out. They include a home, a job, friends and integration in the community. They also include hope, relearned optimism and self-sufficiency.[9]

Release

A patient is typically released from hospital when he or she is deemed to no longer meet the criteria for a form 3 or 4 placement. A release can be made at any time within the period of a placement; there is no need to wait until the placement expires. When a patient continues to meet the form 3 criteria but an adequate support system exists, he or she may be released on a CTO, as discussed above.

When a patient who is the subject of a CTO improves or recovers to the point where he no longer meets the form 3 criteria, the CTO can be terminated.

Mental Health and the Criminal Justice System

When discussing issues relating to mental health, it is important to look at the criminal justice system. Although difficult to identify an exact number, it is apparent that many individuals who are involved with the criminal justice system are suffering from some form of mental disorder. When using the broadest definition of mental disorders, the number can be quite high as it includes substance abuse and anti-social

---

8 A Jablensky, N Sartorius, G Ernberg & M Anker, "Schizophrenia: Manifestations, Incidence and Course in Different Cultures: A World Health Organization Ten-Country Study" (1992) 20 Psychological Medicine Monograph Supplement 1, online: <https://doi.org/10.1017/S0264180100000904>.

9 *Ibid.*

personality disorders.[10] Much of the public's attention is related to the less frequent mental health disorders of schizophrenia and psychotic disorders, which can result in much higher profile criminal cases.[11] As well, the vast majority of those suffering from mental health disorders are victims, not offenders.[12]

Even though a 2001 study found that in fact less than 3 percent of violent offences were attributable to people with only a serious mental illness, the public's perception is that mentally disordered persons are dangerous.[13]

A 2015 sampling of incoming male offenders to federal custody suggests very high prevalence estimates for certain disorders (see Table 5.2). It is estimated that mental health issues are two to three times more common in prison than in the general community. Close to half of incoming male offenders have alcohol dependence or substance use disorders, while more than one-third of offenders meet the criteria for concurrent disorders, indicating high rates of co-morbidity. Though known prevalence is high for many mental health disorders, the actual rates could be even higher.[14]

TABLE 5.2   Prevalence of Mental Health Disorders Among Incoming Male Federal Offenders

Mental Health Disorder	Prevalence Rate (%)
Mood disorders	16.9
Primary psychotic	3.3
Alcohol or substance use disorders	49.6
Anxiety disorders	29.5
Pathological gambling	5.9
Borderline personality disorder	15.9
Anti-social personality disorder	44.1

Sample of incoming federal offenders ($N = 1,110$ men)

Source: JN Beaudette, J Power & LA Stewart, *National Prevalence of Mental Disorders among Incoming Federally-Sentenced Men Offenders* (Research Report R-357) (Ottawa: Correctional Service of Canada, 2015).

---

10 Public Safety Canada, *The Prediction of Risk for Mentally Disordered Offenders: A Quantitative Synthesis*, by James Bonta, Julie Blais & Holly A Wilson (Ottawa: Public Safety Canada, 2013).

11 James RP Ogloff, "Psychopathy/Antisocial Personality Disorder Conundrum" (2006) 40:6-7 Austl & NZ J Psychiatry 519.

12 "The Facts," Mental Health Commission of Canada, online: <http://strategy .mentalhealthcommission.ca/the-facts>.

13 Julio Arboleda-Flórez, Heather L Holley & Annette Crisanti, *Mental Illness and Violence: Proof or Stereotype?* (Ottawa: Health Canada, 1996), online: <http://www.phac-aspc.gc.ca/mh-sm/pubs/ mental_illness/index-eng.php>.

14 Howard Sapers, *Annual Report of the Office of the Correctional Investigator 2014–2015* (Ottawa: Office of the Correctional Investigator, 26 June 2015), online: <http://www.oci-bec.gc.ca/cnt/rpt/ annrpt/annrpt20142015-eng.aspx>.

The criminal justice system has created four categories for persons suffering from mental health disorders: mental health diversion, mental health courts, the "not fit to stand trial" designation, and the finding of "not criminally responsible" (see Table 5.3).

TABLE 5.3   Mental Health Categories Within the Criminal Justice System

Category	Summary
Mental health diversion	Designed for low-risk offenders Offenders diverted away from the criminal justice system into more suitable and appropriate programs
Mental health court	Specialized courts designed to accommodate needs of offenders Still held criminally responsible but dealt with by court that better understands needs of offenders
Not fit to stand trial	At time of first court date, determination that offender cannot appreciate the nature and consequences of court proceedings and cannot instruct counsel Court proceedings put off for period of time
Not criminally responsible	At time of offence, the offender deemed not having required intent to qualify as being criminally responsible for actions and found not criminally responsible on account of mental disorder

Mental Health Diversion

Many individuals who suffer from low-risk mental health disorders can come into contact with the criminal justice system. Ontario has developed diversion programs that are designed for these offenders.

The police are often the first contact for a low-risk offender who might be suffering from a mental health disorder. Depending on the circumstances of the case, the police can choose to charge the offender if an offence has occurred. If no offence has been committed, the police can apprehend the person and take the person to a facility where a determination will be made to admit if the criteria are met. If an offence has been committed, the police can charge the person or divert the person to an appropriate community resource. The officer is more likely to charge the person if the offence involved some degree of violence.

The *Youth Criminal Justice Act* (YCJA) directs police officers to consider using **extrajudicial measures** when diverting a young person away from the criminal justice system.[15] A young person is defined in the YCJA as a person between his or her 12th and 18th birthday at the time of the offence. Section 4 of the YCJA outlines the principles and objectives of extrajudicial measures. Section 6 of the YCJA states that officers "shall consider" extrajudicial measures prior to laying a charge. The officer

extrajudicial measures
a form of diversion designed to deal informally with youth involved in criminal activity, as an alternative to prosecution through traditional criminal procedure; run by the police for low-risk offenders

---

15   *Youth Criminal Justice Act*, SC 2002, c 1.

can take no further action, warn, administer a caution, or refer the young person to a community resource. In the past few years, police have diverted more young persons away from the criminal justice system than have commenced charges.[16]

If the officer decides to charge the offender, the matter will go to court where the Crown attorney has the discretion to proceed with the matter or to divert the case. In Ontario, if the offender suffers from a mental health disorder, and the Crown believes that the disorder is the underlying cause for the criminal behaviour, the case may proceed by way of diversion.[17] The circumstances would not involve serious violence. In these cases, the criminal court proceedings are put off for a period of time in order for the person to complete a community program. If the candidate successfully completes the required program, the Crown will withdraw the charges.

Section 10 of the *Youth Criminal Justice Act* directs the Crown to consider using **extrajudicial sanctions** if a young person was not offered extrajudicial measures by the police. The Crown will put the matter over for a period of time (usually three months), with the young person directed to a community program. If the youth successfully completes the program, the Crown will withdraw the charge.

It is important to note that in order to qualify for **diversion**, the offender must accept responsibility for his or her criminal actions, and that any admissions made by the offender in a diversion program cannot be used against that person in any later proceedings.

It is difficult to gauge the success of these diversion programs as actual data is difficult to come by. However, the use of diversion programs for low-risk offenders who suffer from mental health disorders has been effective in providing more appropriate treatment and responses than the conventional criminal justice system.

extrajudicial sanctions
diversion programs under the YCJA run by the crown attorney for low-risk youth; designed to address criminal behaviour more serious than the type that warrants a warning, caution, or referral

diversion
a program designed to divert individuals away from the formal criminal justice system

Mental Health Court

Ontario established the mental health court, known as Courtroom 102, in 1998 in the Old City Hall Court in Toronto. The goal of the mental health court is to apply the legal rules and consequences of the criminal justice system within the mental health context, appreciating and appropriately dealing with the mental health disorder in question.

The individuals who work in Courtroom 102 are all familiar with and appreciate the mental health component to a case. Specially selected judges, duty counsel, and Crown attorneys, as well as other court officials, are better trained to deal with the criminal cases that involve mental health disorders. Studies have shown positive results with respect to recidivism rates.[18]

---

16   Statistics Canada, *Police-Reported Crime Statistics in Canada, 2015*, by Mary Allen, Catalogue No 85-002-X (Ottawa: Statistics Canada, 20 July 2016).

17   Kathleen Hartford, Robert Carey & James Mendonca, "Pre-arrest and Diversion of People with Mental Illness: Literature Review and International Survey" (2006) 24:6 Behav Sci Law 845.

18   Brian Case et al, "Who Succeeds in Jail Diversion Programs for Persons with Mental Illness? A Multi-Site Study" (2009) 27:5 Behav Sci Law 661.

Toronto has a Community Youth Court that takes a more problem-solving style of conflict resolution when dealing with young persons who have been identified with mental health disorders.

Mental health diversion and the mental health court are more commonly used but less known because of the lower profile nature of the cases. The following two categories are used less frequently but are more well known because of the higher profile nature of the cases.

Not Fit to Stand Trial

For an accused person to stand trial, the accused must be able to understand the nature and consequences of the trial proceedings. The accused person must also be able to communicate with and instruct legal counsel. This determination is made by a psychiatrist who makes a report to the court at the time the accused is brought to court. If the accused is deemed to be unfit, the court can order the accused to remain in detention or treatment until such time that the accused is deemed to be fit to return to court. A stay of proceedings can be issued if the accused is not likely to become fit, if the accused does not pose a significant threat to public safety, and if a stay is in the interests of the administration of justice.[19]

If the accused person is deemed to be unfit to stand trial, the court can order the accused into treatment for a period not to exceed 60 days. If the accused improves and is able to attend court, he or she will be sent back for trial. The Supreme Court of Canada affirmed the "limited cognitive capacity test" in *R v Whittle* in 1994.[20] The court held that, "provided the accused possesses this limited capacity, it is not a prerequisite that he or she be capable of exercising analytical reasoning in making a choice to accept the advice of counsel or in coming to a decision that best serves her interests."[21] The court must hold an inquiry not later than two years after the verdict of unfitness was rendered and every two years thereafter until the accused is either acquitted or tried, to decide whether there is sufficient evidence to put the accused on trial.

The courts must balance the objectives of the fitness rule and the constitutional right of the accused to choose his or her defence and to have the trial within a reasonable time, and the consequences of "unfit" determination must be considered.

Not Criminally Responsible (NCR)

In Canada, the *Not Criminally Responsible Reform Act* was created in an attempt to provide fair and humane treatment for persons suffering from mental disorders along with public safety.[22] For a person to be convicted of a criminal offence, the state must

---

19 Bill C-10, *An Act to Amend the Criminal Code (Mental Disorder) and to Make Consequential Amendments to Other Acts*, 1st Sess, 38th Parl, 2005, c 22 (first reading 8 October 2004).

20 *R v Whittle*, [1994] 2 SCR 914.

21 *Ibid* at 934.

22 *Not Criminally Responsible Reform Act*, SC 2014, c 6.

prove not only the wrongful criminal act but also a guilty mind. Thus, the legislation reflects the possibility that a person committed the act but was not criminally responsible on account of mental disorder (NCRMD). As well, provincial review boards were established for monitoring the treatment and confinement of persons found NCR on account of mental illness.

Section 16 of the *Criminal Code* states:

> No person is criminally responsible for an act committed or an omission made while suffering from a mental disorder that rendered the person incapable of appreciating the nature and quality of the act or omission or of knowing that it was wrong.[23]

The *Criminal Code* also says that the onus of proof for criminal responsibility is on the party that raises the issue in court (s 16(3)) and requires proof on the balance of probabilities (s 16(2)).

Whether or not the issue of fitness to stand trial is raised, the issue of mental illness may still be raised. It must be shown that the accused person was suffering from a "disease of the mind" that prevented the accused from understanding the consequences of his or her actions at the time of the offence. A verdict of NCRMD is not the same as a finding of guilt or a conviction.

A finding of not criminally responsible can lead to a court sentence, or the matter can be deferred to a review board. The court may give the following dispositions:

- detention in hospital (in a secure setting)
- conditional discharge
- **absolute discharge**

absolute discharge
a sentencing order that imposes no penalty on an accused—a finding of guilt but is deemed not to have been convicted

The courts have stated that if the offender does not pose a significant threat to the community, there should be a finding of absolute or conditional discharge.[24] If a person is ordered into secure treatment, the order must be reviewed by the review board. In November 2014, the Government of Canada passed legislation amending the *Criminal Code* provision relating to NCRMD with the introduction of the *Not Criminally Responsible Reform Act*. This action was in large part a response to the high-profile Vince Li case. The Li case involved a man suffering from a serious mental health disorder beheading another person who was asleep next to him on a bus. Li was determined to be NCRMD; after being ordered into secure treatment, and after a number of years being successfully treated, Li was gradually released back into the community.[25]

---

23   *Criminal Code*, RSC 1985, c C-46.

24   RD Schneider et al, "Canadian Landmark Case, *Winko v. British Columbia*: Revisiting the Conundrum of the Mentally Disordered Accused" (2000) 28:2 Am Academy Psychiatry & L 206.

25   *R v Li* (09 March 2009), Winnipeg (MBQB); "Vince Li, Man Who Beheaded Passenger on Greyhound Bus, Given Absolute Discharge," *CBC News* (10 February 2017), online: <http://www.cbc.ca/news/canada/manitoba/vince-li-discharge-1.3977278>.

The *Not Criminally Responsible Reform Act* states in its summary that:

… the paramount consideration in the decision-making process is the safety of the public and to create a scheme for finding that certain persons who have been found not criminally responsible on account of mental disorder are high-risk accused. It also enhances the involvement of victims in the regime and makes procedural and technical amendments.

Some of the key components of the Act are as follows:

- Public safety comes first when courts make decisions with respect to any accused person found NCR.
- For even greater public safety, the legislation creates a new high-risk designation process for those NCR accused persons who are found by a court to pose a higher risk of committing future acts of violence. Upon being designated by a court as high risk, an NCR accused would be held in custody in a hospital and could not be released by a review board until the high-risk designation has been revoked by a court.
- The legislation outlines possible extension by a review board of the period between reviews (up to three years), the denial of unescorted passes into the community, and the condition that escorted passes could be granted only for medical reasons and subject to sufficient safeguards to protect public safety.
- The legislation also enhances the safety of victims by ensuring that they are specifically considered when decisions are being made about mentally disordered accused persons; ensuring that they are notified when such an accused is discharged and where they intend to reside, if the victims so desire; and allowing for non-communication orders between the accused and the victim.[26]

---

26 Department of Justice Canada, News Release, "Federal government actions leading to better protection of Canadians and their communities" (11 July 2014), online: <http://news.gc.ca/web/article-en.do?nid=867529>.

KEY TERMS

absolute discharge, 75

diversion, 73

extrajudicial measures, 72

extrajudicial sanctions, 73

power of attorney, 63

rights adviser, 66

substitute decision maker, 63

SUGGESTED SOURCES

Canadian Mental Health Association,
<http://www.cmha.ca>, or the Ontario or Toronto
branches at <http://ontario.cmha.ca> and
<http://toronto.cmha.ca>

Centre for Addiction and Mental Health,
<http://www.camh.ca>

Community Mental Health Evaluation Initiative,
<http://ontario.cmha.ca/documents/
community-mental-health-evaluation-initiative>

Consent and Capacity Board,
<http://www.ccboard.on.ca>

Ontario Mental Health Foundation,
<http://www.omhf.on.ca>

Ontario Ministry of Health and Long-Term Care,
<http://www.health.gov.on.ca>

Office of the Public Guardian and Trustee,
<http://www.attorneygeneral.jus.gov.on.ca/english/
family/pgt>

Psychiatric Patient Advocate Office,
<http://www.ppao.gov.on.ca>

REVIEW QUESTIONS

1. Why do social service workers need to understand the legislative framework of Ontario's mental health system?

2. Explain how a person who arrives voluntarily at a hospital emergency room might find himself or herself admitted to hospital for mental health treatment even if this is not his or her wish.

3. What is Brian's Law and how did it change the criteria for ordering a form 1 assessment?

4. What is a community treatment order? Under what circumstances might one be made?

5. List the four categories/designations in the criminal justice system that accommodate persons with mental health disorders.

6. List the possible outcomes of an NCRMD verdict.

Child Protection Law, Notes, Reports, and Records

6

LEARNING OUTCOMES

After completing this chapter, you should be able to:

■ Describe the general principles of the *Child, Youth and Family Services Act, 2017* (CYFSA).

■ Explain the roles that social service workers may play in working with the CYFSA.

■ Understand the duty to report neglect and abuse, and describe the triggering circumstances for that duty.

■ Understand the general principles of safety and risk assessment.

■ Describe the various levels of intervention mandated by the CYFSA and understand how a level is chosen.

■ Be aware of contemporary issues in child protection, such as using community resources, advocacy on behalf of children, and cultural sensitivity.

■ Understand the importance of note-taking in social service practice.

■ Describe ways of improving the clarity and understandability of notes.

■ Demonstrate an awareness of confidentiality concerns in making notes and writing reports about clients.

■ Describe how your notes might be used in court.

■ Understand the court process and your role as a social services worker at court.

Introduction

Before the 18th century, protecting children was viewed as simply one facet of raising them and the responsibility of parents. While neglecting or harming one's children was often denounced as morally wrong, parents had the final word over how children were provided for, supervised, and disciplined. In extreme cases of abusive treatment, a relative might intervene, taking a child at risk into his or her own home, but the courts and the government were rarely involved.

Gradually, as the result of pressure from children's advocates—sometimes educators, clergy, or related organizations—the government began to set limits on parental decision-making authority. Nowadays, if a child is at risk from parental harm, the decision to remove the child from the nuclear family is generally made not by extended family members or neighbours, but by government agencies, and these agencies take responsibility for the care of children in need of protection.

At the time of writing, in Ontario, the *Child and Family Services Act* (CFSA) continues to govern the process for taking children in need of protection into custody and set standards for their care.[1] It also creates a duty of care for all people to report evidence of suspected abuse or neglect of a child.

In December 2016, the Ontario legislature tabled Bill 89, *Supporting Children, Youth and Families Act, 2017*.[2] In June 2017, the Act received royal assent. Bill 89 will repeal the CFSA and enact the *Child, Youth and Family Services Act, 2017* (CYFSA) in its place on a day to be named by proclamation of the lieutenant governor. The sections of the new Act relating to 16- and 17-year-olds will be rolled out by the end of 2017, thereby amending the CFSA. The CFSA will be fully repealed in 2018. As such, references in this chapter are made to the CYFSA.

The new Act makes many commitments, such as moving toward a child-centred practice, acknowledging the voice of young people, and addressing systemic racism.

As well, the new Act refers to First Nations, Inuit, and Métis children and young persons, and gives rights of notice and participation to a representative chosen by each of the child's or young person's bands and First Nations, Inuit, or Métis communities.

The terms *society ward* and *Crown ward* are no longer used. Instead, the new Act refers to children who are in *interim society care* and *extended society care*, respectively. The new Act does not refer to children being abandoned or to runaways. And the new Act speaks of bringing children to a place of safety, instead of being apprehended, and of dealing with matters, not dealing with children.

The CYFSA strengthens the voice of children and youth. As well, the new Act broadens the definitions to include First Nations, Inuit, and Métis children to ensure that more Indigenous children are provided specialized recognition within the child welfare system.

In 2016 the Katelynn Sampson inquest provided recommendations that included "Katelynn's principle," which holds that the child should be at the centre of our child

---

1 *Child and Family Services Act*, RSO 1990, c C.11.

2 Bill 89, *An Act to enact the Child, Youth and Family Services Act, 2017, to amend and repeal the Child and Family Services Act and to make related amendments to other Acts,* 2nd Sess, 41st Leg, Ontario, 2017 (assented to 1 June 2017), SO 2017, c 14.

welfare, justice, and education systems. In practice, that would mean children would be consulted directly on decisions affecting them. The CYFSA reflects some of the inquest's recommendations, broadening the definition of a child's best interests to include the child's views and wishes (given due weight in accordance with the child's age and maturity). Other highlights of the new Act include the following:

- Raising the age of protection from 16 to 18 to increase protection services for more vulnerable youth in unsafe living conditions, to support their education, and to reduce homelessness and human trafficking

- Making services more inclusive and culturally appropriate for all children and youth, including Indigenous and Black children and youth, to ensure every child receives the best possible support

- Putting a greater focus on early intervention, to help prevent children and families from reaching crisis situations at home

- Improving accountability and oversight of service providers, including children's aid societies and licensed residential service providers, so that children and youth receive safe, consistent, and high-quality services across the province[3]

Social service workers can be involved with child protection in a variety of ways. For example, those who work in recreation facilities, women's shelters, hospitals, or other centres with child clients may be confronted with evidence of child abuse or neglect, which they will be required to report. Many social service workers also work with children who have already been taken into care, perhaps supporting foster parents or working in children's residences. In these settings, social service workers may be required to support children or parents in accessing and using programs and services in the context of a plan of care. They may also help clients to prepare for hearings and other administrative processes.

Purposes and Principles

The most important purpose of the CYFSA, as expressed in section 1, is

> to promote the best interests, protection, and well-being of children.

This principle has remained the same as in the old Act.

The requirement that legislation be applied according to the best interests of the child is not unique to the CYFSA. This phrase is used in family law statutes as well, with respect to issues of custody and access. Best interests do not necessarily mean what the child wants, although a child's wishes may be considered, particularly in the case of older children. The new Act attempts to strengthen the voice of the child and youth.

---

3   Ministry of Children and Youth Services, News Release, "Ontario Passes Legislation to Strengthen Child Welfare and Improve Outcomes for Youth Province: Putting Children at the Centre of Decision-Making" (1 June 2017), online: <https://news.ontario.ca/mcys/en/2017/06/ontario-passes-legislation-to-strengthen-child-welfare-and-improve-outcomes-for-youth.html>.

Similar to the old legislation, the CYFSA imposes a duty of care on all people to report child abuse and neglect. It governs the process for taking abused children into custody and sets standards for their care. It also provides for counselling and other services for children and their families for the purpose of preventing abuse and neglect.

The additional purposes of the CYFSA (s 1(2)) are expanded to include the following:

1. While parents may need help in caring for their children, that help should give support to the autonomy and integrity of the family unit and, wherever possible, be provided on the basis of mutual consent.

2. The least disruptive course of action that is available and is appropriate in a particular case to help a child, including the provision of prevention services, early intervention services and community support services, should be considered.

3. Services to children and young persons should be provided in a manner that,

i. respects a child's or young person's need for continuity of care and for stable relationships within a family and cultural environment,

ii. takes into account physical, emotional, spiritual, mental and developmental needs and differences among children and young persons,

iii. takes into account a child's or young person's race, ancestry, place of origin, colour, ethnic origin, citizenship, family diversity, disability, creed, sex, sexual orientation, gender identity and gender expression,

iv. takes into account a child's or young person's cultural and linguistic needs,

v. provides early assessment, planning and decision-making to achieve permanent plans for children and young persons in accordance with their best interests, and

vi. includes the participation of a child or young person, the child's or young person's parents and relatives and the members of the child's or young person's extended family and community, where appropriate.

4. Services to children and young persons and their families should be provided in a manner that respects regional differences, wherever possible.

5. Services to children and young persons and their families should be provided in a manner that builds on the strengths of the families, wherever possible.

6. First Nations, Inuit and Métis peoples should be entitled to provide, wherever possible, their own child and family services, and all services to First Nations, Inuit and Métis children and young persons and their families should be provided in a manner that recognizes their cultures, heritages, traditions, connection to their communities, and the concept of the extended family.

7. Appropriate sharing of information, including personal information, in order to plan for and provide services is essential for creating successful outcomes for children and families.

Much like the CFSA, the secondary purposes of the new CYFSA reflect strong support for the preservation of the family unit and a commitment to assisting children within the context of family relationships. Choosing the "least disruptive" course of action requires consideration of the child's existing environment, including, in addition to the family unit, the community and educational setting and the physical environment.

The secondary purposes also recognize the importance of culture, religion, heritage, traditions, regional differences, and community values. To the extent possible, a child's ties to these should be preserved even when the child is in need of assistance or protection. For example, a child in care should be given a chance to attend services at a place of worship for his or her own faith. Attempts are often made to place children with foster families who share their culture.

The needs of Indigenous children are specifically referenced in recognition of historical inequities and the tragedy of residential schools. First Nations, Métis, and Inuit children should receive, where possible, services from organizations that are managed and operated by their own community with respect for its heritage and traditions. This is a reversal of earlier government policy, which aimed to assimilate Indigenous children by taking them out of their homes and communities and placing them in residential schools. In those schools, children were stripped of their language and culture; many were also subjected to physical, emotional, or sexual abuse. The effects continue to be felt generations later.

Approved Agencies and Children's Aid Societies

The CYFSA permits the government to provide services directly or to fund service providers to do so. Approved agencies are corporations that work as agents for the government in providing these services.

Children's aid societies are specially designated approved agencies. There are more than 50 children's aid societies in Ontario, most associated with municipalities. Many also receive funding from private sources. Because of its size and diversity, Toronto has four children's aid societies:

- Catholic Children's Aid Society of Toronto
- Children's Aid Society of Toronto
- Jewish Family & Child Service of Toronto
- Native Child and Family Services of Toronto

Under the CYFSA, children's aid societies are mandated to provide protection to children under the age of 16, and to 16- and 17-year-olds in certain circumstances. The specific functions of a children's aid society include the following:

- Provide guidance, counselling, and other services to families to protect children or prevent child abuse and neglect.
- Investigate allegations or evidence that children under 16, or in the society's care or under its supervision, may be in need of protection. Children who are 16 or 17 may also be found to be in need of protection, and additional circumstances or conditions applicable only to that age group may be prescribed to make that determination. However, they may not be brought to a place of safety without their consent.
- Provide care and supervision for children assigned or committed to the society's care.
- Place children for adoption in appropriate circumstances.

Duties of Service Providers

The duties of service providers set out in the legislation emphasize the importance of procedural fairness when making decisions that affect families in such a fundamental way. In particular, children's aid societies must implement procedures for the disclosure of information to parents and, where appropriate, to children, and provide parents and children with the opportunity to challenge decisions that affect their rights and interests. Part X of the CYFSA, which relates to personal information, is modelled on provisions in the *Personal Health Information Protection Act, 2004*.[4]

> This Part sets out extensive rules for the following: the collection, use and disclosure of personal information by the Minister and by service providers; the determination of whether an individual has the capacity to give, withhold or withdraw consent to the collection, use or disclosure of their personal information; the authorization of a substitute decision-maker to give, withhold or withdraw consent on behalf of an individual; the maintenance and protection of personal information by service providers; individuals' rights of access to service providers' records containing their personal information and to require service providers to correct that information; individuals' rights to make a complaint to the Information and Privacy Commissioner in respect of any contraventions of this Part; the Information and Privacy Commissioner's powers and duties under this Part.

Respecting and promoting procedural fairness is a critical aspect of social service practice. In order to do your job fully, you need the trust of your clients, and it is difficult to establish and maintain that trust if the client's rights have not always been respected. Failure to follow procedures may also result in administrative decisions being overturned by a court and even disciplinary action against the decision-maker.

Voluntary Services

Services may be provided to children and families on a voluntary basis or pursuant to a court determination that the child is in need of protection. The range of voluntary services available will vary from community to community. Some may be provided by a children's aid society and others by different kinds of agencies. Voluntary services can include parenting classes and programs designed to address developmental problems, disabilities, behavioural problems, addiction, domestic abuse, or divorce.

Temporary Care Agreements

A person who is temporarily unable to care for a young child or children may enter into a written agreement with a children's aid society for temporary care. The time limit for such an arrangement is one year for children under six and two years for children aged six or over.

Some children's aid societies may offer parent relief programs through which an exhausted or ill parent of a young child or children can rely on volunteers or staff to care for the children overnight, in either the parent's home or the caregiver's home. These arrangements are typically very temporary (up to a limited number of nights).

---

4   *Personal Health Information Protection Act, 2004*, SO 2004, c 3, Schedule A.

A **temporary care agreement** may also be used where a parent needs to take time in an addiction rehabilitation program. Where a parent recognizes that he or she is unable to cope and that a court will likely order that the child be removed to a place of safety, the parent may agree to place the child in the care of a children's aid society and reserve the right to active participation.

How exactly a parent will participate in a child's care during a voluntary placement will vary among different children's aid societies and will depend on the reasons for the child's placement in care and parental factors. In almost all cases, the children's aid society will, at minimum, provide opportunities for parents and children to visit each other. Social service workers may be called upon to assist parents in remaining involved in their children's care and in improving their parenting skills with a view to having the children back home.

The CYFSA deals with society agreements with 16- and 17-year-olds. It states in section 77:

> (1) The society and a child who is 16 or 17 may make a written agreement for services and supports to be provided for the child where,
>> (a) the society has jurisdiction where the child resides;
>> (b) the society has determined that the child is or may be in need of protection;
>> (c) the society is satisfied that no course of action less disruptive to the child, such as care in the child's own home or with a relative, neighbour or other member of the child's community or extended family, is able to adequately protect the child; and
>> (d) the child wants to enter into the agreement.

The agreements can be for up to 12 months and extended as long as the total does not exceed 24 months up until the young person's 18th birthday. Either party to the agreement can terminate the agreement with written notice (s 77(2) and (4)).

Duty to Report Suspected Child Abuse or Neglect

A report of suspected child abuse or neglect is often the trigger for all further actions under the CYFSA. Reports may come from friends, neighbours, teachers, relatives, or even parents. Actions under the CYFSA may include bringing a child to a place of safety, but more often the children's aid society provides less intrusive programs to support parents, and parents accept assistance voluntarily. All societies encourage parents who are struggling with parenting problems to seek support from a local children's aid society.

When to Report

The CYFSA makes it mandatory for anyone to report a reasonable belief that a child—any child—has suffered or is at risk of suffering from abuse or neglect (s 125(1)). Essentially, a person has a duty to report a suspicion, based on reasonable grounds, that a child has suffered or is at risk of suffering one of the following:

temporary care agreement
where a parent recognizes that he or she is unable to cope and that a court will likely order that the child be removed to a place of safety, the parent may agree to place the child in the care of a children's aid society and reserve the right to active participation

1. The child has suffered physical harm inflicted by the person having charge of the child or caused by or resulting from that person's,

     i. failure to adequately care for, provide for, supervise or protect the child, or

     ii. pattern of neglect in caring for, providing for, supervising or protecting the child.

2. There is a risk that the child is likely to suffer physical harm inflicted by the person having charge of the child or caused by or resulting from that person's,

     i. failure to adequately care for, provide for, supervise or protect the child, or

     ii. pattern of neglect in caring for, providing for, supervising or protecting the child.

3. The child has been sexually abused or sexually exploited by the person having charge of the child or by another person where the person having charge of the child knows or should know of the possibility of sexual abuse or sexual exploitation and fails to protect the child.

4. There is a risk that the child is likely to be sexually abused or sexually exploited as described in paragraph 3.

5. The child requires treatment to cure, prevent or alleviate physical harm or suffering and the child's parent or the person having charge of the child does not provide the treatment or access to the treatment, or, where the child is incapable of consenting to the treatment under the *Health Care Consent Act, 1996*, refuses or is unavailable or unable to consent to, the treatment on the child's behalf.

6. The child has suffered emotional harm, demonstrated by serious,

     i. anxiety,

     ii. depression,

     iii. withdrawal,

     iv. self-destructive or aggressive behaviour, or

     v. delayed development, and there are reasonable grounds to believe that the emotional harm suffered by the child results from the actions, failure to act or pattern of neglect on the part of the child's parent or the person having charge of the child.

7. The child has suffered emotional harm of the kind described in subparagraph 6 i, ii, iii, iv or v and the child's parent or the person having charge of the child does not provide services or treatment or access to services or treatment, or, where the child is incapable of consenting to treatment under the *Health Care Consent Act, 1996*, refuses or is unavailable or unable to consent to, treatment to remedy or alleviate the harm.

8. There is a risk that the child is likely to suffer emotional harm of the kind described in subparagraph 6 i, ii, iii, iv or v resulting from the actions, failure to act or pattern of neglect on the part of the child's parent or the person having charge of the child.

9. There is a risk that the child is likely to suffer emotional harm of the kind described in subparagraph 6 i, ii, iii, iv or v and the child's parent or the person having charge of the child does not provide services or treatment or access to services or treatment, or, where the child is incapable of consenting to treatment under the *Health Care Consent Act, 1996*, refuses or is unavailable or unable to consent to, treatment to prevent the harm.

10. The child suffers from a mental, emotional or developmental condition that, if not remedied, could seriously impair the child's development and the child's parent or the person having charge of the child does not provide the treatment or access to the treatment, or where the child is incapable of consenting to the treatment under the *Health Care Consent Act, 1996*, refuses or is unavailable or unable to consent to, treatment to remedy or alleviate the condition.

11. The child's parent has died or is unavailable to exercise custodial rights over the child and has not made adequate provision for the child's care and custody, or the child is in a residential placement and the parent refuses or is unable or unwilling to resume the child's care and custody.

12. The child is younger than 12 and has killed or seriously injured another person or caused serious damage to another person's property, services or treatment are necessary to prevent a recurrence and the child's parent or the person having charge of the child does not provide services or treatment or access to services or treatment, or, where the child is incapable of consenting to treatment under the *Health Care Consent Act, 1996*, refuses or is unavailable or unable to consent to treatment.

13. The child is younger than 12 and has on more than one occasion injured another person or caused loss or damage to another person's property, with the encouragement of the person having charge of the child or because of that person's failure or inability to supervise the child adequately.

The duty to report is triggered as soon as the person making the relevant observations has reasonable grounds to suspect that harm has occurred, is occurring, or is threatened. This is a fairly easy threshold to meet, since it does not require certainty in the mind of the person reporting but only a reasonable suspicion. For example, a social service worker who observes bruises on a child's body that are not consistent with normal play should make a report, even in the absence of any other evidence and, in some cases, despite an "innocent" explanation by the child.

The low threshold for reporting means that many reports will be baseless. Society employees are trained to assess reports and to conduct investigations in order to make such determinations. The low threshold encourages people to leave it up to the experts. When in doubt, report.

The above sections do not apply to 16- and 17-year-olds, but a person may make a report in respect of a child who is 16 or 17 if either a circumstance or condition described in paragraphs 1 to 11 above or a prescribed circumstance or condition exists.

How to Report

Once a person has reasonable grounds to suspect any form of abuse or neglect listed in the Act, the duty to report is triggered. The specifics of that duty, as expressed by the legislation, are the following:

- Report without delay.
- Report to a children's aid society.
- Explain the reasons for your suspicion.
- Report directly—do not rely on your supervisor or subordinate.
- Report any new observations that occur after your initial report.

While all reports should be made promptly, the timing of the report will be influenced to some degree by the perceived seriousness of the harm observed or the presence of an ongoing threat. For example, if an adult is observed in the act of beating a child, it will usually be appropriate to call the police immediately, before calling a children's aid society. Note that even when the police are called, you are nevertheless obligated to report to a children's aid society.

Where the circumstances are more ambiguous, it may be acceptable to wait and see whether an observation is simply an isolated incident of inadequate parenting (all parents have the occasional bad moment) or part of a pattern. However, it is never appropriate to ignore signs of abuse or neglect in the hope that they will be resolved on their own, or reported by someone else.

When calling to make a report, it's useful to be prepared with notes about your observations and suspicions. It is important to be calm, objective, and open, and to refrain from using the reporting process as a personal attack on the suspected abuser. If your report sounds malicious or exaggerated, the credibility of your information will be tainted. Regardless of your feelings about the abuse or neglect you have witnessed, a coherent, impartial, and factual report is likely to be most helpful to the child.

The requirement that reports be made directly means exactly that. It is not possible to delegate your duty to report to someone else, even to your supervisor. You must make the call yourself. In many cases, it will be appropriate to advise another person of your suspicions, and in some cases, to consider that person's advice with respect to reporting. However, the duty to report is always yours personally, and if you fail to make a report in circumstances where you should have, you may be charged with an offence.

Special Duty

While everyone has a duty to report, the consequences of failing to report are more severe for people who perform professional or official duties with respect to children. The Act provides that if a person

- works with children, such as a teacher, youth worker, recreation worker, or employee of service agencies;
- obtains information triggering a duty to report in the course of professional duties; and
- does not make a report,

that person can be charged with an offence and, if convicted, fined not more than $5,000.

The list of professionals who are liable to be fined does not specifically include social service workers, but many social service workers are employed in at least one of the listed job categories.

Investigation

When a report is made to a children's aid society the society is obligated to investigate. Usually, the first step is to interview the person who made the report. The investigation may proceed from that point on a **consensual** basis, with the parents giving permission to interview and assess the child, and the suspected abuser consenting to an interview as well. Where the society suspects that a child may be in need of protection, it will typically refer the case to a review team.

consensual
something that is agreed to and/or permitted by the party to whom it is done or who participates in it

Review Team

A review team must be made up of at least one legally qualified medical practitioner and others qualified to perform psychological, developmental, educational, or social assessments, as appropriate for the particular case. If the child's parents consent, the child may be assessed by the review team without being brought to a place of safety by a children's aid society. If a problem is uncovered, the parties involved may agree to the provision of services by the society or another suitable agency. Voluntary services may be provided with the child remaining in the home, or with the child moved to a foster home or other facility.

Of course, the children's aid society will not always have the cooperation of parents. Where a society cannot adequately review a child's case because the parents will not consent to an assessment, the child may need to be brought to a place of safety—that is, taken into the custody of the children's aid society.

Homemaker Option

Where a children's aid society has sufficient suspicion to begin the process of bringing the child to a place of safety, it can elect, instead of actually bringing the child to a place of safety, to have a **homemaker** remain with the child in his or her home. A homemaker may live with the child for up to 30 days. If the parent is still not able to care for the child after 30 days, the child is typically brought to a place of safety. Reliance on a homemaker is not appropriate in situations where a child is suffering abuse. Placement of a homemaker in the home tends to be used in circumstances where, for some extraordinary reason, a good parent is temporarily unable to care for a child and there are no relatives available to help out; for example, a parent may suddenly fall ill, be delayed while travelling out of the country, or be detained in criminal custody pending a bail hearing.

homemaker
a person who works in the home of a vulnerable child in an effort either to support a struggling parent or to care for the child during the parent's temporary absence

Child Protection Proceedings

As a social service worker, you need to know and understand the various stages in child protection proceedings, including court procedure, so that you can inform and reassure clients who are experiencing this process.

Example
You work in a women's shelter and have a client whose child was brought to a place of safety as a result of a domestic assault in the child's presence. The child's mother is shocked that her child was taken, panicked about the situation, and anxious to have the child returned. You can assist by explaining why the child was removed from her care—that exposing a child to domestic violence constitutes child abuse, which the mother was unable to prevent—and that there will be a court hearing to determine whether the child needs protection. The client should understand that child protection hearings can be quite lengthy, extending over several days, and that it is unlikely that her child will be returned immediately following the first court appearance. It is also very important, in a case such as this, to advise the client to seek legal representation.

Grounds for Bringing a Child to a Place of Safety

As stated earlier, children's aid societies have a mandate to provide protection to children under the age of 16 and, in some circumstances, to 16- and 17-year-olds. A child in need of protection is defined in the Act, and it lists criteria very similar to those listed in the section relating to the duty to report. This makes sense, because the intent of the section is to impose a duty on people to report information that suggests that a child is in need of protection. The circumstances in which a child may be in need of protection include the following:

- physical, sexual, and emotional abuse
- risk of physical, sexual, or emotional harm
- risk of sexual abuse or molestation
- denial of necessary medical or psychological treatment
- failure to address behaviour of a child that would result in criminal charges if the child were 12 years of age or older

Additional grounds for bringing a child to a place of safety include the following:

- A child already in the care of the children's aid society has left or has been removed from care without authorization.
- A child under 12 has committed an act that, if the child were 12 or older, could form the basis for a criminal charge.
- A child who is under 16 has "withdrawn from the care and control" of parents, guardians, or agencies approved under the Act).

Situations where children have been brought to a place of safety and placed in the care of a children's aid society include, but are not limited to, the following:

- A young teenager with a newborn child does not appear to have appropriate support services available to assist her in caring for the child. The children's aid society considers the child to be in need of protection and has the baby removed from the mother's care at birth.
- A children's aid society has grounds to believe that a parent in a primary care-giving role is using illicit drugs.
- A domestic assault occurs within the family home with the child present at the time of the assault.
- A physician has found marks on a child, resulting in concerns by the children's aid society that inappropriate disciplinary measures are being used in the home.
- The home has not been cleaned by the caregiver for a significant period of time, resulting in concerns for the hygiene and health of the child.

Bringing a Child to a Place of Safety With or Without a Warrant

Generally, a warrant is required before a child may be brought to a place of safety. Pursuant to the Act, a justice of the peace may issue a warrant authorizing a child protection worker to bring a child to a place of safety if the justice of the peace is satisfied, on the basis of a child protection worker's sworn information, that there are reasonable and probable grounds to believe that the child is in need of protection and that a less restrictive course of action is not available or will not protect the child adequately.

However, if a child protection worker believes, on reasonable and probable grounds, that there is a substantial risk to the child's health or safety during the time necessary to obtain a warrant from the court, the child may be brought to a place of safety immediately. Although this provision is consistent with the primary purpose of the CYFSA—to promote the best interests, protection, and well-being of children—the effect is to give a children's aid society a significant degree of power to bring children to a place of safety and remove them from their home, without first having to establish before a justice of the peace or a court that, on a balance of probabilities, there is a need for bringing the child to a place of safety.

In some instances, the court has ordered the return of the child to the previous caregiver subject to restrictions imposed on the caregiver. In those circumstances, the least disruptive alternative was considered appropriate, in accordance with the other purposes of the Act.

A "place of safety," is defined under the Act as a hospital, a foster home, or another place designated as a place of safety (often, a group home established for the temporary care of children awaiting child protection proceedings).

A review team is assigned to every child brought to a place of safety. Within five days, one of three options must be chosen under the Act:

- Return the child to the parent(s) or guardian.
- Bring the case before the court for a child protection hearing.
- Have a temporary care agreement put in place.

The purpose of a child protection hearing is to make a legal determination as to whether the child is in need of protection and to provide for the child's care. Until such a determination is made by a court, the child may not be placed in the care of a children's aid society, and the society may not deliver services without parental consent.

It is often difficult to balance the best interests, protection, and well-being of a child with the autonomy and integrity of the family unit and the least disruptive course of action available to assist a child. The process is extremely disruptive to the family. In the effort to protect a child, and to err on the side of caution in ensuring that a child is protected, the integrity and autonomy of the family is often threatened, as well as the emotional security of the child, who may not be accustomed to being apart from his or her caregiver.

As a social service worker, you may wish to inform a client who is involved in child protection proceedings that, if appropriate, the child may be placed with a family member pending the resolution of the proceedings. Any family member willing to care for the child should present a plan of care to be assessed by the children's aid society.

Participants in the Child Protection Hearing

Parents of the child may be parties to the proceedings; that is, they may present evidence and make arguments. Additionally, any person who has cared for the child continuously for the six months before the hearing, such as a foster parent, may participate in the hearing.

A child aged 12 or over who is the subject of the hearing is generally entitled to attend unless the court thinks that being present would cause the child emotional harm. A child under 12 is generally not entitled to attend the hearing unless the court decides otherwise, on the basis that the child is capable of understanding the hearing and is unlikely to suffer emotional harm as a result.

A child may be represented by a lawyer; however, most children don't have the means to retain a lawyer. In certain cases, the court will decide that the child *should* have legal representation and will make an order that he or she is to be represented by the Children's Lawyer. This is generally done where the court thinks that the child's interests as expressed by the child do not coincide with either society's view or the parent's view of those interests. An example is a case in which an older child expresses a strong desire to remain in the care of an abusive parent.

A social service worker may be called as a witness in a child protection case, particularly if he or she was the one who made the original report. In most cases, giving evidence as a social service worker is a fairly simple matter of truthfully answering the questions asked—without exaggerating, fabricating, or concealing anything, and without making inappropriate or biased judgments about people or facts.

Dispositions

The purpose of a child protection hearing, as mentioned above, is to determine whether a child is in need of protection, and to provide for the child's care. In some cases, the court will make a care order based on a plan of care that has been prepared by a children's aid society. A plan of care must include the following:

- a description of the services proposed to be provided to the child
- an estimate of the time needed to achieve the results hoped for
- a description of the criteria the society will use to determine that those results have been achieved

Social service workers employed by children's aid societies may be involved in the preparation of plans of care and may be required to testify in court about them. In making an order, a court need not endorse or follow a plan of care exactly as proposed, but the plan of care is often a useful starting point in preparing a court order.

Best Interests of the Child

The decision to make a child protection order must be based on the best interests of the child. There are several factors to be considered in determining the child's best interest, including:

- the child's physical, mental, and emotional needs
- the child's physical, mental, and emotional level of development
- the child's cultural background
- the child's religious faith (if any)
- the child's existing family relationships and the importance, for the child's development, of a positive relationship with a parent and a secure place as a member of a family
- the child's views and wishes

Though the court must consider a child's ethnic and cultural background in all cases, the court has a special responsibility with respect to First Nations, Inuit, Métis, and other Indigenous children. Any person who makes an order with respect to an Indigenous child in need of protection must "take into consideration the importance, in recognition of the uniqueness of Indian and native culture, heritage and traditions, of preserving the child's cultural identity."

If a court is convinced that a child is in need of protection, before it may make an order removing the child from the home, the court must be satisfied that less disruptive alternatives would be inadequate to protect the child). This is consistent with the overall purposes of the CYFSA: to promote the best interests, protection, and well-being of children, and to consider the least disruptive course of action that is available and appropriate in a particular case.

Where the children's aid society proposes to keep a child in care, it must explain why adequate protection cannot be assured if the child is returned to his or her home, and what efforts, if any, will be made to maintain the relationship between the child and the parents or guardian. If the society proposes to remove the child permanently, it must inform the court of its plans for a long-term stable placement for the child.

Care and Protection Orders

In some cases, where a child has been brought before the court with the participation of the parents, or with his or her own consent, the court can make a **consent order**. This is an agreed plan for the child's care, developed with input from the parents and/ or the child, and consented to by them.

Most child protection orders are not agreements but rather are imposed by the court. The court has three options when making an order for care on behalf of a child without the parents' consent:

- a supervision order
- an order of interim society care
- an order of extended society care

consent order
an agreed plan for a child's care, developed with input from the parents and/or the child, and consented to by them

SUPERVISION ORDER

supervision order
a directive that allows a child to remain in the care of the parents or guardian under the supervision of a children's aid society for a period of 3 to 12 months

A **supervision order** allows the child to remain in the care of the parents or guardian. The children's aid society provides supervision for a period of 3 to 12 months, giving guidance to the parents or guardian and making sure that the child is safe and well cared for.

INTERIM SOCIETY CARE

interim society care
an order that provides for a child's placement in residential custody for a maximum of 12 months

If the court determines that a child cannot be adequately protected at home, but that it is appropriate for the child to continue to have contact with the parents or guardian, the court will typically make an order of **interim society care**. An order of interim society care provides for a child's placement in residential custody for a maximum of 12 months.

A child who is in society care has the right to visit his or her parents. If the parents (and sometimes others, such as grandparents) wish to visit the child, they must apply to the court for an access order. The court will permit access only if it is determined to be in the best interests of the child. If the child is 16 or older, he or she must consent to the access.

consecutive order
interim society care followed by supervision

The court can also make a **consecutive order** of interim society care followed by supervision (after the child has been returned to the care of the parents or guardian) for a total period not exceeding 12 months.

In some cases, where a child has been placed in interim society care, the court may subsequently determine that it would not be appropriate to return the child to the care of the parents or guardian. In these circumstances, the court can make an order of extended society care in respect of the child.

EXTENDED SOCIETY CARE

extended society care
an order in which the court determines that it is unlikely that the parents or guardian will ever be able to care for the child adequately

If the court determines that it is unlikely that the parents or guardian will ever be able to care for the child adequately, the court will make an order of **extended society care**. When a child enters into extended society care, it is not expected that the child will ever be returned to the care of the parents or guardian. A child who has entered into extended society care may subsequently become available for adoption without the consent of the parents or guardian.

In general, access orders are not made for youth who have entered extended society care. If circumstances were so extreme as to result in extended society care, access is unlikely to be in the child's best interests. Access could also jeopardize the child's chances to be placed in a stable home environment.

An extended society care order ends on the day the child turns 18. An interim society care order or supervision order that has not already expired is also terminated when the child reaches 18.

As was the case in the previous legislation, the new Act can provide continued care and support to persons who are 18 or older and eligible for prescribed support services.

RESTRAINING ORDER

In some cases, instead of or in addition to a supervision or society care order, a court may make a restraining order. A restraining order protects the child from another person by restricting the access of that person to the child. A restraining order can be an appropriate solution where the child has been abused by a person other than the custodial parent, such as a member of the extended family, a family friend, or a neighbour.

REVIEW OF ORDERS

Time-limited disposition orders made by the court (supervision orders, society care orders, and consecutive orders) must be reviewed prior to their expiration. The society is required under the CYFSA to commence a status review application and to serve it on all parties entitled to notice of the proceeding. On status review, the court may terminate the order that was made previously or make a further order of the same kind or another kind.

Status reviews of extended society care orders must be carried out at least once per year. There is one restriction on the making of a further order by the court: An interim care order cannot be made on a status review of an extended care order.

Kinship Care

An alternative to society care orders, which should be considered if appropriate, is the placement of a child in the care of a relative, friend, or neighbour, or, in the case of First Nations, Inuit, Métis, or other Indigenous children, a member of the child's band. This type of placement is made with the consent of the person who will be taking charge of the child.

Kinship care refers to placement of an at-risk child (or children) in the care of grandparents, aunts, uncles, other close relatives, or even non-relatives, such as god-parents, with whom the child has a kinship bond. An arrangement to place a child in kinship care can happen at two different stages in a child welfare case. It can happen with the consent of parents—for example, as part of a voluntary intervention by a children's aid society—or after a formal order has been issued to place the child into society care.

kinship care
placement of an at-risk child (or children) in the care of grandparents, aunts, uncles, other close relatives, or even non-relatives, such as godparents, with whom the child has a kinship bond

Differential Responses

Child welfare organizations in many US and Canadian jurisdictions are beginning to embrace the benefits of adopting a program of differential responses to child welfare cases, depending on the particular circumstances. The Centre of Excellence for Child Welfare (CECW), an agency funded by Health Canada, describes differential response as follows:[5]

> Differential response models, sometimes referred to as "alternative response models" or "multi-track systems," … include a range of potential response options customized to meet the diverse needs of families reported to child welfare. Differential response systems typically use multiple "tracks" or "streams" of service delivery. While some jurisdictions may initiate up to five tracks, as is the case with Michigan, most differential response systems employ two streams with the investigative track handling high-risk

---

5   Nico Trocmé, Della Knoke & Catherine Roy, eds, *Community Collaboration and Differential Response: Canadian and International Research and Emerging Models of Practice* (Ottawa: Centre of Excellence for Child Welfare, 2003) at vii.

cases. High-risk cases include all reports of sexual abuse, serious physical or emotional harm, chronic neglect and cases in which criminal charges may be laid. Less urgent cases are shifted to an alternative "assessment" or "community" track, where the focus of intervention is on brokering and coordinating services to address the short and long-term needs of these children and families.

In Canada, the only province or territory to have formally implemented a differential response model is Alberta. In Ontario, however, research studies and draft papers have been completed on the subject, including a paper by the Ontario Association of Children's Aid Societies (OACAS).[6] While the OACAS suggests that the CFSA implicitly permits the development of a differential response model, changes to the regulations would likely be required to fully support this initiative.

Responsibilities Toward Children in Care or in Receipt of Services

Once a child has been found to be in need of protection, a duty arises, on the part of the children's aid society and its employees, to actively protect the child. Failure to provide protection and service to a child as required by the CYFSA could lead to loss of the designation as a child protection agency or loss of a licence to run a children's residence.

There is also the potential for a civil lawsuit arising out of failure to protect a child. The Act specifically permits the Children's Lawyer to bring a civil suit for damages on behalf of a child against his or her abuser. The definition of abuse for this purpose is set out in section 136(2) of the Act:

> No person having charge of a child shall, …
>> (b) by failing to care and provide for or supervise and protect the child adequately,
>>> (i) permit the child to suffer abuse, or
>>> (ii) permit the child to suffer from a mental, emotional or developmental condition that, if not remedied, could seriously impair the child's development.

Under the Act, a civil suit could be brought against an individual social service worker or against a children's aid society or other child protection agency or residence. In some circumstances, a social service worker may even face criminal prosecution for failure to prevent the injury or death of a child.

Child welfare experts have suggested that social workers and social service workers who perform their duties in good faith and to the best of their abilities within the standards of their profession can generally expect to be free from criminal or civil liability. However, it is clear that law enforcement personnel will respond to the human cost of mistakes, and to the public outrage that follows serious harm to a child under agency supervision.

---

6 Differential Response Sub-Committee of Ontario Children's Aid Society Directors of Service, *A Differential Service Response for Child Welfare in Ontario* (Toronto: Author, 2004).

Notes, Reports, and Records

Accurate and timely note-taking is a crucial skill for social service workers. It is important for workplace efficiency, and it is critical to protect against liability.

Clients have access to all mental health and medical records regarding their care unless the treatment professional has reason to believe that access to the information contained in the clinical record may be harmful to the client or a third party.[7]

Documenting work in progress is a necessary component of keeping organized and prioritizing when dealing with heavy client caseloads. Information that is undocumented may be quickly forgotten or inaccurately recalled. By taking a few extra minutes to jot down notes summarizing all phone calls and meetings with clients, as well as internal discussions about clients, you will be able to pick up a file several weeks later and, at a glance, update your knowledge of the case. If co-workers are involved with the same client, "notes to file" are a valuable communication tool, keeping everyone informed. "To do" lists and action points are also helpful to keep you focused on what needs to be done.

In the event that you are asked to justify your decisions or actions with respect to a client, reliable and detailed notes will back you up. Your notes are evidence that you considered the issue carefully and fully, and responded in a competent and responsible manner. Without this document trail, you put yourself at risk of allegations of negligence.

Besides generating notes for personal or internal agency use, social service workers may also need to produce reports designed to be read by others, such as social workers, judges and lawyers, or government administrators. While internal **notes** are primarily designed as memory aids for the social service worker or to provide information to colleagues, **reports** have different and often quite specific purposes. A social service worker's duty both to respect client privacy rights and to communicate honestly with agencies entitled to receive reports means that considerable judgment is required in preparing external reports.

Standards of Practice for Record-Keeping

The Ontario College of Social Workers and Social Service Workers sets out the following requirements for record-keeping:[8]

> The creation and maintenance of **records** by social workers and the social service workers is an essential component of professional practice. The process of preparation and organization of material for the record provides a means to understanding the client and planning the social work and social service work intervention. The purpose of the social work and social service work record is to document services in a recognizable form in order to ensure the continuity and quality of service, to establish accountability for and evidence of the services rendered, to enable the evaluation of service quality,

notes
documentation primarily designed as memory aids for the social service worker or to provide information to colleagues

reports
documents written by persons who have direct knowledge of or experience with a client, an event, or a set of circumstances that are designed to be read by a third party

records
material prepared and organized to provide a means to understanding the client and planning the social work and social service work intervention

---

7   *McInerney v MacDonald*, [1992] 2 SCR 138.

8   Ontario College of Social Workers and Social Service Workers, *Code of Ethics and Standards of Practice Handbook* (Toronto: OCSWSSW, 2008), at 19.

and to provide information to be used for research and education. College members ensure that records are current, accurate, contain relevant information about clients and are managed in a manner that protects client privacy and in accordance with any applicable privacy and other legislation.

Note-Taking

General Considerations

In taking notes, you are creating a written record of certain events. Before you begin, you should ask yourself the following questions:

- Who will read these notes?
- What will the reader be hoping to learn from them?
- Is the reader familiar with the context, or must I provide background information?
- What are the privacy implications of making these notes?
- What is my own purpose for making these notes?

In the simplest scenario, you will be keeping notes for your own future use. In that case, you should make notes in the format that you find most useful, without worrying about providing background information. However, it is important to keep in mind that in some circumstances, notes recorded for personal use may need to be made available to others, such as colleagues or perhaps the client. Your notes may even be used in a legal proceeding; for example, you may be required, in your professional capacity, to give testimony based on your notes in a court of law. For this reason, any notes relating to the practice of your profession should be accurate, and free from offensive or inappropriate content that would reflect badly on you or on the agency where you work.

If you are keeping notes that are intended to be read by others—for example, in a setting where clients are served by multiple professionals—there will be additional considerations. For example, you will need to consider whether what you write is understandable to the intended reader and whether the notes provide sufficient information.

In the course of your practice, you may encounter situations in which legal issues arise. These can include harassment by another resident in a group home, disciplinary action against staff members, use of restraints to manage a client, and the witnessing of abuse involving a client.

In these situations, it is prudent to take notes so that you can substantiate your actions and your reasons for taking them, in case the incident forms part of a subsequent investigation or legal claim. This type of note-taking is especially challenging, and the keys to getting it right are to be thorough, honest, accurate, and neutral. Sometimes notes taken in these contexts need to be used at a later time to generate a report.

Usefulness and Understandability

Your notes will be useful only to the extent that they can be understood by the reader and that they provide all the information that is required. In reviewing your notes for understandability, you may find the following checklist helpful.

1. Did you make the notes as soon as possible after receiving the information? Timeliness in making notes promotes accuracy.

2. Do your notes follow a well-organized structure—for example, chronological order?

3. Are your notes dated? If you make notes in a shared notebook or file, are they marked as yours?

4. Did you write out, in full, any pertinent details and check the accuracy of the information recorded (including the spelling of names, addresses, and phone numbers)?

5. If you used abbreviations, did you work from a list of accepted or recognized abbreviations, or provide explanations of what they refer to?

6. Did you make it clear which portions of your notes are direct quotations of another person's words by using quotation marks?

Generally, it is not appropriate to attempt to answer the question "Why?" Often, you will be reporting on the actions of others, and you cannot be sure that you understand the motivations for someone's actions, or the underlying causes of an event. Attempting to do so can make you appear less than impartial, if the matter is ever reviewed, or can inappropriately narrow the scope of an investigation.

Making useful, understandable notes requires careful consideration of what information should and should not be reported, and how it should be reported. Some guidelines are suggested in the following section.

Choices About Information

Notes should be focused and concise. Including unnecessary or excessively detailed information will only reduce the readability and impact of important content. For the purpose of building a rapport with your clients, you may sometimes listen to their ideas about quite irrelevant matters, but those conversations need not be recorded. Personal comments should also be avoided; if you must note something negative about a client, you should do so in language that is professional and as neutral as possible.

To illustrate the choice of appropriate information, consider a situation where you are making notes of a client interview to determine employability. Information obviously worth recording would be details about education and work experience, and about the kind of work sought. It would also be useful to note factors that could restrict the client's availability for certain kinds of employment; for example, "She has school-age children and might have difficulty working afternoon and night shifts" or "He was fired from a job that involved sales, which he says he hates." Anecdotes about friendships in previous workplaces are probably not important. You should avoid value judgments, such as "He claimed to have excellent customer service skills, but I think he was just being arrogant." Instead, keep it factual.

Finally, it can sometimes be useful to note gaps in information or to note that you have not observed something that you expected to observe. This can serve as a reminder, to yourself or to colleagues, of matters that should perhaps be investigated further. In the context of the employability interview described above, you might discover that there is a gap of a few years in the client's employment history and that the client is reluctant to provide information about what he or she was doing during that time. Since the reason could affect your client's eligibility for a particular job (for example, if your client was serving time in prison), further attempts should be made to obtain an explanation from the client.

Revising Notes

Sometimes it is necessary to make changes in your notes—for example, if you discover an error or if you want to include additional information. When and how you make such revisions will depend on the kind of work you do and the format you use for recording information. However, in all circumstances, you should follow certain procedures in altering your notes.

The first rule is that, unlike personal notes, notes made for professional purposes should never be destroyed.

The second rule is that, since your notes may be used by others, you should make your changes clear. For example, in handwritten notes or a typewritten copy, use a single line to strike out, and write the correction above or after this line. It is good practice to date and initial any changes of substance (as opposed to trivial changes such as corrections in spelling), particularly if your notes are part of a file to which several people contribute.

Some professionals use notebooks with numbered pages, both for easy reference and for security of the record, since it is immediately evident if an entry has been torn out. If you use this type of note-taking system, never tear out a page; it may appear that you are trying to hide something. Instead, strike through the page with a diagonal line. You should not be reluctant to correct inaccuracies, but you should do so by crossing out in a way that doesn't obliterate the entry, or by adding new, more accurate information on another page.

If you make notes in an electronic format (on a computer), the safest way to make a change is to save the previous entry as a draft, and work from a new version of the document, saving any previous versions for your records. Alternatively, you can use a word processing program that "tracks" changes. These programs often note changes using strikethroughs or different colours and can save the date and time of the change. Many of these programs are designed to manage documents that are accessed by more than one user, tracking the deletions and additions of each.

Privacy Considerations

The introduction of the federal *Personal Information Protection and Electronic Documents Act* and the Ontario *Personal Health Information Protection Act, 2004* added a new layer to the issue of protecting clients' privacy.[9] It is difficult to give specific recommendations about privacy protection here, because social service workers work in a wide range of settings. However, some general guidelines can be suggested.

- Be aware of concerns about privacy and the confidentiality of client information.

- Be familiar with your employer's policy with respect to client privacy.

- If you need to request, share, or use personal information about a client, ensure that the appropriate releases have been obtained.

- Never share your notes unless you have been given permission to disclose them from every person mentioned in them. (Your office may have obtained releases to permit certain kinds of disclosure; inquire whether this is the case.)

- If you are authorized to disclose your notes, make sure you understand the scope of that authorization: to which client(s) and to what information it applies, and to whom the information can be disclosed.

- If in doubt about your right to disclose certain information, withhold the information until you have checked with a supervisor or obtained a new release from the client.

Typically, in a setting where you are expected to take notes to facilitate the provision of client services, there is a certain expectation of privacy associated with the content of those notes. In many cases, people who have interests that are opposed to your client's interests (for example, the other party in a lawsuit) will not be able to gain access to your notes. There are, however, exceptions. Unlike the communications between a lawyer and a client, what is said between you as a social service worker and your client is not considered privileged (protected from disclosure in court). Also, some statutes or court orders can force you to disclose the content of communications with a client. You might also, under certain circumstances, feel a moral obligation to disclose information to a third party, such as if you believe your client is suicidal.

As a result, you should never promise a client confidentiality unless you are certain that you can guarantee it. You should also not allow the client to be lulled into a false sense of security about talking with you. In some cases, it is necessary to warn a client ahead of time that there are certain kinds of information that you cannot keep to yourself. This gives a client the opportunity to decide whether to censor what he or she chooses to tell you.

If you know that a party who is opposed to your client could gain access to your notes, you should use extra care when deciding what information to include in them.

---

9   *Personal Information Protection and Electronic Documents Act*, SC 2000, c 5; *Personal Health Information Protection Act, 2004*, SO 2004, c 3, Schedule A.

This means that you can use discretion in recording unfavourable or unflattering details, but it doesn't allow you to omit information that you ought to record.

It is possible that in a criminal matter involving sexual assault, the lawyer for the accused will request that the victim disclose certain information about past history that will assist in the accused's defence. This is a right for the accused to make a full and fair defence under section 7 of the *Charter of Rights and Freedoms*.[10] Victims have protections against disclosure of information related to past history. It is possible that social service workers will be asked to appear at court along with any relevant notes relating to their client's past history. In such cases the worker has the right to object to the disclosure of confidential client records. The court will balance the legal rights of the defendant and the rights of the victim. The judge will conduct an **"in camera" hearing** to determine whether the production of records is necessary based on the interests of justice.

> **"in camera" hearing**
> a court hearing conducted privately with no public access

The court will look at society's interest in encouraging the reporting of sexual offences, in encouraging treatment for complainants of sexual offences, and in the integrity of the trial process. The judge determines which records are relevant and how the record will be produced, viewed, and edited.[11]

Report-Writing

Report-writing differs from note-taking in two key ways:

- Reports are prepared specifically for use by persons other than the writer.
- Reports are usually written for a specific purpose other than just the creation of a written record.

Reports may also differ in other ways, including the following:

- A report may be prepared in collaboration with other colleagues, professionals, etc.
- The organization or content of a report may be formally prescribed, instead of being left to the preference of the writer.
- The writer may be required to express opinions and/or make recommendations.

While the range of reports that social service workers may encounter in their work is almost limitless, the general function of those reports is universal: They provide a formal framework by which a person who has direct knowledge of or experience with a client, event, or set of circumstances can communicate that knowledge or experience to a third party (a supervisor, an administrator of an agency, a committee, etc.).

---

10   *Canadian Charter of Rights and Freedoms*, Part I of the Constitution Act, 1982, being Schedule B to the *Canada Act 1982* (UK), 1982, c 11.

11   *R v O'Connor*, [1995] 4 SCR 411; *R v Mills*, [1999] 3 SCR 668.

The following examples indicate the kinds of reports that social service workers may be required to contribute to or write:

- *Human resources reports*: A social service worker who supervises other employees may be required to report to a senior manager on the performance of those subordinates.

- *Reports in family relations contexts*: A social service worker who works in a supervised access program may be asked to prepare a report for a court on how well this approach is working for a particular family and whether there are any problems.

- *Reports for use by care workers or health care professionals*: A social service worker may be asked to observe a candidate for long-term care and report on the extent of the candidate's need for assistance with daily living.

- *Reports in the corrections context*: A social service worker who counsels offenders serving custodial sentences may be asked to prepare a report about some aspect of an inmate's progress or behaviour for use in an early release assessment.

- *Reports in the context of making social benefits decisions*: A social service worker who is an intake officer for a social benefits program, such as Ontario Works, may be required to prepare regular reports for program administrators on whether individual clients are complying with participation requirements.

When preparing a report, you will benefit from having thorough and clear notes from which to work. If there is a prescribed format, you should be careful to follow it. This may mean converting content that is organized in one way in your notes into a different format for the report. You may also have to supplement the information in your notes with additional background information, if the intended readers of the report do not have your knowledge of the context—the client, the issue or event, and the circumstances. In effect, you must put yourself in the reader's shoes and ask yourself what the reader needs to know.

Often, you will be required to strike an appropriate balance between your duty to the client, or to your employer, and your obligations as the author of the report. For example, if you are an intake officer with Ontario Works, and you are preparing a report for benefits about an applicant whom you feel is not prepared to comply with participation requirements, you may have a duty to express that opinion even though it would disappoint the applicant. Your duty to your employer and the goals of the program supersede your obligations to the applicant.

Similarly, if you are working as a parole officer, or in a program for inmates of a correctional facility, you may be required to report on a client's suitability for early release. If you have concerns about the client, you must report them, even if doing so appears to be against the client's interest. In such situations, where you are required to draw unfavourable conclusions about a client, explain your reasons truthfully and briefly; avoid unnecessary elaboration. Ideally, well in advance of making your report, you will have laid the groundwork with the client, advising him

1. that you are required to make reports about him in the course of your work;
2. that your reports must be truthful and accurate; and
3. that there are important limits on the confidentiality of communications between you and him.

The general guidelines for writing reports are similar to those for note-taking and can be summarized as follows:

1. In making reports, you should always be scrupulously honest.
2. You should be neutral in your comments unless an opinion is specifically required.
3. You should use appropriate and professional language:
   a. Avoid labels or comments that could be construed as racist, sexist, elitist, or otherwise discriminatory.
   b. No matter how strong your private opinions, refrain from making judgmental or damaging remarks about anyone, even a person whose behaviour toward your client is extremely offensive and upsetting.
   c. Avoid comments that could reflect poorly on you as a professional or on your employer.
   d. Avoid any comments that might suggest bias or a desire to cast blame on another party.

Finally, you should remember that your reports, or your notes, may be viewed by the client at some later time. Therefore, you should take care always to communicate with the sensitivity that is expected of you as a helping professional.

Documentary Evidence in Legal Proceedings

Evidence, in the context of civil litigation or criminal proceedings, is anything that tends to support or disprove a conclusion. In many legal proceedings, a significant portion of the evidence presented takes the form of written documents, collectively referred to as "documentary evidence."

Generally, a document filed with the court is not by itself considered sufficient proof of its contents. In most cases, the court requires a witness to attend in court to give oral testimony about the document—who made it, when it was made, and whether its contents reflect the truth. For example, in a case involving child abuse, a court presented with allegations of child abuse written in a private letter from one person to another will not automatically accept the letter as evidence. In order to establish the reliability of the evidence, the party seeking to have it admitted by the court must call the writer of the letter to testify about the letter and its contents.

It is important for social service workers to understand the role of documentary evidence in legal proceedings and court or tribunal procedures for testing the reliability of such evidence. From time to time, cases arise where notes and other written records created by social service workers are brought forward as evidence for or against a party in the case. In these circumstances, the social service worker who prepared the document may be called to testify in court or at the hearing.

A social service worker may also be called to give oral testimony in a case involving a client or the social service worker's employer, and she may rely on her notes and reports to refresh her memory. This section provides some suggestions that you may find useful if your professional work places you in either of these situations.

Using Your Notes in Court

If you are required to give testimony in court, you will be permitted to bring your notes with you and to consult them as a memory aid. To avoid fumbling with your notes on the witness stand, carefully review them on the day before your court appearance so that you can quickly locate the information you need.

When you testify, you must ask the judge's permission before you refer to your notes, and you will not be permitted to simply read from your notes. The lawyers who question you will want you to describe your current recollection of the events in question; your notes are intended to remind you of important details you may have forgotten.

If you choose to rely on your notes in court, the judge will likely allow the other party's lawyer to examine them and perhaps make photocopies. If your notes relate to more than one client, you have a duty to protect the information about the clients who are not the subject of the court case. You can do this by providing the other party's lawyer with only those pages that apply to the relevant client. If you use a notebook from which it is not possible or acceptable to remove pages, you can use elastic bands to separate the notes that you are required to disclose from the notes that you need to keep confidential.

If you are asked a question and your truthful answer differs from what you have written in your notes, you must give that truthful answer and be prepared to explain to the court why your notes, in your opinion, are not accurate.

Being Cross-Examined on Your Notes

If your notes have been provided to the opposing party's counsel as part of the disclosure process, they may have been entered as an exhibit in the case and may form part of the public record. If this has happened, it is likely that you will be subject to **cross-examination** on the content of your notes by the other party's lawyer. Make sure you have a copy of the notes in front of you before this cross-examination begins. If you don't have them, tell the judge so that you can be provided with a copy.

Your credibility as a witness—the degree to which the judge and jury believe you—can directly affect the weight that will be given to your evidence. For this reason, you will be most helpful to your client if you deliver your testimony in a straightforward way, without excessive elaboration or attempts to hold back information.

cross-examination
the opportunity for opposing counsel to ask a witness questions

If you are asked about a passage in your notes that you cannot immediately recall, do not rush your answer, even if the cross-examining lawyer is pressuring you. Take a moment to think, and, if necessary, ask permission to consult your notes; then, once you're sure, answer the question. It is in the interests of justice for you to answer accurately, not instantly, and you need to avoid making a mistake that the opposing lawyer can use to cast doubt on your credibility.

Since the objective of cross-examination is to undermine the other party's case, the cross-examining lawyer may attempt to find inconsistencies in your testimony, or between your testimony and your notes, so that it appears that you are lying or fabricating information. Rather than react defensively, stay calm, and remember that your duty is to be truthful. If you have made a mistake in an earlier statement, if you have made a mistake in your notes, or if you simply don't remember something, you must say so. But also keep in mind that it is never appropriate for counsel to badger or harass a witness, nor are you obliged to answer the same question twice. If this happens, pause to allow the lawyer for your side to object, or state that you are feeling bullied, or that you have already answered the particular question. Your statement will form part of the court record.

Affidavits

affidavit
a sworn written statement by a witness that replaces testimony

Child protection law has been increasingly using **affidavit** evidence. An affidavit is a sworn written statement by a witness that replaces testimony. It is generally limited to direct knowledge. Hearsay or information conveyed by others is sometimes allowed. Affidavits are drafted by lawyers and should reflect the witness's tone.

KEY TERMS

SUGGESTED SOURCES

Canadian Child Welfare Research Portal (CWRP), <http://cwrp.ca/about>

Office of the Children's Lawyer, <https://www .attorneygeneral.jus.gov.on.ca/english/about/artcl/ fjsd_ocl.php>

Office of the Provincial Advocate for Children and Youth, <https://www.provincialadvocate.on.ca>

Ontario Association of Children's Aid Societies, <http://www.oacas.org>

Rock, Nora, *Child Protection and Canadian Law: A Service Perspective* (Toronto: Emond Montgomery, 2005).

Samuels, Marilyn & Elayne Tanner, *Managing a Legal and Ethical Social Work Practice* (Toronto: Irwin Law, 2003).

REVIEW QUESTIONS

1. What is the paramount purpose of the CYFSA?

2. List four kinds of observations that would trigger a duty to report under the CYFSA.

3. List three possible dispositions that can be made once a child is determined to be in need of protection. How do they differ?

4. Are communications between a client and a social service worker protected by privilege?

5. If a social service worker has recorded confidential personal information about a client in her notes, and a third party requests access to those notes, what should the social service worker do?

Family Law and Adoption

7

LEARNING OUTCOMES

After completing this chapter, you should be able to:

- List the federal and provincial statutes that codify family law in Ontario.

- Understand the key principles that govern custody, access, and support in Ontario.

- Explain the legal importance of the best interests of the child.

- Explain the role of the Children's Lawyer.

- Describe the role of a family support worker with respect to access to Ontario Works benefits.

- Understand the work of the Family Responsibility Office.

- Understand the basic laws of adoption.

- Understand the types of adoption.

- Describe the rules of consent and disclosure for adoption.

Introduction

Divorce, family property, and child custody and access are among the most common types of litigation undertaken by Canadians. The Canadian divorce rate has hovered near the 50 percent mark in recent decades, and most research suggests that common law partnerships break up at least as often as marriages.

Divorce and separation affect many families in the peak child-raising years. Family breakdown has significant negative economic, practical, and emotional consequences for all members of the family.

Social service workers may be involved with separating families in a variety of ways. They may work in shelters for the victims of family violence, as employees of children's aid societies, in the office of the Children's Lawyer, or in any of a myriad of other roles supporting children. In these settings, clients may need basic information about a range of legal issues that arise early in a separation, such as the right to live in the matrimonial home.

Social service workers may also encounter clients who have begun to adjust to a separation but need help with parenting skills. An example of a social service worker's role at this stage might be supporting **supervised access** by a parent to his or her children at a special access and exchange centre.

supervised access
by a parent to his or her children at a special access and exchange centre

While social service workers may be called on to provide basic legal information to their clients, it is very important for them to avoid providing any kind of legal advice. Each case of separation and divorce has its own individual circumstances, and most social service workers lack the training to determine the best course of action for their clients. Even advice that might seem, to the social service worker, to be a matter of common sense may ultimately be detrimental to a client's case.

For example, a social service worker who is concerned about the safety of a separating wife in her home may think that the wife should wait until the husband goes to work and then have the locks changed. However, the law provides that both spouses have an equal right to live in the matrimonial home unless a court order has been obtained granting one spouse the right of exclusive possession.

Likewise, where there are children involved, advising a client to leave the matrimonial home, with or without the children, may also have significant legal consequences. Before a parent leaves with the children, a court order for interim custody should be obtained. If the parent leaves without the children, this may be viewed under the law as abandonment.

A person contemplating separation should review the options carefully with a lawyer before taking any action. Any improper action that a party takes has the potential to be raised by the other party as an issue in the course of subsequent proceedings.

"Common sense" advice can have serious legal ramifications with respect to access as well. For example, it might seem reasonable to recommend that a child with a cold should stay at home instead of going out on a scheduled visit with her father. But this could be interpreted as impeding the father's access and could influence a court to determine that the mother is uncooperative and not a good candidate for custody.

In short, it is essential that a social service worker make no recommendations that could be perceived as legal advice to a client in a family law matter. A social service worker who oversteps these boundaries risks being sued if the client follows her advice and suffers economic or other harm as a result.

Figure 7.1 provides some examples of the difference between legal information (which, if accurate, is acceptable to give) and legal advice, which must be avoided. Social service agencies can help their staff to avoid giving legal advice by preparing a standard handout with basic legal information. An agency can ask a family lawyer to review and approve the handout, so that social service workers can feel comfortable providing it to their clients.

FIGURE 7.1   Examples of the Differences Between Legal Information and Legal Advice

Legal Information	Legal Advice
• Explaining the importance of obtaining legal advice and providing referral to lawyers	• Recommending that a client leave the home
• Providing contact information for local Legal Aid offices	• Recommending that a client change the locks in the home
• Advising clients of the range of issues they may encounter, such as custody and access, support, division of property, occupancy of the matrimonial home, and personal safety	• Recommending that a client refuse to relinquish the children
• Explaining the services provided by supervised access and exchange centres	• Suggesting that a client pay less support
	• Recommending that a client withdraw money from a joint account to keep it from the other spouse

Family Law Issues

Family law has evolved to address the wide range of needs of separating parties and their children:

- Divorce law addresses the "status" issue of whether (and when) the parties can consider themselves single again (and remarry, if they wish).
- Family property law determines the appropriate division of assets and real property brought into and accumulated during the union.
- Family support law is designed to ensure that economically dependent family members who are unable to fully support themselves after family breakdown receive economic help from those who supported them during the union.
- Custody and access law is designed to ensure that the day-to-day care of children and the children's ongoing relationships with parents are arranged in a manner that reflects the children's best interests.
- Family law also addresses the issue of the personal safety of spouses and children.

Like most other areas of law, family legislation evolved from the common law, and many of the directions it has taken reflect common law court decisions. Most modern family law, however, is statute-based. While court decisions dictate the *application* of statutory provisions, our federal and provincial/territorial legislation forms what is intended to be a complete and exhaustive code for dealing with the issues families face after the partners separate.

Family law issues are not resolved only by courts; in fact, handling family matters without going to court is encouraged under our family law. While a court order is needed for a divorce to be final, many couples, whether they were legally married or simply living together, resolve all or most of their family law issues outside court. This can happen by direct negotiation between the parties, who (sometimes with the help of lawyers) draft an agreement, or a contract, to manage their post-separation relations. It can also happen through **mediation**, when a trained, neutral professional supports the parties in working out their issues and achieving an acceptable agreement. Mediation and other forms of alternative dispute resolution are discussed in greater detail in Chapter 11.

Mediation is sometimes said to take place "in the shadow of the law." This means that parties enter into mediation knowing that if their negotiations break down, they will have no choice but to go to court, where resolving problems is more expensive and the parties lose some control over the process (because a judge makes the final decisions). The threat of court can encourage mediated solutions, and the state of the law (for example, the child support formulas used in the court) can serve as guideposts to help the parties know "what's fair," even if this law is never directly applied to their own situation by a court.

mediation
a form of alternative dispute resolution in which a trained, neutral professional supports the parties in working out their issues and achieving an acceptable agreement

Family Legislation

Family law in Canada is complicated somewhat by the historical division of constitutional powers between the federal government and the provinces and territories. While the property aspects of family law fall squarely within provincial and territorial jurisdiction, marriage and divorce were assigned to federal jurisdiction under the *Constitution Act, 1867*.[1]

This means that when a married couple separate and want the marriage to be legally dissolved, the ensuing divorce is governed by the federal *Divorce Act*, but property issues are resolved under provincial and territorial family law legislation.[2] When an unmarried, cohabiting ("common law") couple separate, however, the legal consequences of the separation are governed by provincial and territorial family law statutes.

---

1 *Constitution Act, 1867* (UK), 30 & 31 Vict, c 3, reprinted in RSC 1985, Appendix II, No 5.

2 *Divorce Act*, RSC 1985, c 3 (2nd Supp), as amended.

Divorce

The *Divorce Act*, a federal statute, governs the dissolution of formal marriages in Canada. Unless an existing marriage is dissolved, marriage partners are not eligible to be married again. Marriage breakdown is the only ground for divorce in Canada. Marriage breakdown can be proven using evidence of any of the following:

- one year's separation
- adultery
- cruelty

The great majority of Canadian divorces are granted on proof of one year's separation. A couple seeking a divorce can apply for a divorce order before the year of separation is up, but the divorce cannot be granted until the one-year mark. The *Divorce Act* requires couples (at least in the absence of cruelty or abuse) to consider reconciling, and failing that, to attempt to come to an agreement about issues of support and custody through a mediated process before entering into litigation.

The *Divorce Act*, a federal statute, provides for divorce where the marriage has broken down. Generally, the parties must be separated for a year before a divorce is granted. Divorce is granted on a "no-fault" basis, which means that the court is generally not interested in the conduct of the parties. The *Divorce Act* includes provisions governing spousal support, child support, and custody and access.

It is important to understand that divorce based on separation of at least a year is considered to be "no-fault." This means that it is not relevant for the court to know how the parties treated each other or who left and why. This may be a difficult concept for some marriage partners to grasp, particularly when they are struggling with feelings of anger or loss. Social service workers can help these clients to express and deal with their emotions in a clinical setting, and encourage them to approach legal issues dispassionately.

Same-Sex Marriage

Today in Ontario, partners of the same sex can be formally married. For a few years before same-sex marriage was recognized, cohabiting arrangements between same-sex partners were recognized under the *Family Law Act* for the purpose of some post-separation legal issues, but formal marriage was unavailable to lesbian and gay couples.[3]

Beginning in the late 1980s, a number of gay and lesbian couples in Ontario brought lawsuits challenging their exclusion from access to formal marriage. These legal challenges were usually raised on the basis of discrimination or violation of rights under the *Canadian Charter of Rights and Freedoms*.[4] The Ontario Court of Appeal ultimately ruled that it is against the law to prohibit gay and lesbian couples from marrying, and same-sex marriages became legal in Ontario.

---

3   *Family Law Act*, RSO 1990, c F.3.

4   *Canadian Charter of Rights and Freedoms*, Part I of the *Constitution Act, 1982*, being Schedule B to the *Canada Act 1982* (UK), 1982, c 11.

Around the same time, similar legal challenges were being brought in other provinces and territories. In July 2005, the federal parliament clarified the law by enacting legislation that makes it legal for same-sex couples to marry anywhere in Canada. Same-sex married couples can also obtain a divorce under the *Divorce Act*.

It is important to note that the change to the law does not compel any religious group to endorse or perform same-sex marriages. For example, a Catholic priest cannot be required to officiate at such a ceremony.

Distribution of Family Property upon Separation

When a married couple separates, there is legislation in place in every province and territory to govern the division of their net family property.

In Ontario, the *Family Law Act* establishes rules for the calculation and division of family property so that the couple's property can be divided equitably between them upon separation. Under the Act, a spouse does not acquire an ownership interest in property owned by the other spouse, but does have a right to an **equalization payment** if the parties separate. The equalization payment equals one-half of the difference between the net family property of each spouse, calculated as follows:

> **equalization payment**
> in a separation agreement, equal to one-half of the difference between the net family property of each spouse

1. Start with the value of the property owned by each spouse at the time the parties separate, including land, vehicles, bank accounts, and business interests; then

2. Subtract from this amount
   a. debts and liabilities on the date of separation;
   b. the net value of property owned on the date of marriage (property owned minus debts and liabilities); and
   c. excluded property (gifts and inheritances, damage awards for personal injury, and property excluded by a spousal agreement).

The *Family Law Act* governs the division of the couple's property upon separation by providing for a payment from one spouse to the other in order to equalize the value of their assets. The Act also provides for equal interests in the matrimonial home, regardless of ownership, and for spousal and child support.

Once this calculation is completed for each spouse, the equalization payment is determined by subtracting the smaller net family property amount from the larger. The spouse with the larger net family property amount must pay half the difference to the other spouse, thereby "equalizing" the net family property.

Matrimonial Home

> **matrimonial home**
> property that the spouses ordinarily occupied as their family residence at the time of separation

The *Family Law Act* creates special rules for deciding what happens to the matrimonial home. The legislation defines a **matrimonial home** as property that the spouses ordinarily occupied as their family residence at the time of separation. Unless and until a court orders otherwise, both spouses have an equal right of possession of a matrimonial home, and neither spouse may sell the matrimonial home without the consent of the other. Depending on the circumstances, one party may be temporarily granted the exclusive right to live in the matrimonial home (exclusive possession), one party may buy out the other, or the home may be sold and the proceeds divided equally.

Custody and Access

Custody generally refers to the legal arrangement for the day-to-day care of and decision-making with respect to a child. Having custody of a child means having the authority to make decisions about matters such as education, medical treatment, and religious observance. **Access** generally refers to the arrangement by which the parent who does not have custody is permitted to spend time with the child. Although these terms are still used in family law statutes, their meaning is elastic.

Similarly, expressions like "sole custody" and "joint custody" do not have rigid definitions. Sole custody generally refers to a situation where one parent has decision-making power, and joint custody generally refers to shared decision-making. However, involvement in decision-making need not be all or nothing. Instead of describing an arrangement as sole or joint custody, better terminology may be "parenting plan." In a parenting plan, the rights and responsibilities of each parent may be mixed and matched, according to the family's particular needs. For example, one parent might make decisions about day-to-day medical concerns, and the other parent might make decisions regarding religious observance.

Shared decision-making requires considerable contact between the separated parents. For joint custody to work properly, the parents must be able to negotiate contentious issues and also accommodate each other's schedules. If the parents have joint custody but are incapable of calm and rational discussion, a parenting coordinator may be used as a mediator or an arbitrator to assist the parents in making decisions.

Parenting coordinators can sometimes be social service workers, and they are trained to assess what is in the best interests of the child. If the parenting coordinator is unable to facilitate a compromise between the parents, he or she is empowered, either by the court or by agreement between the parties, to make a binding decision. This helps to diminish conflict and reduce expenses by keeping the parties out of court.

Social service workers may also be involved in exchange programs, which provide a neutral location where parents can drop off and pick up their children. These programs can help to minimize conflict that might arise if one parent had to go to the other parent's residence (for example, if a parent did not get along with the other parent's new spouse) or if the dropping-off parent has a history of entering the other parent's home uninvited.

Both custody and access are governed by legislation: the federal *Divorce Act* and, in Ontario, the *Children's Law Reform Act* (CLRA).[5] Under the *Divorce Act*, either (previously married) parent can automatically apply for custody or access, and other individuals can apply if they have the permission of the court. Under the CLRA, a parent (whether previously married or a former common law partner) "or any other person" can apply.

custody
generally refers to the legal arrangement for the day-to-day care of and decision-making with respect to a child

access
generally refers to the arrangement by which the parent who does not have custody is permitted to spend time with the child

---

5 *Children's Law Reform Act*, RSO 1990, c C.12.

The *Children's Law Reform Act* governs custody and access on the basis of the best interests of the children. As noted above, custody generally means the authority to make decisions about things like education, medical treatment, and religious observance. Where parents share decision-making, custody is joint. Access generally describes the arrangement by which the parent who does not live with the child spends time with the child.

Best Interests of the Child

According to both statutes, custody and access arrangements are to be based on the best interests of the child. Where both parents want custody, the court is required to decide the issue not on the basis of which parent is more "deserving," but on the basis of what will be best for the child.

There are many factors to be taken into account in making custody decisions, and it is very important that clients have the benefit of a lawyer's advice when shaping a parenting plan to be negotiated or litigated between the parties. The court will generally favour an arrangement that fosters stability in the child's life, and it will give weight to historical caregiving patterns. For example, if the child has been cared for by a full-time stay-at-home mother who intimately knows the child's needs, habits, schedules, and preferences, the court will be more likely to award custody to the mother, even if the divorce means that both parents will have to go out to work.

The court will also consider the will and ability of each parent to support and foster a good relationship between the child and the other parent. For example, if one parent obstructs the other parent's access to the child, or speaks negatively to the child about the other parent, the court may try to address this by limiting the time the obstructive parent spends with the child.

It is more or less settled in Canadian law that the opinion of children with respect to custody and access is a factor that can properly be considered by the courts in making decisions. However, the extent to which children should be directly involved in the legal process is much more controversial.

Allowing or encouraging children to testify in court raises a number of concerns. In many cases, children are quite hesitant to express any opinions at all, for fear of displeasing one parent or the other. Where a child who is unwilling to express an opinion reports feeling pressured to do so, a social service worker may have sufficient reason (ideally, after consulting with a lawyer) to advocate for the child's right not to comment.

Where one parent seems to be placing undue pressure on a child to take part in a family law dispute, the court (and/or a mediator) will typically address this concern from the perspective of the best interests of the child; that is, it will allow participation by the child only to the extent that this seems to be in the child's best interests. In extreme cases, a parent's attempts to pressure a child might be viewed as evidence of the parent's unwillingness to further the child's best interests (thus going against an award of custody).

However, where a child is willing, or even eager, to participate in the legal process as a witness, many experts now believe that it is not necessarily damaging, and it may in fact be beneficial, to allow the child to do so.

Finally, in some situations, the court will consider the emotional ties and the preferences of the child. Particularly in the case of an older child, the child's own wishes about living arrangements will often influence the court's decision. The older and more mature the child is, the more influence his or her preferences are likely to have in the court's determination.

With respect to access arrangements, in the great majority of cases, it is considered to be in the child's best interests to maintain a relationship with both parents. The court will even go so far, in some cases, as to award access to a parent against the child's own expressed wishes. Such a decision is always controversial. It is usually made where the court believes that the child's current attitude toward the parent is probably temporary, perhaps coloured by negative feelings arising out of the separation process. If there is no apparent risk of child abuse or neglect, courts are generally very supportive of access.

Custody and Access Assessment

If custody and access issues are contentious and there are "clinical issues," meaning mental health concerns regarding one or both parents and/or the child or children, the court may appoint an assessor to provide it with expert advice. An assessor is a person with technical or professional skill, such as a psychologist or social service worker, who will interview the parents, children, teachers, and mental health professionals involved with the family, and submit a report with recommendations to the court. The parties will be required to pay for the assessment.

If the parties do not have the resources to pay for an assessment, the court may recommend involvement by the Children's Lawyer.

The Children's Lawyer

The provision of a court-ordered or government-funded lawyer for children in Ontario dates back to 1826, when a private lawyer was appointed to serve as guardian *ad litem* (at law) for children who needed legal representation. That role is now filled by the **Children's Lawyer**, an office within the Ontario Ministry of the Attorney General.

The Children's Lawyer represents children in a range of cases, such as contested wills and personal injury lawsuits. In custody and access cases, the Office of the Children's Lawyer may appoint a lawyer to represent the child, or in cases involving young children, appoint a social service worker to undertake an investigation and make recommendations based on the child's best interests.

A child may become a client of the Children's Lawyer only by court order; however, the Children's Lawyer may decline to take the case where it determines that the issues are minor or that the parties can afford to pay for a private custody and access assessment.

In some cases, before the Children's Lawyer is appointed, the child will be accompanied to court by a social worker, a social service worker, or a family support worker from a family support program.

Children's Lawyer
a court-ordered or government-funded lawyer for children, who represents children in a range of cases, such as contested wills and personal injury lawsuits; in custody and access cases, the Office of the Children's Lawyer may appoint a lawyer to represent the child

Supervised Access

Where the court has concerns about the child's safety in the care of a parent, it can award supervised access. The supervision is often provided by a social welfare agency and involves the presence of a social worker or social service worker during the parent's visits with a child. Examples of reasons for ordering supervised access include the following:

- substantiated suspicions that the access parent will abduct the child
- believable allegations of prior child abuse, whether emotional, physical, or sexual, or evidence of such abuse
- believable allegations or evidence of child neglect or a belief on the part of the court that the parent is not fully capable (for example, by reason of substance addiction or mental illness) of caring for the child
- the child's expressed fears or reservations about the access

When supervised access goes well, the parent under supervision may eventually be successful in having the access order changed to allow unsupervised visits.

Enforcement of Custody and Access Orders

Where one or both parties are not following the terms of a custody or an access agreement or order, the CLRA provides mechanisms for enforcement. In some cases, social service workers may need to bring the relevant provisions of the CLRA to the attention of separated or divorced clients who are having problems working with the other spouse:

- Where one party, contrary to the terms of a custody or access order, is withholding a child from the other party, the court can make an order under section 36 allowing the person from whom the child is being withheld (or his or her representative) to "locate and apprehend" the child.
- The court can also issue an order under section 37 restricting removal of the child from the jurisdiction. This order can be enforced by requiring the uncooperative party to place property in trust or post a bond, pending the return of the child at the end of an access visit, or by requiring surrender of the child's passport to the court for safekeeping.
- Under section 38, the court has a broad power to punish those who exhibit "wilful contempt of or resistance to its process or orders in respect of custody of or access to a child." Disregard for the court's orders can result in a fine of up to $5,000 and/or 90 days' imprisonment.

spousal support
a spouse can claim support under the *Divorce Act* provided that the couple was legally married; in Ontario, a common law partner can claim support under the *Family Law Act*

Spousal Support

A spouse who was economically dependent during the marriage or common law relationship may be able to claim **spousal support**. Spousal support is separate and distinct from child support.

A spouse can claim support under the *Divorce Act* provided that the couple was legally married. In Ontario, a common law partner can claim support under the *Family Law Act* provided that the couple

- cohabited continuously for three years or more, or
- had a child together while cohabiting with some degree of permanence.

Eligibility to claim spousal support does not mean that support will automatically be granted. Both spouses have a duty to be self-sufficient. If self-sufficiency is not possible, in determining whether an award should be made, and the amount of any award, the court will consider factors such as a disability, the needs and means of each spouse, and any economic disadvantage attributable to the marriage, such as primary responsibility for child-rearing. Generally, spousal support awards tend to be smaller—or denied—for spouses who are employed or readily employable, and support may be time-limited.

Other factors affecting spousal support awards include the age of each spouse and the duration and nature of the union. If the partners are young and childless, and have lived together for only a few years while both worked, it is unlikely that one party will be awarded significant support from the other. On the other hand, in the case of a breakup of a long marriage, in which the spouses assumed traditional breadwinner–homemaker roles, the likelihood that support will be awarded is high. When a couple with young children separate during or just after a period in which one parent bore a disproportionate share of child-care responsibilities, the caregiving parent may be entitled to support in order to prepare for entering or re-entering the workforce.

Where a person has a viable claim for support but has not pursued that claim, access to social security benefits (such as Ontario Works benefits) may be denied until he or she has attempted to collect support. In some jurisdictions, local social service workers and provincial/territorial government offices can help the individual to pursue an application for support. Similar assistance may also be available where a former spouse has been awarded support and the other party defaults on the agreement and is in arrears. In Ontario, the former spouse can pursue arrears of support through the Family Responsibility Office.

Child Support

Both the *Divorce Act* and the *Family Law Act* provide for **child support** orders. Under the *Divorce Act*, both parents are required to contribute to the support of a "child of the marriage." This term includes not only the biological children of the two partners, but also adopted children, stepchildren to whom one of the partners has stood *in loco parentis* (in place of a parent), and children born outside the marriage union.

The *Divorce Act* requires parents to pay support until a child is 16 years old, and beyond that age if the child is incapable of supporting himself or herself (for example, because of an intellectual deficit).

The *Family Law Act* requires both parents to support a child up to the age of 18, and beyond if the child is enrolled in a full-time program of study. However, where

child support
the requirement of both parents, under the *Divorce Act*, to contribute to the support of a "child of the marriage," including the biological children of the two partners, adopted children, stepchildren to whom one of the partners has stood *in loco parentis* (in place of a parent), and children born outside the marriage union; paid by one parent to the other, and is an issue separate from custody and access

a child is 16 or older and has withdrawn from parental control (a factual determination, proven through evidence), parents are no longer required to provide support.

Child support is paid by one parent to the other and is an issue separate from custody and access. Child support is the right of the child, and a parent can be ordered to pay it even if that parent has not been given legal access to the child or if access has been given and later suspended. By the same token, access rights are not affected by a failure to pay support. This means that a parent is not permitted to restrict the access of the other parent in retaliation for refusal to pay arrears of child support.

Because support is the right of the child, children are permitted to take their parents to court to obtain it. While most children's family law rights are pursued by one parent or the other, the *Family Law Act* (s 33(2)) allows a child to bring an application for support in his or her own right (through a litigation guardian). Where there is no litigation guardian available to do this, the child can sometimes seek representation by the Children's Lawyer.

The amount of child support ordered by the court used to be calculated from scratch on a case-by-case basis, factoring in such issues as the child's needs and the supporting parent's ability to pay. In recent years, however, Ontario moved to guidelines that set out what is essentially a mathematical formula for calculating a particular support payment based on the payer's income. The guidelines were designed to simplify the process of quantifying child support and to reduce litigation.

Domestic Contracts

domestic contract
a valid contract that provides for different rights on separation than those that are described in legislation; the contract may take precedence over the legislation

Married and common law couples may avoid the application of family law rules on breakup of the relationship by means of a **domestic contract**. Where a couple have negotiated a valid contract that provides for different rights on separation than those that are described in legislation, the contract may take precedence over the legislation. Part IV of the *Family Law Act* provides that domestic contracts and agreements to amend domestic contracts must be in writing, signed by the parties, and witnessed. There are three kinds of domestic contracts:

marriage contract
type of domestic contract made by a couple who are married or who intend to marry

- A **marriage contract** may be made by a couple who are married or who intend to marry. The contract can address ownership or division of property other than the matrimonial home, support obligations, and the right to direct the education of children but not the right to custody of or access to children.

cohabitation agreement
type of domestic contract made by a couple who are cohabiting or who intend to cohabit

- A **cohabitation agreement** is similar to a marriage contract but made by a couple who are cohabiting or who intend to cohabit. If the parties to a cohabitation agreement marry, the agreement is deemed to be a marriage contract.

separation agreement
type of domestic contract made between a couple who are married or cohabiting with the intention of separating or who are already separated

- A **separation agreement**, made between a couple who are married or cohabiting with the intention of separating, or who are already separated, may include provisions governing each party's rights and obligations after separation, including ownership or division of property, support obligations, the right to direct the education of children, and the right to child custody and access.

Domestic contracts are important because they can allow each partner in the relationship to maintain a measure of control over his or her life, and valid contracts are generally respected by the courts. However, a child's right to support cannot be bargained away, and a court will not enforce a provision regarding custody and access that it considers contrary to a child's best interests. In addition, a court may rule that a domestic contract signed under duress or without independent legal advice is unenforceable.

Family Violence

Spousal Abuse

Spousal abuse (whether physical or emotional) can precede a breakup or be precipitated by the departure of a spouse. In general, the point of separation and the months following are the most dangerous time in terms of potential for violence. Social service workers who encourage victims of domestic abuse to leave the relationship must recognize the heightened risk that separation presents. The *Family Law Act* recognizes this reality and provides for police involvement in certain situations.

The police will generally not become involved in the enforcement of an order or a settlement agreement, unless the order specifically provides otherwise. For example, an order providing for pick-up and drop-off times will not be enforceable by the police unless the order actually states that it is. If a child is not delivered according to the order, the normal recourse is to go to court. The court will hear such a case immediately, and the non-compliant party may be charged with contempt of court. If the police are called, they will talk to the parties and try to calm everyone down, but they are not generally authorized to enforce a civil order.

If an order does provide for police enforcement, or if there is a concern about possible violence or harm to a child, the police will intervene. The *Family Law Act* also provides for the arrest without warrant of a spouse who has violated a restraining order issued under the legislation.

Child Abuse

Child abuse is discussed in Chapter 6, but it is useful to understand how child abuse allegations are addressed in the context of a couple's separation.

Often, when a couple separates, at least one ex-spouse is plunged into a state of emotional distress and insecurity. Coping with separation is difficult for anyone, but having to deal, at the same time, with a child's distress is a significant complicating factor. Separation can trigger a wide range of reactions, including a deep sense of betrayal, intense anger, and an instinct to protect the children from the other spouse (whether or not they are actually at risk).

Where child custody is a contentious issue between the parents, criticism of the other partner's fitness to be a parent can occur. Sometimes criticism escalates into allegations of child neglect or of physical, emotional, or sexual abuse.

Child abuse allegations made in the context of a separation create an enormous challenge for all concerned. Allegations of abuse that appear to have some foundation automatically require the involvement of child protection agencies in what is no longer a routine divorce.

Where a parent makes an allegation of abuse involving the other parent, the person to whom the allegation is made—including the complainant's lawyer—has a duty to report to a children's aid society under section 72 of the legislation.[6] The children's aid society will then investigate the allegation.

The Family Responsibility Office

Ontario's Family Responsibility Office is part of the Ministry of Community and Social Services. It was created under the provincial *Family Responsibility and Support Arrears Enforcement Act, 1996*.[7]

The Family Responsibility Office (FRO) receives and registers a copy of every family support (spousal and/or child support) order made by Ontario courts, and assists in the enforcement of those orders in cases of non-compliance (that is, where the full amount of support has not been paid as required by the order). It is possible to opt out of the services of the FRO, but both parties (the payer and the payee) must agree to do this.

The FRO charges administrative fees for some of its services and uses various mechanisms to enforce support orders. The most prevalent method is to arrange for support to be deducted from the payer's wages or salary by his or her employer, forwarded to the FRO, and then transferred to the payee.

Social service workers should be familiar with the function and procedures of the FRO, because they may be asked to assist clients in ensuring compliance with a support order. For example, a client may need help in contacting the office, filling out forms, and gathering the documents necessary to support a request for enforcement of support.

Family Support and Ontario Works Benefits

The Ontario Works social security program provides financial and other assistance to Ontario residents who, because of unemployment, disability, or other difficulties, lack sufficient income to support themselves and their dependants. A person's application for Ontario Works benefits may be denied, or benefits may be reduced, if program administrators determine that the applicant is entitled to claim financial support from other sources, including family support (child support, spousal support, or both) from a former spouse. In a case like this, it is generally necessary for the applicant to pursue his or her right to family support in court before qualifying for Ontario Works benefits.

---

6   *Child and Family Services Act*, RSO 1990, c C.11.

7   *Family Responsibility and Support Arrears Enforcement Act, 1996*, SO 1996, c 31.

Adoption Law

The rules for adoption vary among provinces and territories. In Ontario, the governing legislation was the *Child and Family Services Act*. The new *Child, Youth and Family Services Act* will be applied when proclaimed into law.

Adoption allows for the legal means to take on the responsibilities as a parent of a child who is not one's biological child. Residents of Ontario who are 18 years of age can become an adoptive parent.

Types of Adoptions

There are five types of adoptions: public, private, international, adoption of a step-child, and kinship adoption.

Public adoptions involve children who are in extended society care (formerly known as Crown wards). Individuals who are interested in public adoptions must work with a children's aid society. Once approved by the children's aid society, there is no set time period for the adoption to occur. Public adoptions can take between six months and two years or longer to complete and there is no cost.[8]

Private adoptions are handled by private agencies or individuals licensed by the government. Private adoption practitioners conduct homestudies and supervise all private adoption placements. Since most private adoptions involve newborn children, the time frame is based on the birth parents' views and wishes once the homestudy is completed. The costs for a private adoption can be between $15,000 and $25,000 with additional costs possible.[9]

Private agencies licenced by the government and private adoption practitioners handle international adoptions. The costs can be between $20,000 and $50,000, with waiting times varying depending on the country you are adopting from.[10]

Applications to the Ontario court can be made if individuals are interested in adopting a step-child or other relative (kinship adoption). Unless a judge makes an order, an assessment by an adoption practitioner is not needed.[11]

public adoptions
adoptions involving children who are in extended society care (formerly known as Crown wards); individuals who are interested in public adoptions must work with a children's aid society

private adoptions
adoptions handled by private agencies or individuals licensed by the government

---

8   "Public adoption process" (last updated 3 November 2016), online: Ministry of Children and Youth Services, <http://www.children.gov.on.ca/htdocs/English/adoption/decided-to-adopt/public.aspx>.

9   "Private adoption process" (last updated 19 July 2016), online: Ministry of Children and Youth Services, <http://www.children.gov.on.ca/htdocs/English/adoption/decided-to-adopt/private.aspx>.

10   "International adoption process" (last updated 8 July 2016), online: Ministry of Children and Youth Services, <http://www.children.gov.on.ca/htdocs/English/adoption/decided-to-adopt/international.aspx>.

11   "Adoption of a stepchild and kinship adoption" (last updated 30 January 2017), online: Ministry of Children and Youth Services, <http://www.children.gov.on.ca/htdocs/English/adoption/thinking-of-adopting/types.aspx#kinship>.

homestudy
the assessment of a family
or individual who is
considering an adoption

Homestudies are mandatory and are conducted by children's aid societies and private adoption practitioners. A **homestudy** is the assessment of a family or individual who is considering an adoption. Homestudies in Ontario have been standardized into a format called SAFE (structured analysis family evaluation). Topics covered in a SAFE homestudy include the motivation to adopt, personality, skills, childhood, and parenting beliefs of the potential adoptive parents. While the adoption practitioner is learning about the applicants during the homestudy, the applicants are also learning about adoption in Ontario.[12]

The adoption process can be a challenging one. Social service workers can help individuals through this process by providing them the relevant information and assisting with accessing legal assistance.

Best Interests of the Child

The *Child, Youth and Family Services Act* in Ontario requires the best interests of the child as the paramount consideration for adoptions. Other factors that must be considered include the child's physical, mental, and emotional needs; cultural background; religious faith; and other factors listed in the Act. The child's views and wishes, if they can be reasonably ascertained, must also be considered. In Ontario, consent is required for children over the age of seven unless the court determines that consent should be dispensed with.

Consent and Disclosure

In Canada, parental consent for adoption cannot be given prior to the birth of the child. In Ontario, the legislation says that consent cannot be given until the first week after the birth of the child and cannot subsequently be withdrawn after 21 days. Written consent must be given without coercion, with the birth parent fully understanding what she is consenting to, and must be free and informed.

Since 2008, Ontario has opened adoption records, allowing adopted adults and birth parents to apply for adoption orders and birth registrations.[13] Social services workers can assist individuals to access information and legal assistance regarding issues of disclosure.

---

12 "Adoption Homestudy" (n.d.), online: Adoption Council of Ontario, <https://www.adoption .on.ca/adoption-homestudy>.

13 Access to Adoption Records Act (Vital Statistics Statute Law Amendment), 2008, SO 2008, c 5.

KEY TERMS

access, 115
Children's Lawyer, 117
child support, 119
cohabitation agreement, 120
custody, 115
domestic contract, 120
equalization payment, 114
homestudy, 124
marriage contract, 120
matrimonial home, 114
mediation, 112
private adoptions, 123
public adoptions, 123
separation agreement, 120
spousal support, 118
supervised access, 110

SUGGESTED SOURCES

Adoption Council of Ontario,
  <https://www.adoption.on.ca>

Justice for Children and Youth, <http://jfcy.org>

Ministry of Children and Youth Services,
  <http://www.children.gov.on.ca>

Office of the Children's Lawyer,
  <https://www.attorneygeneral.jus.gov.on.ca/english/
  about/artcl/fjsd_ocl.php>

Ontario Association of Children's Aid Societies,
  <http://www.oacas.org>

REVIEW QUESTIONS

1. Does family law legislation apply to couples who were never legally married?

2. What is the overriding principle that guides a court's decisions on custody and access?

3. Are all spouses entitled to spousal support? Are all children entitled to child support? Explain.

4. What is the matrimonial home, and how does the law treat it differently from other property?

5. List three contexts in which a social service worker may work with family members who are going through separation or divorce.

6. Describe three types of adoptions.

Education Law

8

LEARNING OUTCOMES

After completing this chapter, you should be able to:

- Understand the key principles of the *Education Act*.

- Describe the government's approach to violence and harassment in schools, and the relevance of this approach to social service workers who work with students.

- Understand the approach when dealing with student suspensions and expulsions.

- Describe the process for schools dealing with unacceptable behaviours.

- Describe the process by which a student is deemed eligible to access special-needs programs and resources.

Introduction

School boards and individual schools may employ social service workers and youth workers to provide counselling to students. Other social service workers may find themselves dealing with aspects of the education system in the course of providing services to homeless youth or families in crisis. As well, social service workers may work with students who have been expelled from school and who require counselling and other support so that they can continue their education.

Ontario statutes that govern education include the *Education Act* and its "safe schools" amendments, and the *Education Quality and Accountability Office Act*.[1]

The duty to report suspected child abuse or neglect, created by the *Child, Youth and Family Services Act*, is also important to anyone working in schools.[2]

Ontario's *Immunization of School Pupils Act* and the *Health Protection and Promotion Act* require schools to take measures to avoid outbreaks of disease, by, for example, requiring proof of student immunization status, reporting outbreaks, and taking steps to prevent the transmission of communicable diseases within the school population.[3]

Public and Private School Systems

Like most developed countries, Canada funds public education. Each province and territory administers its own education system, and many responsibilities are further delegated to regional school boards. The Ontario *Education Act* and the regulations made under it set out the legal framework for the education of Ontario's children.

The Ontario public school system is divided into two streams: secular public schools and Catholic schools (run by "separate" school boards). The funding of Catholic schools is largely a historical practice and is provided for under Canada's *Constitution Act, 1867*.[4]

The government's funding of Catholic schools and not other religious schools has long been a controversial issue. Section 2 of the *Canadian Charter of Rights and Freedoms* provides that everyone has the freedom of conscience and religion.[5] Many parents, if given the choice, would prefer that their children receive a government-paid education in a school of their own religious denomination, such as a Protestant, Jewish, or Muslim school. The unfairness of funding only Catholic schools has attracted attention at the international level: In 1996, the United Nations Human Rights Committee ruled that Canada was in violation of the International Covenant on Civil and Political Rights because of government funding of Roman Catholic schools and not those of other faiths. In response to the ruling, some Canadian provincial governments implemented partial funding to certain non-Catholic religious schools. Ontario has no such system.

---

1   *Education Act*, RSO 1990, c E.2; *Education Quality and Accountability Office Act, 1996*, SO 1996, c 11.

2   *Child, Youth and Family Services Act*, 2017.

3   *Immunization of School Pupils Act*, RSO 1990, c I.1; *Health Protection and Promotion Act*, RSO 1990, c H.7.

4   *Constitution Act, 1867* (UK), 30 & 31 Vict, c 3, reprinted in RSC 1985, Appendix II, No 5.

5   *Canadian Charter of Rights and Freedoms*, Part I of the *Constitution Act, 1982*, being Schedule B to the *Canada Act 1982* (UK), 1982, c 11.

The Education Act

The *Education Act* creates a framework for the administration of public education in Ontario and covers the following topics:

- responsibilities of parents and students within the education system
- consequences of a student's violation of the safe schools provisions
- means by which parents and students can seek access to special-needs services

Compulsory Attendance

Under the *Education Act*, all children are required to attend school at the age of six, and must attend school or an equivalent learning program approved by the Ministry of Education until the age of 18. Students who turn 18 after the beginning of the school year but prior to December 31 can leave school prior to the commencement of that school year. Failure to enroll a child in school or to take reasonable steps to ensure his or her daily attendance is an offence punishable by a fine under the Act. Students between 12 and 15 years old who miss school regularly can be charged with **truancy**. The penalties can include a fine or the possibility of a probation order. If a student is put on probation, one of the terms will be a requirement to attend school. If the student breaches the probation order further, consequences including custody can occur. Social service workers can assist young persons with the issue of truancy and should direct the youth to a lawyer or legal clinic for legal assistance.

There are exceptions to compulsory attendance at a public school, such as illness, religious holiday, attendance at a private school, and **home-schooling**. The home-schooling exemption under section 21(2)(a) allows absence from school for children who are "receiving satisfactory instruction at home or elsewhere." Private schools and home-schooling must comply with basic curriculum standards set by the province or territory.

Home-Schooling

Home-schooling has always been a controversial subject, probably because a parent's decision to home-school children is a rejection of the public school system. Parents who are critical of the public system are unlikely to provide instruction closely consistent with that system's curriculum. Home-schoolers tend to focus on different educational values and priorities than those of public schools. The instruction provided by parents who home-school their children is subject to review by the provincial/territorial school attendance counsellor. To confirm that a home-schooled child is eligible for exemption from school attendance under section 21(2) of the *Education Act*, the counsellor can launch an inquiry into the parent's home-schooling program under section 24 of the Act.

Social service workers may have clients who are home-schooling their children and who need assistance in obtaining the ministry's approval of their home-schooling program. As well, social service workers may have clients who are 16 or 17 who wish to attend other learning programs and need information and assistance ensuring that the program is approved by the ministry.

truancy
the act of missing school regularly, usually without reason; students between 12 and 15 years old who miss school regularly can be charged with truancy, penalties for which can include a fine or the possibility of a probation order

home-schooling
exemption to the *Education Act* that allows absence from school for children who are receiving satisfactory instruction at home or elsewhere; must comply with basic curriculum standards set by the province or territory

Youth Who Are Not Living at Home

If you have legally withdrawn from your parents and still live in the same school district as your parents, you can attend the school in that district. If you are no longer in the same district as your parents, you can attend school in another district as long as you are paying rent in that school district. If someone other than your parents has obtained legal custody of you, you can attend a school in the district where the person who has legal custody of you lives. Social service workers can assist young persons with their school registration as these issues can be a challenge for the young person. As well, social service workers should direct the youth to a lawyer or legal clinic for information and assistance.

Absence and Children at Risk

A child's non-attendance at school can sometimes be a warning sign that something is not right at home. In some cases, children who are subject to neglect may not make it to school because there is simply no parent taking charge of waking, dressing, and feeding them, and getting them onto the bus. In more serious cases, abused children may be kept at home so that teachers and others in the community will not be alerted to the situation. Absence from school may even be a warning that a child has been abducted (whether by a parent defying a custody/access order or by a person with criminal intent).

If a social service worker has a child client who is missing school and the reason isn't apparent, the parent or guardian should be asked to explain the child's absence. If the explanation raises a suspicion of child abuse or neglect, the social service worker must report to the children's aid society. In extreme cases, it may also be appropriate to contact the police.

Safety

Schools are responsible for the safety of children on their premises during the school day. This responsibility requires measures such as maintaining school buildings and property in safe condition, monitoring systems such as water quality and ventilation, providing safe transportation to and from school, and planning for emergencies such as fires and bomb threats.

Schools are also responsible for protecting children against interpersonal threats from school personnel or other children. For example, school boards must carefully screen teachers, special-needs education specialists, coaches, counsellors, social workers, social service workers, and other individuals who will have contact with children, to ensure that they do not pose a risk to the safety of those children. Schools must also monitor and control situations such as bullying and fights, where children might harm each other.

In addition, schools must try to protect their personnel from the risk of harm from children (for example, threats or physical aggression against teachers or various forms of harassment).

In 2000, the Ontario government enacted an extensive set of amendments to the *Education Act*, known as "the safe schools amendments." This legislation provided for the creation of a code of conduct to address bullying and other worrisome behaviours in schools.

The safe schools amendments provided that schools can create policies for enforcing the code of conduct. These policies generally included automatic penalties for violation of the code of conduct. Many schools had adopted a policy of **zero tolerance**, which mandated immediate suspension or expulsion for prohibited behaviours, especially acts of violence.

zero tolerance
mandated immediate suspension or expulsion for prohibited behaviours, especially acts of violence

After consultations with all parties, the safe schools policies were revised and came into effect February 2008. Bill 212, *Education Amendment Act (Progressive Discipline and School Safety), 2007* provided a series of changes when dealing with behaviours at school: Some suspensions are no longer mandatory, teachers can no longer suspend students, and principals on their own can no longer expel students. The Act has also been changed to focus on a range of consequences for unacceptable behaviour and to require boards to provide support for students.[6]

The Act also stipulates that the unacceptable activity doesn't have to take place physically inside the school. For example, if a student threatens or harasses another student or a teacher on the Internet while the student or teacher is in his or her own home, that behaviour may qualify as having an impact on the school climate, and a student could be suspended for it.

The legislative changes include the following:

- Principals may no longer expel students. They may recommend expulsion to the school board, but it is the board or a committee of at least three trustees that must decide.

- All suspensions will be subject to a possible appeal.

- The timelines for appeals and hearings will be shortened.

- The board shall take into account mitigating factors when determining whether to expel, and the principal shall take them into account when considering whether to suspend and or recommend expulsion.

- The Act imposes minimum rules for investigation that a principal must follow to try to ensure all those involved, including the accused student, are heard from before a decision is made, and to ensure that investigations begin promptly. This includes provisions that the pupil must receive a copy of the principal's report, including reasons for the decision (in the case of suspensions) and findings (in the case of an expulsion recommendation.)

- The Act eliminates full, province-wide expulsions and requires that students who have been expelled be admitted either into another school or a program, depending on the type of expulsion.

- Suspended students and students expelled from all schools in the school board must be assigned to a program.

- Students who have been expelled from their school only must be assigned to another school rather than a program.

---

6   *Education Amendment Act (Progressive Discipline and School Safety), 2007*, SO 2007, c 14 [Bill 212].

- Boards are required to re-admit students after they have completed the program for expelled students. They remain students of the board during the expulsion period.
- At least three members of the board must preside over an expulsion hearing.
- All expulsions may now be appealed to a board or committee tribunal.[7]

The Act stipulates that some activities may lead to suspension (s 306(1)), as well as activities that must lead to suspension and activities that principals must consider for expulsion (s 310(1)). Table 8.1 outlines these obligations.

TABLE 8.1   List of Behaviours That "May" and "Must" Lead to Suspensions or Be Considered for Expulsion

Activities That May Lead to Suspension	Activities That *MUST* Lead to Suspension and for Which the Principal *MUST* Consider Expulsion
Uttering a threat to inflict serious bodily harm	Possessing a weapon
Possessing alcohol or illegal drugs	Using a weapon to cause or threaten bodily harm
Being under the influence of alcohol	Committing physical assault on another person that causes bodily harm requiring treatment by a medical practitioner
Swearing at a teacher or another person in a position of authority	Committing sexual assault
Committing an act of vandalism that causes extensive damage to school property at the pupil's school or to property located on the premises of the pupil's school	Trafficking in weapons or in illegal drugs
Bullying	Committing robbery
Any other activity for which a principal may suspend a pupil under school board policy	Giving alcohol to a minor
	Any other activity for which a principal may suspend a pupil under school board policy and therefore may conduct an investigation to determine whether to recommend to the board that the pupil be expelled

Source: *Education Amendment Act (Progressive Discipline and School Safety), 2007*, SO 2007, c 14 [Bill 212].

---

7   Ontario, Legislative Assembly, *Amended Submissions of Justice for Children and Youth on Bill 212 for the Standing Committee on General Government*, 38th Parl, 2nd Sess (16 and 18 May 2007).

The Act further outlines other factors that schools must consider when looking into student behaviour. These include the following:[8]

- Every school board and every school must have its own code of conduct, which must be available to the public. The code must incorporate the provincial code of conduct and must include a series of escalating consequences for unacceptable behaviour, referred to as the "progressive discipline approach."

- The continuum of the progressive discipline approach must contain a range of interventions, supports, and consequences that are developmentally appropriate, that include opportunities for students to learn from mistakes, and that focus on improving behaviour. The continuum ranges from in-school supports and interventions to short-term suspensions to long-term suspensions or expulsion.

- Principals must make every effort within 24 hours to inform the suspended pupil's parent(s) in writing of the suspension and include the reason for the suspension, information about any programs for suspended students, and information about the right to appeal and the appeal process.

- Principals and boards must consider all of the factors that might have led to the unacceptable behaviour including the following:
  - The pupil does not have the ability to control his or her behaviour.
  - The pupil does not have the ability to understand the foreseeable consequences of his or her behaviour.
  - The pupil's continuing presence in the school does not create an unacceptable risk to the safety of any person.
  - The pupil's history.
  - Whether a progressive discipline approach has been used with the pupil.
  - Whether the activity for which the pupil may be or is being suspended or expelled was related to any harassment of the pupil because of his or her race, ethnic origin, religion, disability, gender, or sexual orientation, or to any other harassment.
  - How the suspension or expulsion would affect the pupil's ongoing education.
  - The age of the pupil.
  - In the case of a pupil for whom an individual education plan has been developed, whether the behaviour was a manifestation of a disability identified in the pupil's individual education plan, whether appropriate individualized accommodation has been provided, and whether the suspension or expulsion is likely to result in an aggravation or worsening of the pupil's behaviour or conduct.

---

8 People for Education, "Amendments to Ontario's Safe Schools Act" (January 2008), online: <http://www.peopleforeducation.ca/wp-content/uploads/2011/09/Amendments-to-Ontarios-Safe-Schools-Act.pdf>.

- Students and their parents or guardians have the right to appeal all suspensions or expulsions, but the decision of the school board on the appeal is final.

- When a student is suspended for an activity that falls under the mandatory suspension criteria, the principal must conduct an investigation to determine whether to recommend to the board that the student be expelled.

- If a principal suspends a student, the principal is required to assign him or her to a program for suspended pupils provided by the board.

- If a principal recommends expelling a student, the board must hold a hearing that includes the principal, the student, the student's parent(s) or guardian(s), and members of the board to determine if the student should be expelled. If a student is expelled, the board must either find another school for the student or place the student in a program for expelled students.

- A **student action plan (SAP)** must be developed for every expelled student. The SAP is to be developed by the principal, in cooperation with staff, the student, and his or her parent(s), and among other things, must set out a series of goals, measures of success, and strategies and types of support for the student.

student action plan (SAP)
developed for every expelled student; the principal, in cooperation with staff, the student, and his or her parent(s), must set out a series of goals, measures of success, and strategies and types of support for the student

Bullying and Cyberbullying

A recent Quebec study revealed that one in three high school students have been subjected to some form of bullying or cyberbullying.[9]

Bullying and cyberbullying manifests itself in such a broad range of behaviour that it should not and cannot be addressed through a single, stand-alone offence.

Bill C-273 amended the *Criminal Code* in order to clarify that cyberbullying is an offence. However, it does not create a new and distinct crime of cyberbullying. Instead, it amends existing sections of the *Criminal Code* to include electronic manifestations of the respective crimes. Specifically, it amends sections 264 (harassment), 298 (defamatory libel), and 372 (false messages).[10]

Other *Criminal Code* offences that can relate to **cyberbullying** include uttering threats (s 264.1), intimidation (s 423(1)), mischief in relation to data (s 430(1.1)), unauthorized use of computer (s 342.1), identity fraud (s 403), and extortion (s 346).[11]

The Ontario *Accepting Schools Act, 2012* was developed in response to the growing concern about bullying behaviours and several tragic suicides of bullied students.[12] Under the Act, which came into force on September 1, 2012, cyberbullying is defined as bullying by electronic means, and may include the following:

cyberbullying
harassment or abuse of other students or teachers via electronic media such as emails, text messages, or posting comments or pictures on the Internet

---

9   Statistics Canada, "Self-Reported Internet Victimization in Canada, 2009," by Samuel Perreault, in *Juristat* 31:1, Catalogue No 85-002-X (Ottawa: Statistics Canada, 2011).

10   Nevena Urosevic, "Canada: Private Member's Bill Proposes To Amend The 'Criminal Code' To Address Cyberbullying," *Mondaq* (15 January 2013), online: <http://www.mondaq.com/canada/x/216170/Education/Private+Members+Bill+Proposes+To+Amend+The+Criminal+Code+To+Address+Cyberbullying>.

11   *Criminal Code*, RSC 1985, c C-46.

12   *Accepting Schools Act, 2012*, SO 2012, c 5.

- creating a web page or a blog in which the creator assumes the identity of another person
- impersonating another person as the author of content or messages posted on the Internet
- communicating material electronically to more than one individual or posting material on a website that may be accessed by one or more individuals

The Act also requires schools to provide instruction for students on bullying prevention and programs for teachers about bullying prevention strategies. School boards are also required to establish bullying prevention plans for schools.[13]

Non-Consensual Distribution of Intimate Images

In recent years, an increasing number of individuals have been exchanging images through their electronic devices. Young persons will often send and receive images that can be of an intimate nature. At times, these images are sent without the consent of the subject of the image. The following studies illustrate the behaviours.

> With respect to young people, an online survey of 1,280 respondents (653 teens aged 13 to 19 and 627 young adults aged 20 to 26) in 2008 commissioned by the National Campaign to Prevent Teen and Unplanned Pregnancy found that 20 percent of teens and 33 percent of young adults had sent nude pictures of themselves via text or email (a practice referred to as "sexting"). A 2012 study published in the American journal *Archives of Pediatric and Adolescent Medicine* that surveyed 948 high school students in Texas, also found that 28 percent of the respondents had engaged in sexting. A third recent study of 606 high school students at a single private school, representing nearly the entire student body, found that nearly 20 percent had sent a sexually explicit image of themselves, and that 25 percent indicated that they had *forwarded* such an image to others.[14]

Although existing criminal offences may apply in certain situations, they do not address the identified harm and therefore are not adequately responsive to the non-consensual distribution of intimate images. To address this gap, a new criminal offence of non-consensual distribution of intimate images was enacted.

> The amendments to the *Education Act* arising from the *Accepting Schools Act, 2012* will change the way principals, supervisory officers, teachers, and students approach and deal with bullying and cyberbullying. They provide administrators with the legislative

---

13 Promoting Relationships & Eliminating Violence Network (PREVNet), "Legal Consequences of Cyberbullying" (n.d.), online: <http://www.prevnet.ca/bullying/cyber-bullying/legal-consequences>.

14 Canada, CCSO Cybercrime Working Group, *Report to the Federal/Provincial/Territorial Ministers Responsible for Justice and Public Safety: Cyberbullying and the Non-consensual Distribution of Intimate Images* (Ottawa: Minister of Justice and Attorney General of Canada, 2013) at 14.

framework to establish policies to promote positive behaviour, and to identify and address inappropriate student behaviour. The particular issue of equity and inclusiveness continues to be at the forefront of the dialogue on bullying in Ontario schools. The new legislation is meant to create policies and practices that allow every student to feel accepted and supported.[15]

Social service workers who work with schools, with expelled or suspended students, or with early-leavers (students who have not returned to school after expulsion) should familiarize themselves with issues of and responses to violence and harassment in the school environment so that they can better assist their clients.

Special Education

About 10 percent of Canadian schoolchildren struggle at some point in their education with some kind of learning problem. Learning and behavioural problems are often closely related and difficult to distinguish, especially in younger children.

Accommodating learning problems often requires support beyond the capacity (in terms of both time and expertise) of classroom teachers. This means that in order to guarantee access to education for children with learning problems, schools must devote human, material, and physical resources specifically to the needs of these children.

The *Education Act* requires school boards to provide special education programs and services for students who require them, and to implement procedures to identify such students. Pressure on public budgets is often particularly threatening to the allocation of resources to special-needs children.

Funding for Autism

Ontario

In 2005, a group of Ontario parents of autistic children were successful in their lawsuit against the province. The court held that cutting off funding for autism treatment at age six was discrimination based on age and disability, and violated the *Canadian Charter of Rights and Freedoms*. The cost of treatment can be about $60,000 per child.

Then-premier Dalton McGuinty responded to the ruling with concern that the court was mandating the expenditure of money, without identifying a source for the money, and launched an appeal to the Ontario Court of Appeal.[16]

---

15   Kate Dearden, "Canada: Ontario's Anti-Bullying Legislation Is Now In Effect," *Mondaq* (9 October 2012), online: <http://www.mondaq.com/canada/x/200118/Education/ Ontarios+AntiBullying+Legislation+Is+Now+In+Effect>.

16   *Wynberg v Ontario*, 2005 ONSC 8749.

British Columbia

A similar case in British Columbia was eventually heard by the Supreme Court of Canada in 2004. The court determined that the province had the right to set its own priorities for health-care funding and could not be forced to pay.[17]

When it becomes apparent to school staff that a student may have special educational needs, the student's case may be reviewed (following notice to the parents) by an **identification, placement, and review committee (IPRC)**. These committees are established within the Ministry of Education to assist in determining which students require and are eligible for special services. Parents and students can also request referral to an IPRC if the school does not initiate the process.

If an IPRC decides that a student has special needs, there are several options available for meeting those needs. The regulation governing IPRCs requires the committee to consider whether the student's needs can be met in a regular classroom, because this may be preferable for the student from the perspective of normal socialization. Service delivery options for special-needs students can include special education for the whole school day, attendance for part of the day in a class designed to support certain skills (such as reading), or special attention in the regular classroom, either from the regular teacher or from an additional trained staff member. Students with severe hearing or vision disabilities may be referred to a school for the hearing or visually impaired.

identification, placement, and review committee (IPRC) committee established within the Ministry of Education to assist in determining which students require and are eligible for special services

Language Barriers

For some children, the ability to benefit from quality public education is a challenge because of language barriers. Especially in urban centres, the Canadian student population enjoys considerable diversity with respect to culture and language. Canada is a popular destination for new immigrants from all over the world. For many such immigrants, access to quality public education is a high family priority. However, children entering Canadian public schools who are not fluent speakers of English (or, in francophone communities, French) are at a significant disadvantage in the classroom.

In areas where there is a high percentage of children for whom English (or French) is not a first language, remedial programs exist to ease the transition of both children and their parents into English (or French) education. Schools tend to do a good job of identifying children who need this assistance, because struggling students put an increased demand on the time of classroom teachers.

Often, a school's efforts on behalf of a child end up assisting the whole family. In smaller centres, however, or in times of cuts to public funding of education, access to language programs is more limited, and social workers, social service workers, and other children's advocates may need to become more active on behalf of children facing language barriers to education.

---

17 *Auton (Guardian ad litem of) v British Columbia (Attorney General)*, 2004 SCC 78, [2004] 3 SCR 657.

The Education Quality and Accountability Office

The quality and effectiveness of elementary and secondary education in Ontario are evaluated by the Education Quality and Accountability Office (EQAO), established by the *Education Quality and Accountability Office Act, 1996*.[18] The EQAO tests students in grades 3, 6, 9, and 10 to assess levels of literacy and competence in mathematics.

Testing has been promoted as a means to ensure government accountability in the provision of public education, and to increase public confidence in education standards in the public school system. Parent reaction to the testing has been mixed. Some parents believe that the intensive testing is stressful for children and that it is of limited value in identifying specific problems in the education system. Other critics question both the value and the cost of testing in the context of cuts to education, particularly where there is no follow-up funding to remedy problems.

---

18   *Education Quality and Accountability Office Act, 1996*, SO 1996, c 11.

KEY TERMS

cyberbullying, 134
home-schooling, 129
identification, placement, and review committee (IPRC), 137
student action plan (SAP), 134
truancy, 129
zero tolerance, 131

SUGGESTED SOURCES

Justice for Children and Youth, <http://jfcy.org>

Ontario Ministry of Education, <http://www.edu.gov.on.ca>

REVIEW QUESTIONS

1. List at least three capacities in which social workers or social service workers may have dealings with the school system.

2. Why is it important for a social service worker with a child client to pay attention to recurrent or unexplained absence from school?

3. What is the most significant challenge facing children with special needs in the public school system, and how can social service workers respond to this challenge?

4. List some of the behaviours that can be considered cyberbullying and dealt with under the criminal code.

5. What is the purpose of Education Quality and Accountability Office testing?

Income Assistance

9

LEARNING OUTCOMES

After completing this chapter, you should be able to:

- Explain the role of income assistance programs in the context of the social support system.

- Understand the general eligibility criteria for each kind of income assistance program.

- Suggest strategies for improving clients' access to income assistance programs.

- Understand the value of advocacy on behalf of economically disadvantaged clients.

Introduction

Most people pay for their living expenses out of personal income or savings. Where circumstances such as age, poor health, disability, or the lack of available employment make it difficult to earn a living, poverty may be the result. When people with young families cannot earn an adequate income, their children suffer as well.

In an effort to respond to poverty, all three levels of government support a framework of programs providing income assistance or social assistance to residents. Federal programs include Employment Insurance (EI), which provides temporary relief for people who have lost their jobs; Old Age Security (OAS), which provides a modest pension to Canadians who have reached 65 years of age; and the Canada Pension Plan (CPP), which provides an additional pension based on years of employment. Provincial and territorial programs include, for example, in Ontario, Ontario Works and the Ontario Disability Support Program (ODSP), both of which provide income assistance, and Workplace Health and Safety Insurance (WHSI), which provides compensation to individuals who have suffered a job-related injury or illness. Municipalities also contribute by providing administrative support for certain programs.

Some programs, such as CPP, EI, and WHSI, are fully or partially funded by premiums paid by employees and their employers. Other programs, such as Ontario Works and programs for the disabled, are funded solely from the general tax base.

Income assistance programs are useful only when they are accessed successfully by those who need them. Sometimes this can be a complicated and frustrating endeavour. Social service workers can be an important resource to clients by providing information about programs and eligibility, by supporting clients in the application process, and by advocating on behalf of clients for access to benefits.

Social service workers may also work in the administration of income assistance programs. For example, they may be employed at an Ontario Works resource centre, providing referrals to training, helping with resumé preparation, and coaching benefit recipients in interview skills. While these individuals will benefit from knowing about other government-funded income assistance programs, the information in this chapter is directed mainly at those who are working in settings in which they support clients' access to such program and will focus mainly on the Ontario Works, ODSP, and CPP programs.

Ontario Works

Ontario Works is Ontario's primary last-resort income relief program. It is managed by the Ministry of Community and Social Services (MCSS) and provides very modest subsistence-level benefits to Ontario residents who lack adequate means of support.

The province chose the name "Ontario Works" as a reminder that the benefits are intended to support Ontarians temporarily while they seek economic independence through employment. The purposes of the program are set out in the *Ontario Works Act, 1997:*[1]

---

1 *Ontario Works Act, 1997,* SO 1997, c 25, Schedule A.

- to recognize individual responsibility and promote self-reliance through employment
- to provide temporary financial assistance to those most in need while they satisfy obligations to become and stay employed
- to effectively serve people needing assistance
- to be accountable to the taxpayers of Ontario

Ontario Works benefits are **needs- and means-tested**. Before persons can gain access to the benefits, they must prove that they do not have the means (any other source of money) to provide for their basic needs. The needs that the program is designed to pay for are basic **subsistence needs**, such as food and housing. In considering an application for Ontario Works benefits, the program administrators will investigate whether the applicant has any assets, such as a registered retirement savings plan (RRSP), or access to other sources of help, such as spousal support **entitlements** or housing subsidies. If the applicant has, these sources must be exhausted first; otherwise, the applicant may be ineligible for Ontario Works benefits, or benefits paid under the program may be reduced.

Recipients are expected to achieve self-sufficiency as soon as possible and must participate in employment-seeking activities as specified in "participation agreements." Non-compliance may result in ineligibility and cessation of benefits.

Ontario Works was created by the *Ontario Works Act, 1997* and the five regulations made under it, replacing the previous income support program provided under the *General Welfare Assistance Act* (now repealed).[2] The administration of the program is also guided by more than 50 provincial policy directives.

Although Ontario Works is a provincial program, it is partially funded by the federal government and administered by municipal governments. Municipal administration means that although the same set of rules is applied across the province or territory, there are minor differences in how benefits are administered by different municipalities.

needs- and means-tested
assessing someone's situation on the basis of his or her needs (i.e., rent, food, and medical necessities)

subsistence needs
a person's very basic living requirements, such as food and shelter

entitlement
a right to receive a benefit based on objective criteria

Pilot Project

After consultations with interested parties, recently the Ontario government announced a pilot project to introduce basic income guaranteed amounts. The Ontario Basic Income Pilot, which will last for three years will begin in the spring and fall of 2017 in the regions of Hamilton, including Brantford and the County of Brant, Thunder Bay and the surrounding area and in Lindsay. A person in the trial can receive up to $16,989 a year, though the equivalent of 50% of any additional earned income will be subtracted from that figure. So a person who makes $10,000 a year at their job, for example, would receive $11,989 in basic income, for a total income of $21,989. Eligible recipients, who must be between 18 and 64 and considered low-income, will be chosen through a randomized selection process.[3]

---

2   *General Welfare Assistance Act*, RSO 1990, c G.6 [repealed].

3   Chris Weller, "Canada is launching an experiment that will give 4,000 people free money until 2020," *Business Insider* (24 April 2017), online: <http://www.businessinsider.com/ontario-announces-basic-income-plan-2017-4>.

Eligibility

Because government funding for income assistance is limited, fairness demands that applicants for Ontario Works benefits meet strict eligibility criteria. The first requirement is that the applicant must be an Ontario resident. An application for benefits must be made to the Ontario Works office in the municipality (or municipal area) where the applicant lives.

Once Ontario residency is confirmed, to determine whether the applicant is eligible for benefits, the local program administrator assesses all sources of support available to the applicant. These include employment income, business income, compensation settlements (for example, an award of damages for injury in a motor vehicle accident, or workers' compensation benefits), spousal and child support payments, savings, and other assets.

The program provides benefits to "benefit units"—that is, to families living together. For that reason, total family income and assets are taken into account when eligibility is considered. This means, for example, that an applicant may be denied benefits (or may receive reduced benefits) if his or her spouse receives a pension.

An applicant may qualify for Ontario Works benefits even if he or she (or a family member) is currently earning employment income. This can happen, for example, where the applicant is employed part-time, works full-time but at a very low wage, or has childcare costs that offset a large portion of her earned income. If the applicant (or a family member) has employment income, Ontario Works benefits are reduced to reflect the availability of that income.

Cutoff levels for income and assets, which vary depending upon the size of the family, determine whether a person is eligible for benefits, and if so, for how much. For example, the amount of benefits may vary depending on whether a parent is a sole-support parent or is in a spousal (married or common-law) relationship. Where two adults live in the same residence and one of them is seeking to apply as a sole-support parent, program administrators will investigate the nature of the relationship between the adults to determine whether it is a spousal relationship or not.

If an adult applicant lives with his (or her) parents, it can be difficult (though not impossible) for the applicant to obtain benefits. The applicant can qualify if he is financially independent and in need. In some cases, an adult living with parents who are also in need of income assistance will be treated as part of the parents' benefit unit; that is, he or she will receive benefits, but they will be included in the payment to his or her parents rather than paid separately.

In general, children under the age of 18 must be supported by their parents. A financially independent teen living at home will not be paid benefits if Ontario Works views such payments as providing an incentive to the teen to leave home. However, teens who are 16 or 17, living on their own, and not being supported by parents can, in some cases, have themselves declared independent of their parents. This situation could arise, for example, for a teen who has left home because of abuse. Teens under 18 must be attending high school or an approved training program in order to qualify for benefits, and their attendance at school is verified monthly.

Benefit Rates

Benefit rates under the Ontario Works program are based on a number of factors, including family size, age of dependants, housing costs, location, and whether the applicant requires a special diet because of health problems. The calculation of benefits to pay for basic monthly needs other than shelter is illustrated in Table 9.1. Benefits may be higher for recipients who live north of the 50th parallel and do not have year-round road access, and for those who require a special diet.

Added to this basic needs amount is another amount for shelter. The calculation of the shelter benefit takes into account the applicant's actual shelter costs. These can include rent, mortgage payments, taxes, insurance premiums, and the cost of heating, electricity, and water/sewage service, including hot water. However, a limit is set on the amount of the shelter benefit paid under the program. This maximum monthly shelter allowance is adjusted upward as the size of the benefit unit increases (as shown in Table 9.2). For this purpose, the size of the benefit unit means the number of people in the family for whom benefits are paid.

In determining the amount that will be paid to the recipient, the general rule is that the shelter benefit is the lesser of the actual shelter expenses and the maximum benefit. However, the maximum benefit is so low that, in practice, it would be rare for the actual cost of shelter to be lower. Consider the benefit amounts shown in Table 9.2 in relation to the current cost of housing in Ontario. Even allowing for variations between communities, there has been a steep and steady increase in the price of owner-occupied housing in recent years, and the cost of rental accommodation, particularly in larger urban centres, is well above the maximum benefit threshold. Therefore, for many recipients of Ontario Works benefits, there will be a significant gap between actual shelter costs and the monthly shelter allowance.

The total benefits payable under the Ontario Works program are calculated by adding the basic benefit, the shelter benefit (the maximum allowance or the actual shelter cost if it is less than the maximum), and an amount for special diet or northern residence, if applicable.

The benefits payable are different in certain circumstances—for example, where the recipient lives in a women's shelter or a homeless shelter, or where housing and food expenses are paid through a room-and-board arrangement. Also, the benefits are subject to change over time to reflect the cost of inflation. For accurate information about current benefits, it is advisable to consult the statute and the relevant policy directives.

TABLE 9.1 Ontario Works Benefit: Monthly Amount for Basic Needs Other Than Shelter, by Number and Age of Dependants in Benefit Unit

No. of Dependants Other Than a Spouse	Dependants 18 years and over	Dependants 0–17 years	Monthly Basic Needs Amount	
			Single	Couple
0	0	0	$305	$468
1	0	1	342	468
	1	0	589	616
2	0	2	342	468
	1	1	589	616
	2	0	737	780
3	0	3	342	468
	1	2	589	616
	2	1	737	780
	3	0	902	945

For each additional dependant, add $165 if the dependant is 18 years of age or over, or $0 if the dependant is 0 to 17 years of age.

Source: "Ontario Works (OW) Rate Chart," Toronto Employment & Social Services (1 November 2015), online: <https://www1.toronto.ca/City%20Of%20Toronto/Employment%20and%20Social%20Services/Files/pdf/P/ratetable-community%20Nov%202015%20FINAL-s.pdf>.

TABLE 9.2 Ontario Works Benefit: Amount of Maximum Monthly Shelter Allowance by Benefit Unit Size

Family Size	Maximum Monthly Shelter Allowance
1	$376
2	609
3	662
4	718
5	774
6 or more	801

Source: "Ontario Works (OW) Rate Chart," Toronto Employment & Social Services (1 November 2015), online: <https://www1.toronto.ca/City%20Of%20Toronto/Employment%20and%20Social%20Services/Files/pdf/P/ratetable-community%20Nov%202015%20FINAL-s.pdf>.

Employment Assistance

Because the purpose of Ontario Works is to provide last-resort assistance while recipients of benefits work toward employed self-sufficiency, the program incorporates a number of initiatives designed to support the back-to-work journey. These include the following:

- resource centres where participants can work with counsellors to develop resumés and cover letters
- advice and coaching in interview skills
- referrals to basic education and job retraining programs at no cost to the participant (these typically focus on basic and general skills, such as literacy)
- the Community Placement program, which places Ontario Works recipients in unpaid positions in community agencies or programs to assist them in gaining skills, working experience, and confidence
- the LEAP (Learning, Earning, and Parenting) program for young parents (aged 16 to 25) who are attending or who wish to return to high school
- the Employment Placement program, which identifies employers willing to take on employees who are "less job-ready" and require retraining in order to make the transition from welfare to work

Ontario Works strives to assist participants in taking the shortest path to re-entry into the job market. This means that even while the participants are retraining, they must be actively searching for work. Participation in job search activities is closely monitored by the program administrators, and failure to participate may be grounds for the discontinuation of benefits.

LEAP Program

The LEAP program is compulsory for all teen parents aged 16 and 17 who are recipients of Ontario Works benefits and have not completed high school. It is recommended, but not compulsory, for recipient parents aged 18 to 25 who have not completed high school. LEAP provides supports such as child care and alternative education options to allow teens with dependants to complete their education.

The "learning" portion of LEAP involves education, either at a regular school or at a special facility for teen parents. The "earning" portion involves taking part in activities such as school co-op programs, apprenticeship and job-shadowing programs, and summer employment. The "parenting" portion of LEAP refers to participation in a minimum number of hours of parenting training.

Earnings Exemption

As noted above, an applicant may qualify for Ontario Works benefits even though he or she receives income from another source, such as employment income or WHSI benefits. In general, every dollar of income received from other sources is subtracted from the benefit amount for which the applicant would otherwise be eligible.

However, to support a participant's efforts at finding gainful employment and becoming independent, modest earnings received from a job found *while on benefits* are counted on a 50 percent basis.

Application Process

Applying for Ontario Works benefits involves a number of steps. Social service workers can assist clients in applying for Ontario Works benefits and should be thoroughly familiar with the directives.

First Stage: Telephone Screening

As noted earlier, an application for benefits is made through the municipality where the applicant lives. At the initial contact with the program office (which is usually by telephone), the prospective applicant typically receives information from an intake officer about the program, the application process, and the supporting documents that will be required. The applicant is also pre-screened for possible eligibility. After obtaining the applicant's oral consent to disclose personal information, the intake officer asks a series of questions designed to determine whether eligibility is likely. If the answers indicate that the applicant may be eligible, an in-person interview is scheduled.

If the answers elicited on the telephone indicate that the applicant is not eligible for benefits, the intake officer must communicate this conclusion, with reasons, to the applicant while still on the telephone, and must then mail a written copy of the conclusion to the applicant. Within ten days of receiving the reasons, the applicant may submit a written objection and demand an appointment to continue the application process through an in-person interview. A different intake officer must conduct the interview.

Second Stage: In-Person Interview

Once an interview is scheduled, the applicant should begin gathering the documentation needed to support the application.

Applicants can bring a support person, including, if appropriate, a social service worker, to the interview.

There are a number of components to a second-stage interview, including the following:

- an employment information session
- completion of a participation agreement
- completion of the rest of the application
- verification of information gathered at both stages
- a request for additional information related to the first stage, as appropriate
- signing of all forms

The information session includes communication, by the municipal staff, of the principles of the program. These include a statement that social assistance is a last-resort benefit, that people are better off working and being self-reliant, and that the conditions of assistance require that the applicant pursue activities in support of returning to the workforce.

The intake worker will discuss return-to-work programs and strategies available to the applicant, and together they will make a plan for the applicant to undertake these activities while receiving assistance.

The plan will then be incorporated into a participation agreement. The participation agreement puts the applicant's commitment to specific back-to-work strategies in writing. If at any time while the applicant is receiving benefits he or she fails to meet the terms of the participation agreement, Ontario Works can begin to take steps to withhold benefits.

The second-stage interview must take place within four business days of the initial application. More than one interview may be required, especially if the applicant does not have all the necessary documentation available when he or she first comes in. Once the entire process is complete, the applicant, if successful, will complete all the necessary forms.

Documentation

Numerous documents are required for the application, and gathering them can be onerous for many applicants. Social service workers can help their clients with completing forms and organizing documents.

The applicant should be prepared to complete the following Ontario Works forms provided by the Intake Screening Unit:

- Application for Assistance, Part I: Financial Assistance
- Application for Assistance, Part II: Participation Agreement
- Consent to Disclose and Verify Information
- Rights and Responsibilities Form
- Declaration of Support and Maintenance, where applicable
- Application for Temporary Care Assistance, where applicable

The applicant must also bring the following supporting documents to the interview:

- birth verification: birth certificates or passports for the applicant and all other members of the benefit unit ("beneficiaries")
- marital status: divorce or separation documents
- spousal and/or child support: support order or agreement
- immigration status: immigration documents, sponsorship documents, Canadian citizenship card, or certificate
- pension and social assistance income: eligibility for benefits under other programs (for example, EI, WHSI, ODSP, or CPP), with assignment forms where appropriate
- property: copies of deeds and/or mortgages for any property owned by the applicant or beneficiaries
- debts: verification of all debts over $500
- social insurance numbers: identity cards or tax returns

- health cards
- bank account statements
- receivables: details of monies owing to the applicant or beneficiaries and their efforts to recover them
- year and make of vehicles
- funds held in trust
- rental income: payments received from a roomer or boarder (including a family member)
- proof of current income
- accommodation costs: lease/rental agreements (including number of occupants where applicable); verification of insurance and condominium fees

Disputes over Eligibility

internal review
the review of an
administrative decision by
a different decision-maker
within the institution

If an applicant goes through the second stage of the process and is then informed, in writing, that he or she is ineligible for benefits, or is entitled to only a reduced level of benefits, the applicant can request an **internal review** of the decision. While waiting for the review and any subsequent appeal to be completed, the applicant can request interim financial assistance; however, if he or she is eventually found not to be eligible for equivalent program benefits, the applicant will have to repay the full amount of any support received to which he or she is not entitled.

The internal review process is designed to provide an informal, open, and efficient means of addressing disputes over eligibility, and to reduce the number of times applicants seek recourse to the Social Benefits Tribunal (SBT). Internal reviews are intended to provide applicants with as much information as possible to help them understand why they have been found ineligible for program support. The policy directives also reinforce the fact that eligibility decisions that go against an applicant may sometimes be reversed, once all of the relevant circumstances have been assessed in the course of a review.

Internal Review

An applicant can request an internal review by submitting a written, signed request to the municipal administrator. The request must be delivered to the program office within ten calendar days of receipt of written notice of the administrator's decision. In exceptional circumstances, this time period can be extended.

On receiving the request, the administrator decides whether a review is warranted. If the administrator decides that it is, he or she has ten days to complete the review and report the results to the applicant. The person conducting the review cannot be the person who made the original eligibility decision and must be of equal rank or senior to the original decision-maker. If the administrator chooses not to conduct a review, the applicant has a right to appeal the decision directly to the SBT.

The case file and the original decision are examined to determine whether the decision was

- consistent with the Ontario Works legislation, regulations, and policy;
- based on correct application of the legislation, regulations, and/or policy;
- reasonable;
- based on information that was factual and comprehensive;
- based on a correct interpretation of the facts;
- the result of appropriate use of discretionary power; and
- not the result of administrative error.

The person conducting the review must also consider any additional information available at that time. The policy directive notes that internal reviews are an informal process, and that legal representation is not required as a part of that process. However, if the applicant goes on to appeal the review decision, he or she may wish to engage a legal representative at that stage.

From the perspective of social service workers who may be involved in the administration of the Ontario Works program, the legislation and policy directives establish important internal standards for tracking and documenting reviews, including a requirement for program administrators to keep track of certain statistics with respect to reviews and report them to MCSS in accordance with a regular schedule.

To avoid appeals based on a municipality's failure to handle reviews appropriately, municipal staff, particularly officers charged with conducting reviews, should take special care to keep on file all relevant correspondence and other documents. They should also note any oral request for a review; while an oral request must be followed by a written request, in certain circumstances it may permit a time extension. In addition, staff should document the specific procedural safeguards employed, such as ensuring that a different decision-maker handles the review.

Municipal staff should also ensure that the review process is consistent with the principles established by the legislation—namely, that it is informal, open, and informative.

Appeal to the Social Benefits Tribunal

If an applicant is not satisfied with the review decision, or if the ten-day time period following the request has elapsed and the administrator has not conducted a review, the applicant can appeal the original eligibility or quantum decision to the SBT. The applicant has 30 days from the date of completion of the internal review (or 40 days from the date of his request for a review that does not take place) to file an appeal. Appeal forms are available from the Ontario Works office or the municipality.

Before the hearing, both parties (the applicant and the administrator) can make written submissions to the SBT. The SBT encourages this because a written submission provides a useful reference to the issues in dispute. In some cases, the SBT can make a ruling based on written submissions alone, without holding a hearing.

If a hearing is scheduled, it is very important that the applicant attend. Failure to do so without a good reason will result in automatic denial of the appeal, and the applicant will not be able to make another SBT appeal for two years.

At the appeal hearing, the onus of proof is on the applicant; that is, it is up to the person seeking benefits to show why he or she is eligible. In general, the applicant is the first to state his or her side of the case at the hearing. However, if the applicant has no lawyer, the SBT may ask the Ontario Works administrator to make his or her presentation first, so that the applicant can see how the process works and understand what questions need to be answered to prove the case.

The timing of hearings varies. The SBT is required to schedule a hearing within 60 days of receiving notice of the appeal, but the actual date of the hearing could be more than 60 days after filing. The policy directives suggest a range of wait times between about six weeks and three months from the time of filing; however, the current reality is that it may be as much as eight to ten months before a hearing is held. This has the unfortunate effect of discouraging some applicants from making an appeal, either because it is too long to wait for a resolution, or because the applicant is worried about the requirement to pay back months of interim assistance if the appeal is lost.

After the hearing, or after the SBT decides to proceed on the basis of written submissions, the SBT has 60 days to issue a written decision to the parties. If the decision orders that the applicant is entitled to benefits, Ontario Works must comply and provide those benefits. If the applicant's appeal is denied, he has a right to request reconsideration by the SBT. (The administrator can also request reconsideration.)

After a request for reconsideration is made and addressed by the SBT, if either party is still not satisfied with the result and believes that the SBT has misinterpreted the legislation or regulations in making its decision, that party can appeal the decision to the Ontario Divisional Court. The facts of the case are not reconsidered by the Divisional Court, only matters of law. A party who chooses to proceed to court will need legal representation.

Monitoring Eligibility and Discontinuation of Benefits

Ontario Works participants are monitored on a regular basis to ensure that they are complying with the terms of their participation agreement. A participant who leaves Ontario and is away for more than seven days without notifying the program office, or who acquires assets or earns income over eligibility thresholds, or who stops complying with program requirements, will become ineligible for benefits.

Participants are required to report any changes in circumstances, such as getting a new job, about once a month. The participation agreement is updated every three months, and the effectiveness of employment assistance activities is reviewed at that time. Sometimes it is more efficient to conduct these reviews upon achievement of an employment assistance milestone, such as completion of a training program. A complete review of the participant's financial situation, called the consolidated verification process (CVP), is performed once a year. A CVP review consists of an examination of the budgetary needs of the recipient and benefit unit, including any changes in family size, accommodation arrangements, income sources, asset levels, residence in or absences from Ontario, and any other factors that affect eligibility.

If a recipient of benefits fails to comply with Ontario Works requirements, the terms of the participation agreement can sometimes be renegotiated to take extenuating circumstances into account. If the participant fails to comply with the renegotiated participation agreement, he or she becomes ineligible for the benefits originally awarded, and any future benefits are reduced or cancelled. Reduction or cancellation of benefits may be applied either to the primary recipient alone or to other members of the benefit unit.

When an Ontario Works administrator determines that a participant is no longer eligible for benefits because of non-compliance, the participant's benefits may be suspended for three months for a first occurrence and six months for a subsequent occurrence. The reason for the non-compliance is important: Circumstances beyond the person's control, such as illness, childcare responsibilities, addiction, mental health, homelessness, and other personal circumstances, are considered before making a decision to cancel benefits. The consequences of applying this penalty are potentially severe—there is a real possibility that the family will be unable to meet their basic needs if they cannot find other income through employment or personal supports. What is demanded of participants is a reasonable effort, and those who are unable to achieve self-sufficiency should not be cut off from benefits.

It is possible for an adult's benefits to be cancelled while those of a dependant child are continued, because children under 16 are not themselves subject to participation requirements.

If a participant objects to a decision to suspend benefits, he or she can request an internal review and/or appeal to the SBT, as described above.

Ontario Disability Support Program

ODSP was created by the *Ontario Disability Support Program Act, 1997*.[4] It is designed to provide income assistance to adult Ontario residents who, because of long-term health problems or disabilities, are unable to earn enough income from employment to cover their basic living needs. The program is both regulated and administered by MCSS (in contrast to Ontario Works, for which program delivery has been delegated to municipalities).

Eligibility

In order to qualify for ODSP benefits, a person must

- be 18 or older and an Ontario resident;
- meet the threshold for financial need; and
- suffer from a substantial physical or mental impairment that is either continuous or recurrent and expected to last for a year or more.

---

4   *Ontario Disability Support Program Act, 1997*, SO 1997, c 25, Schedule B.

Benefits and Employment Assistance

The level of benefits available under ODSP varies with the recipient's family circumstances. Additional health benefits, such as drug subsidies, are also available.

The Ontario Disability Support Program also offers employment supports, such as special equipment, child care, and transportation, to facilitate employment for those recipients who are able to work.

While some benefit recipients will be completely unable to work owing to their disabilities, others may be able to do certain kinds of work, especially if job modifications or accommodations are made for them. ODSP provides employment assistance services designed to support participants' efforts to enter the workforce.

Unlike the Ontario Works program, the employment program for disabled clients under ODSP is voluntary; there is no obligation for the recipient of benefits to achieve self-sufficiency. However, able-bodied spouses and adult dependants in the same household are required to participate in employment activities through Ontario Works.

While participation in employment assistance services is voluntary, reporting on status is compulsory. Recipients of benefits are required to report once a month on their current status, advising of any changes in employment, home address, accommodation, income, and financial situation.

Recipients are encouraged to earn income if they are able to do so. Income earned is deducted from the benefits otherwise provided on a 50 percent basis; however, the calculation of the deduction takes into account certain expenses related to employment.

In the spring of 2006, the Ontario government announced plans to enhance the provision of employment assistance services to the disabled, including ODSP participants. The planned improvements included, for example, the continuation of health benefits for people who, through employment, have become ineligible for financial assistance but do not yet have employer-sponsored health benefits.

ODSP also offers a "community start-up and maintenance benefit" (CSUMB), a one-time payment, to assist ODSP recipients with a move, or to preserve existing housing. This benefit can be used to pay expenses associated with moving out of an institution, moving out of a home where the recipient is at risk of abuse, moving to accept a job, or moving as a result of eviction for non-payment of rent or utilities. The payment can also be used to pay arrears of rent and prevent an eviction, if necessary. The CSUMB benefit can generally be claimed only once in a 24-month period.

Young disabled people under the age of 18 may also be eligible for benefits under the Assistance for Children with Severe Disabilities program, administered by the Ministry of Children and Youth Services.

Application Process

Applicants for ODSP benefits follow a procedure that is similar to, though typically slightly less formal than, the Ontario Works application procedure. The initial contact and screening are usually conducted by telephone, and if the applicant appears to qualify, he or she is invited to schedule an appointment for a full screening at an ODSP office. As under the Ontario Works program, there are upper limits on the assets and income that an applicant may have in order to qualify for benefits. Income from other adults in the household, such as a spouse, may reduce benefits.

If the applicant qualifies on the basis of financial need, he or she will receive a "disability determination package," consisting of several forms, which must be completed and returned to the Disability Adjudication Unit (DAU) within 90 days of the date of issue. The package includes a "Health Status Report and Activities of Daily Living Index," which describes the applicant's health, capabilities, skills, and limitations, and must be completed by a medical professional. There is a second form authorizing the release of medical information, and a third, discretionary (optional) form in which the applicant is asked to describe what it is like to live with his or her disability. On receipt of the completed forms, the DAU determines whether the applicant is eligible for program benefits. If the applicant fails to meet the 90-day deadline for submitting the package, he or she will be found ineligible. A one-time request for an extension is permitted.

Disputes over Eligibility

An applicant who is found to be ineligible can request an internal review of the decision. If the basis for the finding is the applicant's financial standing, the request for the review is directed to the local ODSP office. If the applicant is found to be ineligible on the basis of disability status, the request is directed to the DAU.

As in the case with the Ontario Works program, an applicant who disagrees with the outcome of an internal review can appeal the decision to the Social Benefits Tribunal.

Federal Income Assistance Programs for Older Canadians

Many people rely on government-funded programs to support an acceptable standard of living after they reach retirement age. There is a trend among Canadian employers to eliminate once-common pension plans for employees. Sometimes these plans are replaced with matched or partially matched contribution savings plans and RRSPs, but in many cases, employers make no provision at all for employees' post-retirement financial needs—apart from their obligation to match employee contributions to the Canada Pension Plan. CPP is just one component of the federal system of income assistance for older Canadians; the other programs include the Old Age Security (OAS), the Guaranteed Income Supplement (GIS), and the Allowance.

Canada Pension Plan

CPP is a federal government–run savings plan created under and governed by federal legislation, the *Canada Pension Plan*.[5] It is designed to provide seniors who have worked in their lifetime with a basic income upon retirement. Eligibility for pension benefits and payments to recipients under the plan are administered by Employment and Social Development Canada (ESDC).

---

5 *Canada Pension Plan*, RSC 1985, c C-8.

Throughout their working years, individuals make contributions to the plan, either through paycheque deductions or, if self-employed, through an annual payment. Employers also contribute by matching the payments made by employees. The government collects and invests the money to fund distributions from the plan to participants during their retirement years.

Contributions

Employees earning salary or wages above a minimum threshold must make CPP contributions. The amount of the contribution is calculated as a percentage of income earned (up to a maximum income threshold) and is deducted by the employer from the employee's pay. These employee contributions are matched dollar-for-dollar by the employer.

Self-employed people must pay both the employee and employer portions.

Benefits

There are three kinds of benefits available through CPP:

- retirement benefits: a monthly benefit payable to the retired person until death
- survivor benefits: benefits payable after the pension holder's death to his or her estate, spouse, or dependent children
- disability benefits: benefits payable to someone who once worked but can work no longer because of a disability

Recipients do not receive CPP benefits automatically, but must apply. To ensure that pension benefits are received as soon as the pensioner becomes eligible, it is wise to apply at least six months before the planned retirement date. Individuals who are eligible for survivor benefits and disability benefits also should apply at the earliest opportunity.

RETIREMENT BENEFITS

The retirement benefits payable under the plan are modest: they are designed to replace about 25 percent of the earnings upon which the contributions were based. As a result, CPP alone will not generally sustain the lifestyle that the pensioner enjoyed while working.

Anyone who has made a valid contribution to CPP is eligible for CPP benefits upon reaching age 65, whether or not living in Canada at that time. People aged 60 to 64 are sometimes eligible to receive benefits if they stop working or their income drops considerably, but eligibility for early retirement benefits depends upon compliance with minimum contribution requirements.

The level of benefits is generally based on the individual's earnings and contributions to the plan and his or her age at retirement. Benefits are indexed to reflect changes in the cost of living over the duration of the pension.

SURVIVOR BENEFITS

Survivor benefits are benefits paid after a pensioner's death to his or her estate, or to a surviving spouse and/or dependent children. A social service worker with a client who is eligible for the survivor benefit may need to assist the client in providing information to ESDC in order to access the benefit.

Children's benefits are payable to children who are either under 18 when their parent becomes disabled or dies, or between 18 and 25 and enrolled in a full-time program of study at a university or college.

DISABILITY BENEFITS

People who contribute to CPP may be eligible for disability benefits if they have a disability that prevents them from working regularly.

Disputes over Eligibility or Benefits

If a pensioner disagrees with a CPP decision, such as a decision denying disability benefits, he or she may request reconsideration within 90 days. A request for reconsideration is made to Employment and Social Development Canada (ESDC) and must be in writing, stating why the applicant disagrees with the decision. When the request is received, a ministry officer reconsiders the decision and either affirms it or makes a new decision.

Old Age Security, Guaranteed Income Supplement, and the Allowance

Old Age Security

ESDC describes OAS as the cornerstone of Canada's income support system for seniors, created under the *Old Age Security Act*.[6] This is because (in contrast to CPP) a person does not need to have contributed to the system in order to receive a benefit.

The basic qualification for OAS is residence in Canada for at least ten years at any time between the ages of 18 and 65. People who have lived in Canada for at least 20 years in this period can qualify to receive OAS while living outside Canada. The amount of OAS benefits is dependent on length of residency in Canada. A person who has lived in Canada for 40 years between the ages of 18 and 65 is eligible for the maximum benefit level, while people who have lived here for less than 40 years receive a smaller pension based on length of residency.

Guaranteed Income Supplement

GIS is a pension benefit paid in addition to OAS in order to assure a minimum standard of living for low-income seniors.

The Allowance

Another benefit available to some seniors is called the Allowance. This benefit is designed to provide income to low-income people aged 60 to 64 (that is, those who

survivor benefit
a benefit paid to the dependants of the benefit recipient after his or her death

---

6 *Old Age Security Act*, RSC 1985, c O-9.

are not yet eligible to receive OAS) who have a spouse or partner who is eligible for OAS/GIS. This benefit takes into account the situation where an older couple's income is low after the retirement of at least one of them, but only one is old enough to access OAS/GIS. If the spouse of a person who is eligible for the Allowance dies, the benefit is increased. This increased benefit is called the Allowance for the survivor.

Promoting Access to Income Support

Social service workers may encounter clients in financial need in a variety of ways. Following are some examples:

- Clients who have recently become disabled may rely on social service workers through health-care support agencies.
- Clients may encounter social service workers at shelters for abused women and children, where they may be fleeing a person who supported them financially.
- Clients may be in financial need as a result of a life crisis (job loss, divorce, death of parents, fire, natural disasters, etc.).
- Clients may be elderly people in various settings, such as nursing homes, who have used up their savings.

In general, Canadians are reasonably well informed about the existence of the "social safety net" and the fact that there are benefits available to them. In many cases, a social service worker may be asked to help clients inquire about the details of the various programs, including how to apply and how to appeal a decision. Social service workers can be of particular assistance in helping clients to fill out forms and track down supporting documents.

Social service workers can also play an important role in helping clients to access emergency assistance—for example, temporary lodging in a shelter, interim Ontario Works benefits, or groceries from a food bank. By maintaining a thorough knowledge of the emergency services available in your community, you can buy time for a client while he or she applies for benefits and awaits the processing of the application.

If there are no emergency services or inadequate emergency services available in the community, social service workers can have an important role in advocating for the development and funding of these services. Clients can even be encouraged to become part of this process (by participating in a clothing/toy exchange, a babysitting co-op, or a ride-sharing program, for example).

In some cases, social service workers will encounter clients who face unusual barriers to accessing income support, such as the following:

- *Clients who cannot legally work in Canada.* Clients whose immigration status excludes them from access to legal jobs in Canada are also not eligible to participate in programs such as Ontario Works or to contribute to the Canada Pension Plan. For these clients, you may need to arrange emergency shelter and living support via charitable organizations designed to support refugee claimants or those whose immigration status is unsettled. Once emergency assistance is in place, the first step is to assist the client in obtaining official refugee or landed immigrant status so that he or she can work in Canada.

- *Clients with communication/comprehension problems.* Some clients may have trouble accessing benefits because of a communication problem. Clients who face a language barrier may need translation services. Clients with a cognitive impairment may need help arranging for a substitute decision-maker (an attorney for personal care or other appointee).

- *Clients with interpersonal/family problems.* Some clients may come from families in crisis, where there is abuse or neglect. These clients may be adults (for example, a battered woman who is part of her husband's Ontario Works benefit unit but who is having her benefits withheld by him) or children (children who are living in poverty but whose parents have not applied for benefits or have had benefits cut off because of lack of compliance with program requirements). These clients may need other kinds of help—for example, assistance leaving the family home and moving into a shelter, or a referral to a children's aid society—before effective steps can be taken to support their access to social benefits.

In these special cases, social service workers will need to draw on their experience with other aspects of client service—first, in eliminating barriers to income assistance, and then, once barriers are overcome, in supporting clients in accessing that assistance. Note that overcoming barriers may require the social service worker to refer a client to organizations and services outside the local community.

As a social service worker, you will often be expected to act as an advocate for your clients. This may mean supporting them in their attempts to access benefits even after a decision has gone against them. For this reason, you will need to have a basic understanding of the processes available to challenge administrative decisions. You will also need to know how to assist a client in obtaining legal assistance where legal representation is necessary to protect or establish an entitlement to benefits.

KEY TERMS

entitlement, 143
internal review, 150
needs- and means-tested, 143
subsistence needs, 143
survivor benefit, 157

SUGGESTED SOURCES

Canada Benefits, Government of Canada, Services and Information, <http://www.canada.ca/en/services/benefits.html>

Ministry of Children and Youth Services, Assistance for Children with Severe Disabilities program, <http://www.children.gov.on.ca/htdocs/English/specialneeds/disabilities.aspx>

Ministry of Community and Social Services, LEAP program, <http://www.mcss.gov.on.ca/en/mcss/programs/social/questions/leap.aspx>

Ministry of Community and Social Services, Ontario Works, <http://www.mcss.gov.on.ca/en/mcss/programs/social/ow/>

Social Benefits Tribunals Ontario, <http://www.sjto.gov.on.ca/sbt/>

REVIEW QUESTIONS

1. List at least two federal income-assistance programs and two Ontario income-assistance programs.

2. What does the name of the Ontario Works program mean, and what values does it reflect?

3. What happens if a person who is receiving Ontario Works benefits begins receiving an income, but one that is not enough to live on (for example, income from a low-paying part-time job)?

4. Can children receive Ontario Works benefits? What about teens living on their own?

5. If an Ontario Works recipient has his benefits cut off (for example, for failing to meet the terms of his participation agreement), and he wishes to challenge the decision to suspend or terminate his benefits, what must he do?

6. Who is eligible to receive retirement benefits under the Canada Pension Plan?

Criminal and Civil Law

10

LEARNING OUTCOMES

After completing this chapter, you should be able to:

- Identify the main statute in Canadian criminal law and other criminal and quasi-criminal statutes (federal and provincial/territorial).

- Understand the concepts of *actus reus* (act or conduct) and *mens rea* (intent).

- Understand the differences between summary conviction, indictable, and hybrid offences, and the trial options available for each.

- Understand the general purpose, objectives, and principles of sentencing.

- Identify different kinds of sentences and describe the main differences among them.

- Understand civil procedure and the rules and legal traditions that govern the conduct of civil trials

- Describe the structure of the Ontario court system.

- Demonstrate a general understanding of pre-trial issues and describe the stages of a criminal trial and list the trial participants.

- Explain the role of evidence in the civil and criminal legal systems, list the types of evidence, and describe the role of witnesses and the types of questions witnesses may be asked.

Introduction

This chapter serves as a broad and basic overview of the general principles of criminal and civil law. Criminal law comprises both substantive law (what constitutes a crime) and procedural law and evidence (the process for bringing an accused to justice). Civil procedure refers to the rules and legal traditions that govern the conduct of civil (non-criminal) trials. Civil actions arise when one party begins legal proceedings against another party in pursuit of a remedy for a harm or expected harm—for example, a wrongful act or omission, or a violation or breach of legal rights.

Social service workers perform several important roles in the criminal justice system. For example, they may work with youth in programs designed as an alternative to traditional criminal procedure. They may also work in the corrections system, within prisons, or in community support programs for inmates. More commonly, social service workers will find that many of their clients are in some way involved with the criminal and civil justice system and dealing with criminal or civil justice issues, either as victims or as offenders.

Regardless of the work setting and the clientele, it is useful for a social service worker to have a general understanding of the criminal and civil justice system.

Criminal Law and the Constitutional Division of Powers

Canada's constitution divides the power to make laws between the federal and provincial and territorial governments. The federal government has jurisdiction over the creation of criminal law, while the provinces and territories have jurisdiction over its administration and enforcement. All criminal laws are enacted by the Parliament of Canada and codified in a small body of federal statutes. The best known of these statutes and the one of broadest application is the *Criminal Code*.[1] The Code defines a wide range of offences, sets the rules of procedure, establishes the penalties that may apply to each specific offence, and provides guidelines for sentencing.

The provincial and territorial courts administer the criminal procedure according to the rules contained in the Code.

In addition to the *Criminal Code*, there are several federal criminal-law statutes that govern subject areas for which the federal government has a discrete enforcement mission, strategy, scheme, or philosophy. Examples of such subject-specific statutes include the *Controlled Drugs and Substances Act* and the *Crimes Against Humanity and War Crimes Act*.[2]

The *Criminal Code* includes many different substantive offences, such as theft, assault, murder, and fraud, and provides for a range of sentences appropriate for each offence. The Code also outlines the procedure for a fair trial, emphasizing that the accused is innocent until proven guilty beyond a reasonable doubt.

Legislatures of both levels of government can create laws that impose penalties for certain acts or forms of behaviour that are considered illegal but not criminal

---

1   *Criminal Code*, RSC 1985, c C-46.

2   *Controlled Drugs and Substances Act*, SC 1996, c 19; *Crimes Against Humanity and War Crimes Act*, SC 2000, c 24.

(provided that the subject matter of the statute falls within the government's jurisdiction). In other words, illegality is not synonymous with criminality. This distinction makes practical sense. For example, the licensing of pets is typically regulated by municipalities; for example, there is currently a by-law in the Durham region that prohibits cat owners from allowing their cats to roam free outside. Since roaming cats are considered to be a nuisance, rather than a safety and security risk, it wouldn't be appropriate to bring the full range of criminal justice system procedures and penalties to bear on a roaming-cat owner. As a result, letting a cat out in that region is illegal but not criminal, and the penalty is minor: The owner must pay a small fine.

Illegal (or "quasi-criminal") offences are contained in a very wide range of provincial/territorial statutes and municipal by-laws. At the provincial/territorial level, these statutes are designed to support the enforcement of activities that fall within provincial/territorial responsibility under the constitution. An example is Ontario's *Highway Traffic Act*.[3]

First Nations, Métis, and Inuit and the Criminal Justice System

Canada's Indigenous—or First Nations, Métis, and Inuit—peoples have a complicated constitutional relationship with the federal and provincial and territorial governments. As descendants of the original occupants of Canada, predating the arrival of Europeans, Indigenous peoples have traditionally characterized their relationship with government as that of two independent nations engaged in negotiating the details of their coexistence in this land. In the last half-century, First Nations have successfully negotiated jurisdiction over a number of aspects of government formerly under federal or provincial/territorial authority; for example, many First Nations, Métis, and Inuit communities now run their own schools, police forces, and other services.

Many people believe that Indigenous peoples have the right to self-government and that this includes the right to administer criminal justice within their own communities. The relationship between members of the First Nations, Métis, and Inuit, and the Canadian justice system has always been fairly rocky. Statistics continue to demonstrate that Indigenous peoples are overrepresented in the prison population (individuals charged, convicted, and imprisoned for crimes). This means that the percentage of Indigenous convicts or inmates in Canada's prisons is higher than one would expect on the basis of the percentage of Indigenous people in our society as a whole. The reasons for this overrepresentation are complex. Many commentators suggest that the poverty and isolation resulting from the marginalization of Indigenous people have led to a higher crime rate. In addition, systemic discrimination and unfairness in the treatment of Indigenous people within the justice system results in more Indigenous people being charged, convicted, and incarcerated compared to non-Indigenous peoples engaging in the same conduct.

---

3   *Highway Traffic Act*, RSO 1990, c H.8.

But these factors aside, many commentators suggest that the Canadian justice system, in theory and in structure, is not compatible with Indigenous cultural ideas about justice. New initiatives designed to remedy problems that Indigenous peoples face within the justice system have tended to focus on creating alternative approaches to justice that better reflect the cultural values of First Nations, Métis, and Inuit peoples.

For example, section 718.2(e) of the *Criminal Code* requires judges, when sentencing Indigenous offenders, to give particular consideration to "all available sanctions, other than imprisonment, that are reasonable in the circumstances." **Restorative justice** as a sentencing principle reflects important Indigenous cultural values: Rather than seeking to punish the offender, it focuses on making **reparation** to the victim and to the community in general for the purposes of healing, rehabilitation, and reconciliation.

In some Indigenous communities, the principle of restorative justice is applied through the use of a **sentencing circle**, a process that involves an open dialogue in a public forum between the offender, the victim, and other members of the community. One of the key purposes of a sentencing circle is to reinforce the expectation that the offender will assume responsibility for his or her actions within the community as a condition of receiving its support.

Social service workers who serve Indigenous clients may be involved in developing or administering alternatives to the traditional criminal procedure that better serve the interests of Indigenous people, or in advocating for the development of such alternatives.

The Basics of Offences: Elements of an Offence and Defences

Elements of an Offence

The *Criminal Code* sets out in every offence provision the specific elements of the offence that must exist in order for a suspect to be charged with a crime. For the accused to be found guilty, the charge must be proven in court through oral testimony or physical evidence, or both.

The elements of an offence, or its substantive part, fall into two categories: the actions or omissions that constitute the offence, and any required mental state, such as intent, recklessness, or negligence. These are known respectively as the ***actus reus***, the physical act or omission involved in committing the offence, and the ***mens rea***, the state of mind or the level of intent attributed to the accused that establishes his or her fault in so acting or failing to act. For example, the offence of assault consists of an action—applying force to another person without that person's consent—and a mental state—applying the force "intentionally." Both of these conditions must be present for an action to constitute an assault.

---

restorative justice
an approach to justice that places an emphasis not on punishing the offender but on taking responsibility for actions, compensating for harm done to victims, and repairing relationships

reparation
a payment made to compensate for harm

sentencing circle
alternative sentencing procedure in which the penalty for a crime is decided through a consultative process involving the offender, the victim, and the community

actus reus
the physical act or omission that when combined with the required intent constitutes an offence

mens rea
the mental element of a crime; the intent required to satisfy the description of an offence

Actus Reus

The *actus reus* of an offence can be an act, a state of being, or an omission.

Most of the offences in the *Criminal Code* are action offences: offences that require the accused to commit a certain act include striking, stealing, and counterfeiting. An action offence may also include a requirement that the action of the accused caused a certain result (for example, the offence of assault causing bodily harm).

Most state-of-being offences are offences of possession, which can include weapons, controlled drugs, and break-in tools. The *actus reus* for such an offence is simply the fact of being in possession and control of the particular item.

In some cases, the law requires a person to take a particular action in a particular circumstance, and it becomes an offence of omission to *not* take the required action. Examples are refusals to obey police orders, such as stopping at a road block or refusing to provide a breath sample when asked to do so. There is also a class of criminal negligence offences in which the failure to act (whether with intent or otherwise) endangers or causes harm to another person.

Mens Rea

Under our law, the availability of criminal sanctions almost always depends upon a legal finding of moral guilt. To determine guilt, the court examines evidence of the accused's state of mind at the time of committing the alleged offence. To be found guilty of a criminal offence, the accused person must have made a choice to do something wrong, made the choice voluntarily or with free will, and known that the act was wrong.

If all of these elements are proven, then the accused is said to have the requisite *mens rea*, or "guilty mind."

Many offences under the *Criminal Code* describe not only physical acts but also the mindset of the accused at the time of committing the act, using modifying words to define the criminal behaviour. Offences may depend not only on the action committed but also on how it is committed—for example, "wilfully," "recklessly," or "with intent to injure."

Intent is a key to *mens rea*. The law recognizes degrees of intent, which range from direct intent (the most serious in a criminal offence) to negligence (the least serious). In general, offences that carry more serious penalties require a higher level of intent: One form of first-degree murder, for example, requires not only a specific intent to kill but also evidence of planning and deliberation on the part of the accused. Second-degree murder requires only the specific intent to kill, while the lesser charge of manslaughter requires a general intent to injure the victim, without any particular thought as to whether the victim would die as a result.

At the lower end of the range of intent are recklessness, wilful blindness, carelessness, and negligence. These lower levels of *mens rea* may be said to describe unjustifiable risk-taking.

Criminal negligence differs from ordinary or civil negligence in that it requires some level of *mens rea*, such as wanton and reckless disregard for the lives and safety of others. A motorist who engages in drag racing on a public road may be criminally negligent even if at the time there is no other traffic and no apparent danger to others. Criminal negligence does not require proof of intention or deliberation; indifference to the possible consequences is enough.

Defences

prosecution
the process of presenting the case for convicting and sentencing a person accused of an offence, undertaken by the Crown attorney

defence
in criminal or civil law, the accused or the party who is responding to a lawsuit; the arguments put forward by an accused or a defendant

When a person is charged with an offence and the case is brought to trial, it is the responsibility of the **prosecution** to prove every element of the charge beyond a reasonable doubt. The accused is not required to present a **defence**. The defence usually presents evidence that casts doubt on one or more elements of the charge. For example, the defence may argue that the accused couldn't have committed the crime because he was somewhere else at the time. By presenting evidence such as an alibi, the defence may raise a reasonable doubt about the validity of the charge.

Most specific defences are designed to prove that the accused did not have the required intent, or *mens rea*, to commit the offence. Recognized defences include self-defence, mental incapacity, consent (especially with respect to sexual assault), and entrapment. If the accused is being tried by a judge and jury, and presents evidence in support of a recognized defence, the judge will need to explain the legal effect of the specific defence to the jury so that jury members can take it into account in their decision to convict or acquit the accused.

The Investigation

The police investigate circumstances in which it appears that someone may have committed an offence. When they have identified a suspect and the information they have collected appears to be sufficient to prove that the suspect committed the *actus reus* and had the *mens rea* on which the specific offence is based, they will generally proceed to lay a criminal charge. Once that has been done, police provide evidence to the Crown attorney, who will decide whether to prosecute the case against the accused person. The prosecution later uses this evidence at trial.

Rights of the Individual

To protect the privacy and security rights of individuals, police investigations are conducted according to strict procedural rules. The rules governing investigations include a person's rights with respect to search, being detained, reasons for detention, rights to legal counsel, and the right to know what the specific charges are against you.

The *Canadian Charter of Rights and Freedoms* has codified a range of rights.[4] Table 10.1 illustrates these Charter rights.

In general, before the police can engage in any investigative action (searches, detentions, collection of samples, etc.) that invades a person's privacy, they must have reasonable and probable grounds to suspect that an offence has been committed, and that the actions that they propose will uncover evidence in support of that suspicion.

---

4   *Canadian Charter of Rights and Freedoms*, Part I of the *Constitution Act, 1982*, being Schedule B to the *Canada Act 1982* (UK), 1982, c 11.

TABLE 10.1   Charter Rights Related to Police Conduct

Charter Section	Charter Right
Section 8	Everyone has the right to be secure against unreasonable search or seizure.
Section 9	Everyone has the right not to be arbitrarily detained or imprisoned.
Section 10(a)	Everyone has the right on arrest or detention to be informed promptly of the reasons therefor;
Section 10(b)	Everyone has the right on arrest or detention to retain and instruct counsel without delay and to be informed of that right;
Section 11(a)	Any person charged with an offence has the right to be informed without unreasonable delay of the specific offence;
Section 12	Everyone has the right not to be subjected to any cruel and unusual treatment or punishment.

Source: *Canadian Charter of Rights and Freedoms*, Part I of the *Constitution Act, 1982*, being Schedule B to the *Canada Act 1982* (UK), 1982, c 11.

There are instances in which the police need to obtain a search warrant. Generally, a search without warrant is presumed to be illegal. In these cases, the police officer would need to justify the search. Searches with warrants are presumed to be legal, and it would be up to the accused person to show why the search was illegal.

The greater the degree of a person's privacy, the greater the degree of certainty required on the part of the police when searching. Searching the trunk of a car, entering someone's home, and searching a person's smartphone are examples of increased privacy concerns.

In 2014, the Supreme Court of Canada ruled in a close 4–3 margin that police can search cellphones without first obtaining a warrant, as long as certain conditions are present. The conditions include a lawful arrest, the search being incidental to the arrest, the search being limited to the specific purpose related to the arrest, and the taking of detailed notes of the search by the police. The dissenting judges in this case disagreed with the majority, citing the privacy interests in the person's cellphone as being paramount.[5]

When evidence is collected in a manner that violates the Charter rights of a person accused of a crime, that evidence is sometimes excluded from use in the subsequent trial of that person.

Any individual who is being treated as a suspect in a criminal matter, and who believes that his or her rights have been or are being infringed, should obtain immediate legal assistance. The consequences of a criminal conviction are serious. If, as a social service worker, you take a call from a client who is in trouble with the law, you should suggest that the client contact a lawyer and, if appropriate, you should help the client to do so by putting him in touch with legal aid or a lawyer referral service.

---

5   *R v Fearon*, 2014 SCC 77, [2014] 3 SCR 621.

Disclosure Requirements

The criminal justice system in Canada is based on the presumption of innocence, and the accused person has the right to know the case that will be made against him or her. The system of disclosure requires the police and the Crown prosecutor to provide to the accused person and his or her lawyer all the evidence in their possession related to the particular offence. The accused is entitled to disclosure in a timely fashion. A delay in the release of disclosure can result in the accused asking for the charges to be withdrawn, citing section 11(b) of the Charter for unreasonable delay.

There is also a continuing obligation on the Crown to disclose new information and evidence to the accused as it is uncovered or discovered.

The disclosure requirement extends through the Crown prosecutor to the investigating police officers themselves. The police have both a statutory and a common law duty to disclose to the Crown prosecutor all relevant information that has been collected during an investigation, even if that evidence could be used to prove the innocence of the person accused of the offence.

If the police fail to do this, the accused is entitled to a remedy. If evidence has been lost or destroyed either by the police or by the prosecution, and this loss affects the ability of the accused to make a full answer and defence, the judge may issue a **stay of proceedings**. This is a ruling that stops further prosecution of the case; that is, the charge against the accused is dropped. To be granted a stay, the defence must establish that the accused's right to a fair trial has been denied or irreparably harmed, or that the non-disclosure was in bad faith or constitutes an **abuse of process**—an improper action or series of actions on the part of the police that undermines the fairness of the criminal procedure. An individual's right to a full and fair defence is included in section 7 of the Charter, "the right to life, liberty and security of the person and the right not to be deprived thereof except in accordance with the principles of fundamental justice."

stay of proceedings
a court order that stops proceedings against an accused

abuse of process
an improper action or a series of actions on the part of the police or prosecution that undermines the fairness of the criminal proceedings

Charges and Elections

Types of Charging Documents

The charging document sets out the criminal charges against the accused and begins the process toward trial. It identifies the specific charges or offences (known as counts) that the accused is alleged to have committed. There are two types of charging documents:

- An **information** is the charging document used for offences tried in a provincial/territorial court or youth court and is usually sworn by a police officer.
- An **indictment** is the charging document used for offences tried in a superior court of criminal jurisdiction and is usually signed by the prosecutor.

information
a type of charging process or document that is used to begin a prosecution of a summary conviction offence

indictment
a type of charging process or document that is used to begin a prosecution, usually of an indictable offence

The *Criminal Code* prescribes the forms that are to be used and the procedures for completing and delivering charging documents. It is essential that the charging document be made out correctly for the charge to proceed to trial.

Classification of Offences

Our criminal justice system classifies *Criminal Code* offences into three categories, according to their seriousness and the procedure used to deal with the charge in court: summary conviction offences, hybrid or dual offences, and indictable offences.

In general, **summary conviction offences** are less serious offences and carry light penalties. Any charge tried by summary conviction is tried in the provincial/territorial court before a provincial/territorial court judge alone, without a jury. No preliminary hearing is held.

Indictable offences are more serious crimes that usually carry stiffer penalties. The court and mode of trial varies according to the offence. In most cases, the accused has the right to a preliminary hearing.

Hybrid or dual offences may be tried as a summary conviction offence or as an indictable offence at the election of the prosecutor. Hybrid or dual offences reflect the fact that the seriousness of an offence can vary greatly. For example, the hybrid offence of assault may involve a slight nudge or a violent punch. The prosecutor will consider the facts of the case before determining whether to proceed by summary conviction or indictment. That decision will determine the court and the mode of trial.

Table 10.2 summarizes the differences in procedure depending on the type of offence.

summary conviction offence
usually a less serious offence that is tried by means of a simplified procedure and that attracts less serious penalties

indictable offence
a serious offence that attracts a significant penalty and that is tried through a more complex criminal procedure

hybrid/dual offence
an offence that can be charged either as a summary conviction offence or as an indictable offence according to the Crown's election

TABLE 10.2   Classification of Offences

	Summary Conviction	Indictable	Hybrid
Court	Provincial/ territorial court	Accused chooses provincial/territorial court or Superior Court	Prosecutor chooses whether to proceed by summary conviction or indictment
Preliminary hearing	No	Accused has right to preliminary hearing if he or she elects to be tried in Superior Court	
Jury	No	Accused has right to have a jury if he or she elects to be tried in Superior Court	
Charging document	Information	Indictment	

Source: *Criminal Code*, RSC 1985, c C-46.

Applying these rules of procedure under the Ontario court system, all summary conviction offences are tried in the Ontario Court of Justice (the provincial court). Indictable offences may be tried in the Ontario Court of Justice or in the Superior Court of Justice, usually at the election of the accused. The court in which a hybrid or dual offence is tried will depend on whether it is treated as a summary conviction or an indictable offence, and on the election of the accused where available.

Choosing the Court and Mode of Trial

Not all charges proceed to trial; the accused may plead guilty or may negotiate a plea bargain with the prosecutor. However, if the accused pleads not guilty, he may have the option of choosing the court and mode of trial to decide the case.

Structure of the Ontario Court System

When clients are required to attend court, social service workers can provide an important support during this process. The legal system, and court in particular, can be intimidating for many clients, and they may find the experience extremely stressful. As well, social service workers may also be called upon to testify in a professional capacity at a trial involving a client. Whether you are directly involved or assisting a client in a court proceeding, social service workers need to understand court procedure and what is expected of a witness.

Criminal offences and some civil disputes are tried in either the Superior Court of Justice or the Ontario Court of Justice. Ontario also has several specialty courts, such as Family Court to deal with family law cases and Small Claims Court to deal with minor civil disputes.

In 1999, the Supreme Court of Canada released an important decision in a case called *R v Gladue*.[6] One of the key findings in *Gladue* was that Canada's justice system at the time relied too heavily on incarceration as a response to criminality, especially in cases involving Indigenous offenders.

One of the responses to the *Gladue* decision was the creation of a special branch of the Ontario Court of Justice, called the Gladue Court. The Gladue Court has three Toronto locations and handles only cases involving Indigenous offenders. Indigenous offenders include status and non-status Indians, First Nations, Métis, and Inuit who identify themselves as such.

The intention in creating a separate court for Indigenous people charged with criminal offences is to provide a venue in which the unique circumstances of these individuals are taken properly into account in the pursuit of justice. Judges and others who work in this court are specially trained in Indigenous issues.

Decisions of the Ontario Court of Justice in respect of certain minor criminal offences and provincial offences may be appealed to the Superior Court of Justice. Decisions of the Superior Court of Justice may be appealed to the Ontario Court of Appeal. The Ontario Court of Appeal hears only appeals; it does not conduct trials. Moreover, it hears only those cases in which there is a legal issue to be clarified or an issue of importance to the public interest. For this reason, a party who wishes to appeal a civil matter must apply to the court for "leave" (permission) to appeal. In criminal cases, the accused may appeal the Superior Court's decision "as of right"—that is, the Court of Appeal cannot refuse to hear the appeal. Most Court of Appeal hearings are before a three-judge panel, although a larger panel may hear certain very significant cases. There are no juries at the Court of Appeal, because the issues being examined involve questions of law rather than determinations of fact.

---

6   *R v Gladue*, [1999] 1 SCR 688.

A party who wishes to appeal a decision of the Ontario Court of Appeal may apply for leave to appeal to the Supreme Court of Canada. The court will review the decision and decide whether to grant or deny leave, depending on whether there are sufficient legal grounds. A decision of the Supreme Court is final.

Criminal Procedure

Criminal Trials

Criminal procedure refers to the rules and legal traditions that govern the conduct of trials of persons accused of criminal offences.

In a criminal trial, the **prosecutor** of the charge is the government, represented by the Crown attorney (the Crown); the person accused of the charge is the **defendant** or accused and is usually represented by a lawyer who specializes in criminal defence law.

Once the police have laid charges and the Crown has decided to prosecute, the accused must go to court and present a defence if he or she hopes to escape a criminal conviction. The alternative is to plead guilty and thus avoid a lengthy trial. Sometimes the defendant can negotiate with the prosecution to plead guilty to a lesser charge. This is called a **plea bargain**. A plea bargain saves considerable time and money and removes the risk inherent in a trial, where the outcome is never certain. Many defendants are willing to accept a plea bargain in order to avoid the risk of conviction on a more serious charge and a heavier sentence.

Rules of Criminal Procedure

The primary source of criminal trial procedures is the *Criminal Code*. While individual courts also have their own procedural rules, the *Criminal Code* prescribes most of the steps in the prosecution of a criminal offence, from charging to sentencing.

Pre-Trial Procedures

Before a criminal trial begins, there are many preliminary steps. When a person is suspected of committing an offence, the alleged offence must be investigated and evidence must be collected. The investigation stage often includes an interview of the suspect and all witnesses. When the evidence is sufficient to support a reasonable belief that the suspect committed the offence, a charge is laid. All of these procedures must be conducted according to strict rules imposed by the common law, the *Criminal Code*, and the *Canadian Charter of Rights and Freedoms*.

Depending on the circumstances in the particular case, various hearings and motions may be held or brought in court, either before or at the start of a trial. Three examples are described below: a bail hearing, a hearing to determine whether the accused is mentally fit to stand trial, and a preliminary inquiry.

BAIL HEARING

The *Criminal Code* sets out detailed procedural rules governing the detention of an accused in custody pending trial. Generally, except in the case of the most serious offences, a person who has been charged with an offence and detained in custody

prosecutor
the Crown attorney prosecuting a case

defendant
in a criminal matter, the person accused of a charge, usually used with respect to summary conviction offences; in a civil matter, the person opposing a plaintiff's claim

plea bargain
a negotiation between the prosecutor and an accused that results in a guilty plea

judicial interim release
also called bail; release
from custody pending
first court appearance

following his arrest is entitled to a bail hearing before a judge or a justice of the peace, "without unreasonable delay" (usually within 24 hours or three days). The *Criminal Code* refers to this as a **judicial interim release** hearing.

Generally, the court will order the release of the accused unless the prosecution can show cause (give reasons) as to why he should be kept in custody or released subject to certain conditions, such as a requirement to stay away from victims or that a bond be posted on the accused's behalf. In determining whether to release an accused while awaiting trial, the court will consider whether the accused will flee the jurisdiction to avoid trial or poses a danger to society, or if the court feels that releasing the accused will result in the public losing confidence in the criminal justice system.

Usually the onus is on the Crown to show cause, but there are some circumstances where the onus is reversed to the accused to show why he or she should be released.

HEARING TO DETERMINE FITNESS TO STAND TRIAL

For a trial to be fair, the accused must be capable of the following:

- understanding what is going on
- understanding the consequences he or she faces as a result of the trial
- understanding, instructing, and receiving advice from his or her lawyer

If the accused is mentally incapable of any of these things, the trial cannot proceed. Where there is a question regarding the fitness of the accused, a hearing may be held before the trial (or at any time in the subsequent proceedings).

The *Criminal Code* states that a person is "unfit to stand trial" if he or she is unable, because of a mental disorder, to conduct a defence or to instruct counsel to do so (s 2).

The trial judge may order an assessment of the accused to assist in determining mental fitness. If the accused is found to be unfit to stand trial, he or she may be committed to a mental institution until such time as he or she is fit to stand trial. In other words, a finding that the accused is unfit to stand trial will not remove the charges or save him or her from possible conviction; it will simply postpone the trial.

PRELIMINARY INQUIRY

A preliminary inquiry may be held where the accused is being tried in the Ontario Superior Court of Justice. It is not automatic but may be requested by either the accused or the prosecution. The purpose of the preliminary inquiry is to provide an opportunity for the Crown and the accused to present evidence and make submissions before a judge sufficient to establish that the accused either should or should not stand trial for the offence charged. Generally, on hearing the evidence, the judge will either order the accused to stand trial or discharge him.

Stages of a Criminal Trial

If the accused is committed to trial on at least one charge, the trial goes ahead. The following is a simplified outline of the stages of a typical criminal trial:

1. The jury is selected.
2. Any pre-trial motions are heard.
3. The charges are read and the plea is entered into the trial record.
4. The prosecution makes an opening statement.
5. The defence makes an opening statement.
6. The prosecution presents its evidence (calling witnesses and/or introducing physical evidence).
7. The defence presents its evidence.
8. The prosecution presents its closing arguments.
9. The defence presents its closing arguments.
10. The judge instructs the jury on how to apply the law.
11. The jury deliberates and delivers its verdict.
12. If the accused is found guilty, the judge hears submissions from the prosecution and the defence and imposes a sentence.

Sentencing

If the accused is found guilty, either after a trial or after entering a guilty plea, the next step is sentencing. The *Criminal Code* provides courts with a range of sentencing options for each offence, including maximum and minimum thresholds. To determine what is an appropriate sentence within the given range, judges consider the sentences imposed in other cases with similar facts. **Precedent** helps to ensure that sentences are consistent and that offenders are treated fairly as compared with others who have committed similar crimes. The court will also apply certain sentencing principles, described below.

precedent
the principle that requires courts to follow the legal rulings made by superior courts in decisions based on similar facts

Purpose and Principles

Purpose

Section 718 of the *Criminal Code* states that the fundamental purpose of sentencing is "to contribute, … to respect for the law and the maintenance of a just, peaceful and safe society." In particular, the sentence that is imposed should aim to achieve one or more of the following objectives:

- to denounce unlawful conduct
- to deter the offender and other persons from committing offences
- to separate offenders from society, where necessary
- to assist in rehabilitating offenders
- to provide reparations for harm done to victims or to the community
- to promote a sense of responsibility in offenders and acknowledgment of the harm done to victims and to the community

Principles

To assist judges in making sentencing decisions consistent with the purpose and objectives in section 718, the *Criminal Code* sets out several principles to be applied in choosing among the available sentencing options. The fundamental principle, in section 718.1, is that the sentence must be proportionate to the seriousness of the crime and the degree of responsibility of the offender.

Section 718.2 sets out additional sentencing principles. These include the requirement that the court consider any "aggravating or mitigating circumstances" when imposing a sentence. Aggravating circumstances are circumstances that make the crime more serious, such as use of a weapon or the vulnerability of the victim. Where these are found to have been present, the court may choose to impose a heavier sentence in the range of available options. Mitigating circumstances are circumstances that indicate a decreased degree of responsibility for the crime or speak to the rehabilitation of the offender, and they may lead the court to impose a lighter sentence.

The other principles to be applied in sentencing, as specified in section 718.2, include consistency (similar sentences for similar crimes in similar circumstances) and consideration of an alternative to imprisonment in appropriate circumstances.

Section 718.2(e) states that "all available sanctions, other than imprisonment, that are reasonable in the circumstances and consistent with the harm done to victims or to the community should be considered for all offenders, with particular attention to the circumstances of Indigenous offenders."

Types of Sentences

The most common sentences imposed are the following:

- imprisonment in a custodial facility
- conditional sentence of imprisonment
- a suspended sentence
- a fine
- discharge, with or without probation

Imprisonment

Where an offender is sentenced to imprisonment, he or she may be held in a federally run penitentiary, a provincially run detention centre, or a territorial correctional centre, depending on the length of the sentence. Sentences of less than two years are served in provincial/territorial institutions; longer sentences are served in federal institutions.

Conditional Sentence of Imprisonment

In some circumstances, a court may impose a conditional sentence of imprisonment to be served in the community instead of a prison. The offender usually lives in his or her own home or the home of a relative. The conditions may place the offender under house arrest but permit him or her to leave home to go to work, attend medical appointments, or shop for necessities; however, the offender's whereabouts will be carefully monitored. If the conditions are breached, the offender may be imprisoned for the remainder of his sentence.

Suspended Sentence

A judge can impose a **suspended sentence** for an offence that does not carry a minimum sentence. A suspended sentence means that the offender is released back into society, subject to certain conditions set out in a **probation** order. If the offender breaches the conditions of the probation order, he or she faces being sentenced on the original offence and forced to serve the sentence.

Fine

A fine may be imposed instead of or in addition to another punishment, such as probation, a conditional sentence, or imprisonment, provided that the offence does not carry a minimum term of imprisonment. Before imposing a fine, the court must consider the ability of the offender to pay it. Failure to pay a fine can result in imprisonment.

Discharge

In some cases, a person convicted of a less serious offence may be discharged on either an absolute or a conditional basis—that is, without having to serve a sentence or pay a fine. An **absolute discharge** has no conditions attached to it and takes effect right away. An accused who receives an absolute discharge is deemed not to have been convicted and has no criminal record in connection with the offence. A **conditional discharge** includes a probation order with conditions that can be in effect for up to three years. After the probation period has passed without violation of the conditions, the discharge becomes absolute. Violation of the conditions can result in a formal conviction and a sentence.

Pre-sentence Report

In deciding the type and length of the sentence to be imposed in a particular case, the judge may hear submissions from both the prosecution and the defence. These take place at a sentencing hearing before the judge.

Sometimes the judge orders a pre-sentence report to assist in the sentencing decision. If ordered, the report is prepared by a probation officer before sentencing and is filed with the court. The report usually contains information on the background and character of the offender, separate from the offence. The report gives the judge insight into the offender so that the sentence can be effective both in punishing the offender for the offence and in promoting rehabilitation. Social service workers who have worked with the offender may be asked to help in preparing a pre-sentence report.

---

suspended sentence
the release of an offender into society, subject to certain conditions set out in a probation order that if breached may result in serving a sentence

probation
a sentence that includes the imposition of terms that if breached may result in a more severe penalty

absolute discharge
a sentencing order that imposes no penalty on an accused—a finding of guilt but is deemed not to have been convicted

conditional discharge
a sentencing order that includes no penalty other than probation

Drug Treatment Court

In 1998, Toronto launched a pilot program aimed at breaking the cycle of addiction and crime. The program, which began as a pilot project and has been extended, is known as Drug Treatment Court. In order to be admitted to the program, participants must be addicted to cocaine, crack cocaine, or heroin; have a history of non-violent drug-related convictions; be willing to accept moral responsibility for their crimes; and be committed to addictions treatment.

The program, which now has counterparts in Vancouver, Edmonton, Regina, Winnipeg, and Ottawa, allows participants to avoid jail time by submitting to treatment, supervision, and weekly urinalysis. Failure to meet program requirements can lead to discharge from the program, followed by sentencing, and often to a jail term. Participants who graduate from the program and reoffend are usually sentenced to probation only.

Social service workers whose clients include people addicted to cocaine, crack, or heroin should be aware of the program so that they can explain it to their clients and suggest that clients participate, if eligible.

Civil Procedure

Civil Actions

Civil procedure refers to the rules and legal traditions that govern the conduct of civil (non-criminal) trials. Civil actions arise when one party begins legal proceedings against another party in pursuit of a remedy for a harm or expected harm—for example, a wrongful act or omission, or a violation or breach of legal rights. The most common civil remedy is damages—monetary compensation for a loss or injury. However, there are other remedies available under civil procedure, such as judicial orders in custody disputes and judicial reviews of decisions of administrative tribunals.

Most civil actions never reach court. It is very common for conflicts that have escalated into lawsuits to be solved or settled through negotiation or mediation at some stage prior to trial. "Settling out of court" is a worthy objective, since trials are often very expensive for all parties (and for taxpayers as well). Litigation also tends to polarize the parties, creating additional animosity. For a business deal gone wrong, this may not be a serious concern; however, in other cases, such as family law disputes, the effect on children can be devastating.

A party to a civil action may be an individual, a corporation, or a public authority such as a municipal agency or a provincial ministry. In civil court, each party, including government parties, appears on its own behalf; that is, there is no Crown prosecutor as in a criminal trial.

plaintiff
the party in a civil lawsuit who initiated the lawsuit

applicant
a person who has initiated a legal process

respondent
the person opposing an applicant in a legal process

Depending on the type of proceeding, the person who has begun the lawsuit is called either the **plaintiff** or the **applicant**, and the person who is opposing it is called either the defendant or the **respondent**. The defendant in a civil lawsuit may, in addition to defending against the plaintiff's claim, file a counterclaim against the plaintiff.

Most Ontario civil trials are presided over by a judge. A party may request a jury to decide questions of fact and/or to assess the amount of damages in some cases. A jury trial is not available in all cases, such as those heard in Small Claims Court or those with respect to family law issues. Jury trials tend to be longer and more costly than trials by judge alone.

Civil Courts

Most civil disputes are tried in the Superior Court of Justice, Family Court, or Small Claims Court.

The Superior Court hears civil trials where the damages being claimed are over $25,000. Small Claims Court hears civil matters where the amount of damages claimed is $25,000 or less. It offers a much simpler court procedure than the Superior Court of Justice, and parties appearing in Small Claims Court often choose not to be represented by a lawyer.

Rules of Civil Procedure

Ontario has issued *Rules of Civil Procedure* in a regulation under the Ontario *Courts of Justice Act*.[7] The rules are very long and comprehensive. The following outline provides an overview of the stages in a civil lawsuit in the Superior Court of Justice.

Before Trial

1. Informal attempts at resolution are often made by the parties.

2. If these efforts are unsuccessful, the plaintiff serves the defendant with a statement of claim and files one with the court.

3. The defence serves and files a statement of defence and, sometimes, a counterclaim.

4. The parties attend a mandatory mediation session to see if they can resolve some or all of the issues without going to court.

5. If the parties have not resolved the case, they begin preparing for trial by

   a. preparing an affidavit of documents (a sworn document containing all relevant documents in the party's possession);

   b. attending at discoveries (meetings to share evidence with the other side); and

   c. answering undertakings (promises, usually to provide information) that have been made in the discovery stage.

6. The parties attend a settlement conference with a judge, who tries to facilitate a settlement.

7. If the matter does not settle, a trial date is set. (The trial must be before a new judge.)

8. The court hears any pre-trial motions or applications (hearings on issues collateral to the subject of the dispute, such as the admissibility of a particular document into evidence).

---

7   *Rules of Civil Procedure*, RRO 1990, Reg 194; *Courts of Justice Act*, RSO 1990, c C.43.

Stages of a Civil Trial

1. The plaintiff makes an opening statement. (Sometimes the defence, usually with leave of the court, makes an opening statement immediately after the plaintiff's.)

2. The plaintiff presents evidence (calling witnesses and/or introducing physical evidence). This is usually the longest part of the trial.

3. The defendant makes an opening statement (unless it followed the plaintiff's opening statement).

4. The defendant presents evidence.

5. The plaintiff has an opportunity to present response evidence (restricted to addressing new issues raised by the defence).

6. The plaintiff makes closing arguments.

7. The defendant makes closing arguments.

8. The judge and/or jury considers the evidence and arguments, and renders a decision.

Evidentiary Standards

In both civil and criminal cases, the party who is required to prove the claim or the charge is said to have the burden of proof, or the "onus." The standard of proof is the degree of proof that the party must produce to be successful. In other words, the standard of proof refers to how convincing the proof must be.

balance of probabilities
the party making a claim (or counterclaim) against another party must prove that the basis for the claim is more likely than not to be valid

In civil trials, the standard of proof is a **balance of probabilities**. This means that the party making a claim (or counterclaim) against the other must prove that the basis for the claim is more likely than not to be valid. This standard applies to the key elements of a civil claim and to the claim as a whole. Before a judgment can be awarded, the trier of fact, taking into account all of the individual facts, must be convinced, on a balance of probabilities, that the legal elements of the claim (or counterclaim) have been established.

beyond a reasonable doubt
the sum of all the facts pointing to guilt must be so convincing that no reasonable person would question that conclusion

In criminal trials, the standard of proof is **beyond a reasonable doubt**. This means that the sum of all the facts pointing to guilt must be so convincing that no reasonable person would question that conclusion. This standard is based on the principle that a person is "innocent until proven guilty." The standard of proof for a criminal charge is high because a criminal conviction carries a heavy stigma in our society, with serious long-term consequences for the offender, including, in some cases, imprisonment.

The burden of proof in criminal trials falls on the prosecution. The defence is not required to present any evidence, although it usually does so. There is no obligation on the accused to prove his or her innocence or even to question the arguments presented by the prosecution.

Being a Witness

Sometimes a social service worker has a client who is required to attend court in a family law, criminal, or other matter, or a social service worker may be asked to testify in a criminal or civil proceeding in a professional capacity—that is, as an expert witness.

The Questioning of Witnesses

Witnesses are generally summoned to appear in court by means of a **subpoena**—a legal document that compels a witness's appearance by force of law.

The party who has called a witness in support of its case calls that witness to the stand and conducts an examination-in-chief. This examination will attempt to draw as much information out of the witness as possible by asking open-ended questions. Questions that contain crucial information and suggest an answer are leading questions and are not permitted in an examination-in-chief.

Often, if a lawyer asks a question that is not permitted under the law of evidence, the other party's lawyer will object. If this happens, the witness should remain quiet and not answer the question until the judge has made a ruling on the objection.

When the lawyer who called the witness has completed the examination-in-chief, the other lawyer gets a chance to examine the witness. This examination of the other party's witness is called cross-examination. In general, a lawyer who is conducting a cross-examination will try to control the content of the witness's answers. This is done by asking leading questions and questions that have very short answers.

For the witness, the key to handling questions in a cross-examination is to listen carefully to each question and reply to exactly what is asked, no less and no more. Lawyers conducting a cross-examination will sometimes try to shake a witness's confidence in his or her own observations or create opportunities for the witness to contradict either his or her own testimony or that of another witness of the examining lawyer. If this happens, the witness may pause before answering in order to give the examining lawyer an opportunity to object to the question.

Preparing for Court

There are a number of other things you, as a social service worker, should do to prepare for giving evidence in court:

1. Review written information relevant to the case, including
   a. any notes you have made about the incidents about which you will be questioned;
   b. if the case relates to a client, the client's file;
   c. your copy of any statement that you have made to lawyers or police; and
   d. any other documents that may be useful in refreshing your memory of the events.

subpoena
a legal document that compels a witness's appearance by force of law

2. Don't make any changes to your notes, but highlight key points for easy reference.

3. Bring your notes to court (along with your curriculum vitae).

4. Confirm the time and exact location of the hearing the day before your scheduled appearance. Be sure you know how to find the hearing room.

5. If you are giving testimony in your professional capacity, speak with a supervisor who has attended this kind of hearing before. What was the experience like? What kinds of questions were asked? Does your supervisor have any suggestions or advice for you?

6. Speak with the lawyer representing the party who has called you as a witness. Ask any questions that you have about the trial process and your role in it. Try to find out what kind of questions you are likely to be asked in examination and cross-examination.

7. If you have some idea of the questions that you may be asked, think about how you will answer.

8. If you are not comfortable speaking in a formal setting, and you expect to be asked to testify on future occasions, consider obtaining training in public speaking.

While a social service worker with general skills may talk to the child witness about court procedures, it is preferable to arrange for a specialist trained in child psychology, and, ideally, a specialist in preparing children to testify in court, to work with the child.

Giving Testimony

The following are some tips to keep in mind when you are on the witness stand:

- Dress neatly and professionally and arrive on time.
- Find out the correct form of address for speaking to the justice or judge, such as "Your Honour," and make sure you use it.
- Keep your notes at hand, but ask the judge's permission first before you consult them.
- Speak slowly, clearly, and audibly.
- Be aware of your body language; don't fidget.
- Be courteous and respectful toward the court and all participants in the proceeding.
- Don't volunteer information; wait until you are asked a question.
- Answer questions truthfully to the best of your knowledge.
- If you don't know the answer to a question, say so; don't guess.
- If you make a mistake, say so.
- In general, it is best to keep your answers brief. If the lawyer wants more information, he or she will ask a follow-up question.
- Don't exaggerate or speculate.

- Avoid slang.
- Avoid using professional jargon unless it is relevant to the matter on which you are testifying or necessary for accuracy.
- If you would like to emphasize a particular answer, it can help to turn toward the judge and address him or her directly.
- Don't express your personal views of the other parties in the case, especially the defendant in a criminal trial or the opposing party in a civil lawsuit. Objectivity makes you more credible; bias makes you less so. Credible testimony is the most helpful contribution you can make to the trial process.
- If the cross-examining lawyer is aggressive, stay calm and try to avoid reacting to upsetting questions.
- Be clear about the difference between your client's interests, your own interests, and the interests of your employer (if applicable).
- Remember that you have a duty at all times to tell the truth. If you are giving testimony about a client, you must act in the best interests of the client as far as is consistent with telling the truth.

KEY TERMS

absolute discharge, 175

abuse of process, 168

actus reus, 164

applicant, 176

balance of probabilities, 178

beyond a reasonable doubt, 178

conditional discharge, 175

defence, 166

defendant, 171

hybrid/dual offence, 169

indictable offence, 169

indictment, 168

information, 168

judicial interim release, 172

mens rea, 164

plaintiff, 176

plea bargain, 171

precedent, 173

probation, 175

prosecution, 166

prosecutor, 171

reparation, 164

respondent, 176

restorative justice, 164

sentencing circle, 164

stay of proceedings, 168

subpoena, 179

summary conviction offence, 169

suspended sentence, 175

SUGGESTED SOURCES

Criminal Lawyers' Association,
   <http://www.criminallawyers.ca>

Law Society of Upper Canada, <http://www.lsuc.on.ca>

Legal Aid Ontario, Community Legal Clinics,
   <http://www.legalaid.on.ca>

Ontario Crown Attorneys Association,
   <http://www.ocaa.ca>

Ontario Ministry of the Attorney General, Ontario Victim
   Services, <http://www.attorneygeneral.jus.gov.on.ca/
   english/ovss/index.php>

REVIEW QUESTIONS

1. What is meant by an "element" of an offence?

2. Why is the concept of *mens rea* (intent) so central to
   the imposition of criminal penalties?

3. What can happen if a court determines that police
   collected evidence in violation of an accused's
   rights under the *Canadian Charter of Rights and
   Freedoms*?

4. Why should social service workers who encounter
   clients in conflict with the law encourage or assist
   those clients in seeking legal advice?

5. In what roles might a social service worker be
   required to appear in court?

Alternative Dispute Resolution and Restorative Justice

11

LEARNING OBJECTIVES

After reading this chapter, you should be able to:

- Explain the concept of restorative justice and distinguish it from the traditional justice system.

- Define alternative dispute resolution.

- Describe the various alternative dispute resolution mechanisms.

- Understand when disputes are more appropriately resolved through the use of dispute resolution mechanisms.

Introduction

The majority of disputes between parties—whether they be individuals, corporations, or government bodies—are not resolved in a courtroom. In general, over 90 percent of civil cases in Ontario settle before trial.

Litigation is a highly formalized, adversarial process. It is expensive and, in most cases, it can only produce a win/lose result: one party's victory is the other party's defeat. Litigation has the potential to alienate the parties; it can turn relatives or friends into enemies and permanently sever business or commercial relationships.

Most conflicts are not so sharply drawn, and the parties could benefit from a more creative, collaborative approach—a solution that benefits both sides.

Alternatives to litigation begin at the very informal, interpersonal level (see Table 11.1). When conflicts arise, there is almost always an opportunity for the parties in conflict to negotiate a solution. For example, where the child of divorced parents is resisting the continual movement from one home to another prescribed by a custody agreement, the parents do not need to take their problem to court. They can, perhaps with the child's input, negotiate a new agreement to govern the child's residence. If appropriate, they can request a consent order formalizing the new agreement, but there is usually no obligation to do even this. Another example is a landlord–tenant dispute, where a tenant has complained to a landlord that there is no running water. To resolve the issue, the parties might negotiate a schedule for repair and possibly a partial rent rebate.

alternative dispute resolution (ADR)
a term used to describe a range of recognized strategies—for example, assisted negotiation, mediation, and arbitration—that are designed to help resolve disputes without recourse to the traditional court system

Where parties have not been able to solve their problems on their own, sometimes a more structured process is needed. **Alternative dispute resolution (ADR)** is a term used to describe a range of recognized strategies—for example, assisted negotiation, mediation, and arbitration—that are designed to help resolve disputes without recourse to the traditional court system. The common element in structured ADR strategies is the involvement of a neutral third party.

Social service workers may be able to assist clients in accessing ADR services. Social service workers may also be engaged directly in ADR in the course of advocating for their clients. Consider, for example, a women's shelter client whose Ontario Works benefits have been suspended because she has failed to live up to the terms of her agreement to participate in job search activities. The client may ask the social service worker to speak to Ontario Works on her behalf, perhaps, for example, to explain that an intensive trauma counselling program that the client has been participating in has taken up more time than anticipated in the previous month. If the social service worker persuades Ontario Works to revisit its suspension decision, she has engaged—successfully—in a form of ADR.

Goals of ADR

ADR comes in many forms, ranging from negotiation at one end of the spectrum to binding arbitration at the other. The goals of ADR vary somewhat, depending upon the particular mechanism that is used. In general, however, ADR is designed to support parties in conflict in their efforts to fashion their own solutions and avoid the expense of litigation. Even binding arbitration, which is similar to court in that the decision-maker imposes a decision on the parties, is less expensive than going to court, and it gives the parties much more control over the process.

Fact-finding—the collection of evidence, and proving one party right and the other wrong—is less important in ADR than in traditional litigation. While the courts strive to deliver answers to legal questions, ADR strives to deliver solutions, and, where possible, to preserve or restore relationships.

TABLE 11.1   Alternative Ways of Resolving Disputes

	Negotiation	Mediation	Arbitration	Litigation
Participation in process	Voluntary.	Voluntary, unless the parties agree otherwise beforehand.	Voluntary, unless the parties agree otherwise beforehand.	Involuntary.
Formality	Usually informal and unstructured although the parties can agree to structure if they wish.	The degree of formality and structure will depend on the mediator and the extent to which the parties accept the mediator's proposals to formalize and structure the process.	Less formal than litigation, but much more formal and structured than negotiation or mediation.	Highly formal, following a process prescribed by the rules of civil practice.
Control of process	Parties control the process and may proceed with or without negotiation "rules."	Mediator and the parties control the process, normally with the mediator proposing rules for the process and the parties agreeing.	Arbitrator controls the process.	Judge controls the process.
Outcome	Private agreement, enforceable as a contract.	Private agreement, enforceable as a contract.	Private decision by arbitrator that is usually binding, unless the parties agree beforehand to non-binding arbitration. Decision may be subject to court review and enforceable by legal action.	Public decision by judge, supported by reasoned analysis and enforceable by the court.

From a more practical perspective, ADR saves money and time by allowing parties to avoid expensive and time-consuming litigation. In disputes where money is on the line, an early settlement leaves more money in the pockets of both parties.

From an interpersonal perspective, ADR may be a healthier way to settle problems than recourse to litigation. The reason is that in ADR, there are no rules of evidence that prohibit the parties from talking about issues that are not legally relevant but are of importance to them. Many conflicts have their roots in hurt feelings. By providing a context of open discussion in which these subjective issues can be raised, ADR presents the opportunity for the healing of damaged relationships and reconciliation of the parties.

Example

Thomas's elderly father, Albert, recently suffered a serious stroke, and was declared incapable of making health care decisions or managing his financial affairs. While Albert is recovering in a nursing home, Thomas obtains a court order making him his father's legal representative. After being advised that Albert will need nursing care for life, Thomas sells his father's house and makes arrangements for a permanent placement in long-term care. Albert's health gradually improves and he is now seeking to challenge the court order that gave his son the power to make these decisions.

If this matter went to court, evidence would be called to establish whether Albert was in fact incapable at the time of the order, whether Thomas's application for the order was proper, and whether the decision to sell the house was within the terms of the order. Little or no court time would be devoted to more subjective issues—for example, Albert's perception that his son's decision was hasty, or Thomas's perception that he had to act quickly to secure a top-quality care placement that was not expected to be available for long.

If, instead, the dispute is resolved through an ADR process, such as mediation, these non-legal issues can be raised and discussed. Albert will have the opportunity to express his resentment over being "parented" by his child, and Thomas will have the opportunity to express his anxiety about his father's welfare. These considerations will become part of the solution that is ultimately proposed. Albert may even withdraw his challenge to Thomas's appointment. Not only will the legal conflict be resolved but the father–son relationship may be preserved.

ADR Mechanisms

Negotiation and Assisted Negotiation

negotiation
the act of "working things out"

Negotiation is the formal word for "working things out." People negotiate with each other on a daily basis. Consider, for example, a driver who lives on a main commuter route into the city and is trying to enter a flow of steady rush-hour traffic from her driveway. If she had to wait for a break in the traffic, she might be there for a very long time. However, most drivers in this situation will negotiate entry into the line of traffic by making eye contact with oncoming drivers. If an approaching driver returns the eye contact, nods, and slows to let the waiting driver in, then the parties have successfully negotiated an exception to the traditional right-of-way rules.

Not all negotiations are this simple. When parties have been thrown into conflict by some kind of negative event, their natural motivation to be generous and reasonable diminishes. Reaching a solution may require the passage of some cooling-off time, a number of failed attempts, and possibly even an apology. Sometimes this process can be facilitated by the parties' delegation of their role in the negotiation to someone who was not part of the dispute, and who therefore lacks the emotional baggage that can slow the process. This is assisted negotiation.

In theory, a negotiator can be anyone with the expertise to understand and resolve the issue in dispute. Sometimes it is appropriate to appoint a lawyer as the negotiator; negotiating on the part of clients is sometimes the most important aspect of a lawyer's work. However, if legal expertise isn't required, someone else may be an equally effective negotiator. A social service worker can provide this kind of assistance as long as it is within the limits of his or her role and training. The extent to which a social service worker is permitted to negotiate with others on behalf of a client should be explicitly addressed in a contract of employment and/or in an employer's policies. Social service workers may not give legal advice and should not negotiate directly with a lawyer who is representing someone in conflict with the social service worker's client.

In addition to these considerations, there are three keys to successful negotiation:

- The client must trust the negotiator.
- The client must give the negotiator specific instructions about the results he or she wants, any concessions or admissions he or she is willing to make, and any limits on the negotiator's freedom to work toward an agreement.
- The negotiator must work within the client's instructions, request clarification of those instructions if any uncertainty develops, and act in the best interests of the client at all times.

Neutral Evaluation and Conciliation

Neutral evaluation and conciliation describes a process in which parties in conflict jointly consult an independent party for an impartial assessment of the dispute. As in the case of negotiation, this happens informally in many everyday situations. For example, a man is shopping for a suit, accompanied by his wife. He tries one on but thinks it makes him look fat. His wife says no, it makes him look distinguished. They see a salesperson nearby and ask him what he thinks: Does this style suit the shopper, or would another style suit him better?

A more formal and serious example of neutral evaluation is a pre-trial conference in a criminal case. The evaluation is made by a judge, but not the one who will preside over the trial itself. At the pre-trial conference, the prosecutor and defence counsel meet with the judge to discuss the issues in the case and, where appropriate, to attempt to narrow the issues for trial. For example, an accused involved in a massive brawl between opposing fans after a hockey game may be charged with both assault causing bodily harm and attempted murder. After listening to both sides, the judge may conclude that the evidence relating to the attempted murder charge is weak, and conviction on that charge is unlikely. The judge may advise the parties that, in the interests of fairness and efficiency, the prosecutor should drop the attempted murder charge and proceed with the assault charge alone. The judge at a pre-trial conference may not make a binding decision, but may make recommendations.

As in the case of negotiation, neutral evaluation and conciliation can be performed by a professional (such as a judge) or by an ordinary person, like the salesperson in the first example. The one factor that qualifies a person as an evaluator of disputes is experience or expertise. The salesperson presumably knows something about suit styles that flatter the customer; the judge has expertise in criminal law and experience with criminal trials. In view of the evaluator's expertise, while the parties are not obligated to act on his opinion, they may well be influenced by it when deciding about next steps.

Social service workers may sometimes be called upon to evaluate situations within their knowledge or experience. Consider, for example, a social service worker who supervises the meetings of a residents' council in a long-term care facility. The residents are brainstorming about ideas for their autumn social. One group of residents would like to have a Hallowe'en party. Another group would like to have a "fantasy draft" hockey pool party complete with betting. When asked which proposal is more likely to win the approval of management, the social service worker may point out, with reasonable confidence, that the long-term care facility will be unlikely to lend its support to any kind of gambling-related activity.

While this kind of advice is clearly within the scope of the social service worker's role, advice-giving situations need to be handled with extreme care. For example, you have a client who wants to apply for subsidized housing, but you think he isn't eligible because he has some assets. Even if you have some experience with housing assistance, it would be inappropriate to talk the client out of making an application, since you cannot be sure how the eligibility criteria will be applied in a particular case. Whenever a client requests an evaluation and the underlying question is whether he should take further steps to pursue a right or entitlement, the correct answer, for a social service worker, should always be either "yes" or a recommendation to consult a lawyer or some other qualified person (such as an administrator at the agency that provides the assistance or entitlements).

Mediation

Mediation involves having the parties meet to discuss their conflict in the presence of an independent third party. The mediator facilitates the discussion, helping to encourage appropriate disclosure and to keep the talks productive. The mediator does not make a decision; instead, the mediator supports the parties in coming to their own voluntary settlement, which is eventually converted into a written settlement agreement that binds the parties.

If the talks are unproductive, the parties can terminate the mediation process. In general, anything that has been said during mediation is without prejudice to any future legal proceedings; that is, it cannot be used against the parties in court. This encourages the parties to be open and candid in expressing their concerns.

There are many different styles of mediation, often depending on the personality and approach of the mediator. Facilitative mediation is a more hands-off style, whereas in evaluative mediation, the mediator is more actively involved, providing opinions about the arguments and proposals advanced by the parties.

Where parties attending mediation have filed court documents and intend to go to court if mediation fails, they are sometimes said to be negotiating "in the shadow of the law." Especially in a situation in which the legal precedents are clear, the mediator may have a general idea of how the court would likely decide the dispute. If one of the parties is unrealistic in his demands, advising the parties of the likely outcome of a trial may help to reframe the negotiations.

In some circumstances, parties are permitted to bring a support person to a mediation session. This support person is not generally a lawyer but rather a friend, a relative, or a counsellor such as a social service worker. Having a support person at a mediation session can help if the party is intimidated by the process, or by the other party; it is sometimes difficult to sit face to face with a person with whom you have an unresolved conflict.

As a social service worker, if you are asked to attend a mediation session as a support person, you should understand that your role is to be there as a resource to your client if needed. It is generally not appropriate for support people to take a significant part in the discussions, or to be very active in providing advice. It is usually better to wait for questions to be addressed to you before you speak. Your client may be helped by your presence alone—by simply having someone else in the room who understands the story from his perspective.

ADR Chambers

ADR Chambers is a unique example of an ADR service provider. Chambers is the word generally used to refer to an office in a court building in which a judge has private discussions with counsel and sometimes witnesses. These discussions are often held in an attempt to resolve issues that are affecting the progress of litigation.

ADR Chambers is so named because its membership began with a group of retired judges. Membership has since grown to include lawyers, but the organization still puts an emphasis on conducting alternative dispute resolution against a backdrop of experience with the traditional legal system. Services offered by ADR Chambers include mediation, arbitration (including provision of a specialized panel to deal with Indigenous issues), neutral evaluation, international dispute resolution, and private appeals.

A private appeal is a hearing before an ADR panel following a decision by a trial court, where the parties agree to pursue an appeal of the decision through ADR Chambers rather than through a provincial or territorial appeal court. When the parties decide to proceed by private appeal, they sign a document stating that they are relinquishing their rights to a regular appeal and that they agree to be bound by the decision of an ADR Chambers appeal panel (usually a panel of three arbitrators). For the parties, one advantage of a private appeal is speed in resolving the dispute: The appeal can be conducted shortly after the trial decision is handed down. Another advantage is a degree of control in deciding who will hear the appeal: Often, each party chooses one panel member, and the two chosen will appoint the third. (For more information, go to <http://adrchambers.com/ca>.)

Mandatory Mediation

Mediation is an alternative to litigation in any civil dispute. Generally, it is chosen at the option of the parties; however, in certain circumstances, the parties are required to attempt mediation before seeking resolution in a civil court. Mandatory mediation became law in Ontario in 1999 when new rules were added to the *Rules of Civil Procedure*.[1] One of these rules requires parties in all case-managed, defended, non-family civil matters scheduled for trial in Toronto, Ottawa, or Windsor to attempt mediation before going to trial. Another rule imposes mandatory mediation in wills and estates cases in the same cities.

---

1 *Rules of Civil Procedure*, RRO 1990, Reg 194.

case management
procedures that have
been established in
cities with busy courts,
with the objective of
alleviating bottlenecks
in the justice system

Case management refers to procedures that have been established in cities with busy courts, with the objective of alleviating bottlenecks in the justice system. Under case management, the parties are required to meet specific deadlines in completing certain stages of the trial process, in an effort to speed up the disposition of cases before the courts.

Where a case is under case management, the parties must choose a mediator within 30 days of the filing of the first statement of defence. If the parties cannot agree on a mediator, the local mediation coordinator chooses one for them. The parties then schedule the date on which mediation will commence. Each party is required to file a statement of issues with the mediator, summarizing the party's case as he or she sees it. The statement of issues must be filed no later than seven days before the scheduled mediation date.

The parties are required to attempt mediation within 90 days of the filing of the first statement of defence. While they are not required to agree to a settlement, they must attend and make an attempt to mediate for at least three hours. Most mediations, whether successful or not, take no more than two days.

The parties share the cost of the mediation. There is a set maximum fee for the first three hours, which varies according to the number of parties involved. After the first three hours, if the parties want to continue, they can negotiate an hourly rate for the mediator's time.

The mediator's fees for the mandatory mediation session cover the following services:

1. One half-hour of preparation time for each party
2. Up to three hours of actual mediation[2]

The mediator's fees for the mandatory mediation session shall not exceed the amount shown in Table 11.2.

TABLE 11.2   Mediator's Fees for Mandatory Session

Number of Parties	Maximum Fees
2	$600 plus GST
3	$675 plus GST
4	$750 plus GST
5 or more	$825 plus GST

Source: *Administration of Justice Act*, Ontario Regulation 451/98, *Mediators' Fees (Rule 24.1, Rules of Civil Procedure)*, s 4(1).

A mediation session is not necessarily held at the court; it can be held wherever it is convenient for the parties. A neutral location—for example, the mediator's office—is usually best. The parties must attend in person, with lawyers if they are represented. Mediation sessions are private; the only people allowed to attend are the mediator, the parties, and their lawyers, unless everyone agrees to the inclusion of another person. The purpose of this rule is to encourage full disclosure of all issues. For many parties, the privacy provided by mediation—not having "dirty laundry" aired in public or

---

2 *Mediator's Fees (Rule 24.1, Rules of Civil Procedure)*, O Reg 451/98, s 3(2).

being required to reveal sensitive business or financial information—makes it an attractive alternative to litigation.

If the parties manage to achieve resolution of the dispute at the mediation session, the terms of resolution are drafted as a settlement agreement, which is filed with the court. The court can then enforce the agreement against a party who fails to honour it, in the same way that a court can enforce a trial judgment. If the parties do not settle, the mediator must prepare a report that states this and file it with the court.

Mediation in Family Law Cases

As noted above, mediation is not mandatory in family law cases. The reason is that in family disputes there is often an imbalance of power between the parties, which makes mediation inappropriate. However, where this obstacle does not exist, family disputes can benefit greatly from mediation. Where there are children involved, ongoing contact between the parties is necessary and important; a process that diminishes conflict rather than polarizing the parties in adversarial positions has significant long-term advantages.

Achieving a settlement through mediation can give family members a sense of having cooperated in the outcome, which can motivate them to honour the terms of the agreement. Mediation can also help family members to resolve non-economic aspects of their conflict, thereby laying the foundation for reasonable relations in the future.

Ontario statutes that recognize ADR are set out in Table 11.3.

TABLE 11.3   Ontario Statutes That Recognize ADR

Workplace Safety and Insurance Act, 1997, SO 1997, c 16
Residential Tenancies Act, 2006, SO 2006, c 17
Professional Engineers Act, RSO 1990, c P.28
Police Services Act, RSO 1990, c P.15
Labour Relations Act, 1995, SO 1995, c 1, Schedule A
International Commercial Arbitration Act, 2017, SO 2017, c 2, Schedule 5
Personal Health Information Protection Act, 2004, SO 2004, c 3, Schedule A
Insurance Act, RSO 1990, c I.8
Children's Law Reform Act, RSO 1990, c C.12
Condominium Act, 1998, SO 1998, c 19

To encourage the mediation of family disputes in appropriate cases, the Ontario government provides and financially supports family mediation services through family mediation programs administered by the courts. These programs offer mediation services with costs charged on a geared-to-income scale. The mediators who work in these programs are certified in accordance with established standards, and they follow guidelines issued by the Ministry of the Attorney General in screening applicants for mediation services.

Arbitration

arbitration
the most formal of ADR
processes, and the closest
to litigation in style;
parties attend before
a neutral person

Arbitration is the most formal of ADR processes, and the closest to litigation in style. The parties attend before a neutral person (or sometimes a panel of three persons) and deliver their arguments. The arbitrator or panel then renders a decision. Unless the parties have agreed otherwise, an arbitral decision is final and binding.

Arbitral decisions are often pursued as part of a larger negotiation. For example, before coming to arbitration, the parties may have already reached agreement about some aspects of the dispute, and the binding arbitration may be needed only to resolve a couple of outstanding issues on which there is an impasse. Thus, like other forms of ADR, arbitration supports party-based decisions even though a final decision may be imposed by the arbitrator.

Evidence given at arbitration hearings is subject to certain rules, but usually these are less formal than the rules of evidence that apply in court. Unless the parties and their arbitrator are working according to an agreed-upon set of arbitration rules, the procedures that will apply in the arbitration are those prescribed by the applicable provincial arbitration legislation. Ontario's *Arbitration Act, 1991* governs such issues as jurisdiction, reviewability of arbitral decisions by courts (like judicial review of the decisions of administrative boards), and the timing of various parts of the process such as the delivery of the arbitrator's order.[3] The *Arbitration Act, 1991* applies to all arbitration prescribed or permitted by statute in Ontario unless the legislation expressly states otherwise.

Arbitration is prescribed by a statute governing the parties or by an agreement between them, or entered into voluntarily as a means of avoiding litigation after the dispute has already arisen.

An example of arbitration prescribed by statute is found in section 7 of Ontario's *Insurance Act*.[4] Section 7 applies in circumstances where a claim arises that could potentially be covered by more than one insurer and a dispute arises as to which insurer is liable to satisfy the claim. In such cases, section 7 requires that the dispute be settled by arbitration instead of litigation. The arbitration process is governed by the rules created by the *Arbitration Act, 1991*.

In the context of the *Insurance Act*, arbitration limits expensive litigation between insurance companies to the benefit of consumers because this cost is inevitably passed on in the form of higher insurance premiums.

Where there is no applicable statute, parties may negotiate an agreement or a contract that sets out terms governing the relations between them. A common example is a collective agreement between unionized workers and company management. The contract may include an arbitration clause requiring that disputes arising in respect of the terms of the contract be resolved through arbitration. An arbitration clause may be included in many kinds of contracts, such as marriage contracts, employment contracts, and commercial contracts.

---

3   *Arbitration Act, 1991*, SO 1991, c 17.

4   *Insurance Act*, RSO 1990, c I.8.

Recognizing When ADR May Not Be Appropriate

While ADR offers clear advantages over litigation in many cases, it is not appropriate to every situation. There are two primary reasons why ADR may not be appropriate in a particular case:

- At least one of the parties is motivated to pursue litigation rather than settle out of court.
- The parties are in unequal bargaining positions, by reason of the historical pattern of their relationship or because of other circumstances, making it unlikely that ADR would produce a fair outcome.

Motivation to Pursue Litigation

In general, parties in conflict are motivated to settle the dispute by ADR; it provides a relatively speedy and inexpensive route to resolution of the issue, and it achieves a reasonable compromise between competing interests. However, in some situations, at least one of the parties is influenced by other considerations that outweigh the potential benefits of settlement.

An analogy is found in the way the justice system deals with crimes. When a crime is committed, a conflict arises between the victim and the perpetrator, and also between the perpetrator and society. However, there is no mechanism in traditional criminal law for "settling" criminal cases. Dropping charges and plea bargaining are close approximations, but generally, our justice system and social values don't readily accommodate the notion of negotiated compromise as an adequate response to an act of criminal wrongdoing. While there is some limited provision in our system for amends to be made between an offender and his victim, the trial of criminal offenders in public courts and the sentences imposed on conviction include an important social penalty—namely, public denunciation of the offender for his or her actions. This need for formal recognition of a person's wrongdoing can make ADR inappropriate in certain non-criminal cases as well. Consider the following example:

Example

Bonita has a job that is interesting and pays well, but she is suffering constant harassment and threats from a co-worker. The co-worker, jealous about being passed over for a promotion, has destroyed Bonita's personal property, calls her at home to harass her after hours, and threatens to spread damaging and untrue gossip about her in the office. Bonita asks management to address the problem, but the company takes no action and the harassment continues. Bonita's mental health suffers, eventually forcing her to resign. Later, she learns from someone in HR that this is the third time that harassment by the same co-worker has driven another employee out of the company.

Given the circumstances, Bonita decides to sue the employer, claiming damages for constructive dismissal. The employer offers to settle the claim out of court by paying Bonita 75 percent of what she might expect to receive through successful litigation (an attractive offer, considering the legal costs of taking the employer to court). However, Bonita feels that in accepting the settlement, she would, in effect, be condoning the employer's tolerance of harassment in the workplace, and also perpetuating such behaviour, insofar as the co-worker's actions would escape public exposure. For this reason, Bonita is unwilling to settle and instead prefers to pursue the claim in court.

ADR is most attractive to parties who can put a dollar value on the resolution they want, and who are not strongly motivated by the desire to set a legal precedent, to make an example of the other party, or to pursue their rights as a matter of principle. As a social service worker, you will encounter many clients who simply want what they are entitled to—access to their children, for example. In the absence of imbalance of power issues, it is often appropriate to support the efforts of these clients to find and use ADR services.

You may also encounter the occasional client who is willing to pursue a test case, enduring the rigours of litigation in an effort to benefit others in his situation. Depending upon the public importance of your client's case, it may not be appropriate to encourage the client to mediate. Instead, you may choose to help the client find an advocacy group or a lawyer who is willing to take on the case on a pro bono basis.

Imbalance of Power

ADR may not be appropriate where there is an imbalance of power in the relations between the parties, or where one party is intimidated by the other. This is very common in families with a history of domestic abuse. Where one party has been subjected to violence or abuse by the other party, the abused party is unlikely to be capable of negotiating with the abuser as an equal. There may be undercurrents of influence between the parties that even a mediator would miss, and this subtle intimidation may cause the abused party to settle for much less than a court would award.

The Ontario Ministry of the Attorney General recognizes the limitations of ADR in such circumstances:

> Mediation is not appropriate for everyone, particularly in cases where there has been violence or abuse. Where one party is afraid of, or intimidated by, their spouse/partner, mediation may not be a good idea.[5]

This concern is reflected in the ministry's guidelines for screening applicants under the government's family mediation program. The criteria to be met include the following:

- Abuse has not occurred that has rendered either party incapable of mediating
- No harm will come to either party or the children as a result of mediating.
- The parties' desire to mediate is voluntary.
- Any inequality in bargaining power can be managed so as to ensure that negotiations are balanced and procedurally fair.
- Parties are psychologically ready to mediate and have the capacity to do so.
- The complexity of the case does not exceed the mediator's education, training, and competence.[6]

---

5 Ontario, Court Services Division, *What You Should Know About Family Law in Ontario* (Toronto: Ministry of the Attorney General, 2012), online: <https://www.attorneygeneral.jus.gov.on.ca/english/family/familyla.html>.

6 "Policies for Government-Funded Mediation Services at the Family Court" (29 October 2015) at "Intake and Screening," online: Ontario Ministry of the Attorney General <https://www.attorneygeneral.jus.gov.on.ca/english/family/policies.php>.

Imbalance of power does not only occur in the divorce context; it can be a factor in any situation involving parties who have a history of conflict. The following are examples of other situations where intimidation or unequal bargaining power may make ADR unsuitable:

- disputes over wills or estates
- disputes between parents and children—for example, where a child is seeking a power of attorney over a parent or authority to make medical decisions on the parent's behalf
- landlord and tenant disputes where the tenant is hard to house because of a criminal record or serious financial problems
- employment matters where there have been allegations of harassment

This is not an exhaustive list; capacity to mediate depends on the facts of the situation and the particular parties involved. In general, however, individuals who are vulnerable because of age, mental health or mental capacity problems, extreme poverty, lack of education, or a history of abuse may not be effective advocates for their own rights in the context of ADR.

Restorative Justice

"Putting things right" is a central goal of ADR, and also the core of the concept of restorative justice. **Restorative justice** is an approach that applies some of the principles of ADR to criminal disputes. It is a philosophy that has broad application within the justice system, and not just in the context of ADR. One of the goals of restorative justice is to repair relationships and restore harmony in the community:

> Restorative justice is a value-based approach to responding to wrongdoing and conflict, with a balanced focus on the offender, victim, and the community. Restorative justice focuses on transforming wrongdoing by healing the harm, particularly to relationships, that is created by harmful behaviour. … By collectively identifying and addressing harms, needs and obligations resulting from wrongdoing, we are able to create healing and put things right again.[7]

Within the core of restorative justice is the concept of transformation. Transformation relates to restorative justice through five key elements: community, capacity, connection, voice, and sacredness.[8]

restorative justice
an approach to wrongdoing and conflict that seeks to repair relationships and restore harmony in the community, focusing equally on the offender, the victim, and the community

Victim–Offender Mediation

In 1974, in Kitchener, Ontario, two teenagers committed acts of vandalism and property damage to 22 properties. Rather than putting the youths only through the conventional court system, the suggestion was made by the probation officer and

---

7 Art Lockhart & Lynn Zammit, *Restorative Justice: Transforming Society* (Toronto: Couto, 2005) at 7.

8 *Ibid.*

volunteer members of the community for the offending youths to meet with each of the victims to be held accountable and repair the harm done. This suggestion was presented to the judge who presided over the case as part of the pre-sentence report. The judge, who was seeking new approaches to justice, agreed to the suggestion of meeting the victims and included this directive as part of the probation order.[9]

The youths met each of the victims and heard their stories. Over a period of time, the youths apologized and restored the amount of expenses incurred by the victims in the form of restitution and fines.

The 1974 Kitchener case was the beginning of the Victim–Offender Reconciliation Program. Victim–offender mediation includes the victim, the offender, and the mediator, in a process described by the Centre for Justice & Reconciliation:

> With the assistance of the mediator, the victim and offender begin to resolve the conflict and to construct their own approach to achieving justice in the face of their particular crime. Both are given the opportunity to express their feelings and perceptions of the offence (which often dispels misconceptions they may have had of one another before entering mediation). The meetings conclude with an attempt to reach agreement on steps the offender will take to repair the harm suffered by the victim and in other ways to "make things right."[10]

The mediation process is voluntary. Neither the victim nor the offender can be forced to participate in the process. The offender must accept responsibility for his or her actions. As well, in Ontario all information provided by the participants is confidential, and no statements can be used later on in any court proceedings.

The trained mediators must ensure that the parties feel safe during the mediation process. Any aspects of fear, anger, and imbalance of power between the participants must be removed for the mediation process to be successful.

If the parties come to an agreement, the resolution will be put in writing with the obligations monitored and enforced.

Conferencing

A family-group conference is similar to a victim–offender mediation. The conference is a meeting of individuals in the community who have been affected by the harmful behaviour. "The conference provides a forum in which the parties to an incident can come together to examine the factors that led to the harmful actions, the impact that behaviour had on the lives of others and possible ways in which order can be restored to the community."[11]

Conferences will include more individuals than only the victim and the offender. Other affected and interested members of the community will participate as well.

---

9   *Ibid.*

10   Christopher Bright, "Victim Offender Mediation" (nd), online: Centre for Justice & Reconciliation <http://restorativejustice.org/restorative-justice/about-restorative-justice/tutorial-intro-to-restorative-justice/lesson-3-programs/victim-offender-mediation/#sthash.X7eCuADb.dpbs>.

11   *Supra* note 7 at 88.

Family members, friends, teachers, social service workers, police officers, and anyone who has a role to play in the event can be included in a conference.

The conference format creates a safe, problem-solving environment that can significantly reduce further harm by addressing the underlying causes of crime, encourage participants to rebuild a sense of community, and reconnect people in trouble with supports necessary for future success.[12]

The conference process is voluntary. All those involved must take ownership of the harm done and accept responsibility for their actions.

Principles of Restorative Justice

Some of the principles of restorative justice include the full participation of victim, offender, and community; the healing of what has been damaged; full and direct accountability; reintegration of the victim and offender; and closure. There is also a focus on the present and future with recidivism rates decreasing.

When Can Restorative Justice Processes Be Used Within the Criminal Justice System?

Victim–offender mediations and group conferences can be used at various stages in the criminal justice system. Community groups and schools can use restorative justice methods within their communities prior to any police or court action. As part of extrajudicial measures and sanctions, police officers and Crown attorneys can implement restorative justice alternatives. As well, restorative justice options can be used as part of a plea bargain arrangement. Restorative justice alternatives can also be part of judicial sentencing.

Benefits of Restorative Justice Practices

Table 11.4 outlines some of the benefits of restorative justice from the victim's and the offender's perspective.

TABLE 11.4   Benefits of Restorative Justice to Victims and Offenders

Victim benefits can include the following:
• has the opportunity to actively participate in the process
• is fully informed about the incident, the offender, and the process
• has a better chance of receiving meaningful restitution
• has the opportunity to resolve the incident in a peaceful manner
• can experience a sense of closure
Offender benefits can include the following:
• has the opportunity to be aware of harm suffered
• has the opportunity to make it right with the victim
• has the opportunity to take responsibility
• can avoid a criminal record
• is fully informed as to process
• has a greater chance to not reoffend

---

12 *Ibid.*

Restorative Justice and Recidivism

Some results from the literature review found that restorative justice programs had a small effect on offender recidivism. Based on 46 studies with nearly 23,000 participants, restorative justice programs, on average, were associated with a decrease of 3 percent in recidivism. Contrary to expectations, the programs were more effective with adults (8 percent reduction) than with youth (2 percent reduction). Providing some form of restitution to victims was the activity most associated with reductions in offender recidivism.[13]

An evaluation of a restorative justice program in the city of Winnipeg was conducted. Unlike an earlier report of this program that had a one-year follow-up, this evaluation followed offenders for three years after completing the program. The program participants were compared to a group of probationers with similar offence and criminal history characteristics who did not participate in the restorative justice program.

The offenders who participated in the restorative justice program had lower recidivism rates than the matched group of probationers. With each year during the follow-up period, the differences in recidivism rates for the two groups widened. At the first year, the restorative justice offenders had a recidivism rate of 15 percent compared to 38 percent for the probation group. At the second year, the respective rates were 28 percent and 54 percent, and by the third year the rates were 35 percent and 66 percent.[14]

The conventional criminal justice system often provokes a sense of alienation for both victim and offender. The stigma of charges can alienate the offender from his or her community. Additionally, if found guilty, the offender may be removed from the community to serve a sentence in a correctional facility or transitional house. Similarly, the victim is often isolated and alienated by this process. Victims often complain that they have no voice in the system. They may emerge from the court process disillusioned and angry.

In contrast, restorative justice initiatives seek to shift the focus to aspects of justice that are often neglected in the traditional system: subjective perceptions of the "crime," victim and community perspectives, compensation and reparations, conflict resolution and creative problem-solving, and the healing of relationships in a way that maintains a sense of community among justice system participants.

---

13   James Bonta et al, "An Outcome Evaluation of a Restorative Justice Alternative to Incarceration" (2002) 5:4 Contemp Just Rev 319.

14   *Ibid.*

KEY TERMS

alternative dispute resolution (ADR), 184
arbitration, 192
case management, 190
mediation, 188
negotiation, 186
restorative justice, 195

SUGGESTED SOURCES

ADR Chambers, <http://adrchambers.com/ca>

Ontario Ministry of the Attorney General,
 <http://www.attorneygeneral.jus.gov.on.ca>

Department of Justice, <http://www.justice.gc.ca>

St. Leonard's Society of Canada,
 <http://www.stleonards.ca>

Restorative Justice, Correctional Service of Canada,
 <http://www.csc-scc.gc.ca/restorative-justice>

Centre for Justice & Reconciliation,
 <http://restorativejustice.org>

REVIEW QUESTIONS

1. Why can it be an advantage to settle a legal dispute out of court?

2. List three ADR mechanisms.

3. What are the keys to successful negotiation?

4. List some of the core concepts of restorative justice.

5. List the stages in a conflict when restorative justice can be used?

6. List some of the benefits to the victim and the offender of restorative justice.

Youth Criminal Law

LEARNING OBJECTIVES

After reading this chapter, you should be able to:

- Summarize the evolution in our society's approaches to youth criminal responsibility and justice.

- Describe the general principles of the *Youth Criminal Justice Act*.

- Explain what is meant by extrajudicial measures.

- List some of the differences in how our criminal justice system treats youths who are accused of offences, as compared with adults.

- Understand the sentencing principles that apply to young persons in conflict with the law.

- Understand some of the sentencing options, including adult sentences that apply to young persons.

- Describe the general rules that govern the treatment of youths in custody.

Introduction

The Canadian justice system recognizes that young people who commit criminal offences are different, in important ways, from adult offenders.

Research has shown the following:

- Young people (children and teenagers) are not mature, intellectually, behaviourally, or emotionally; as a result, they may not be capable of understanding the subtleties of right and wrong conduct or the full consequences of their actions.
- Youth in conflict with the law often have motivations for their criminal actions that differ from those of adults for similar crimes, such as peer pressure or thrill-seeking.
- Despite media suggestions to the contrary, teenagers commit fewer crimes than adults, and teenage offenders are less likely than adults to use serious violence in committing their crimes.
- Young people who commit a first offence while in their teens are less likely to reoffend than first-time adult offenders.
- Sentences based on deterrence tend to be less effective for teenagers than for adults, but reintegrative-focused approaches are more effective for teenagers.
- In general, teen offenders are more sensitive to being labelled as criminals (in the sense that labelling provokes reoffending), and they are also more worried than adult repeat offenders about the effect that a criminal record may have on their future.

Because of these and other factors, Canada's criminal justice system provides for different treatment of young offenders through two statutes, the *Criminal Code*[1] and the *Youth Criminal Justice Act* (YCJA).[2] The starting point is the codification of an age threshold for criminal responsibility with respect to crimes committed by children. Section 13 of the *Criminal Code* provides the following:

> No person shall be convicted of an offence in respect of an act or omission on his part while that person was under the age of twelve years.

While young people aged 12 and older are subject to the offence provisions of the *Criminal Code*, the YCJA applies an additional "protective" layer of interpretation and procedure to the way the justice system manages youth in conflict with the law. For example, consider the following:

- The principles for sentencing youth in conflict with the law are different from those for adult offenders.

---

1   *Criminal Code*, RSC 1985, c C-46.

2   *Youth Criminal Justice Act*, SC 2002, c 1.

- There is greater protection for the privacy of younger offenders, and there are special rules for certain aspects of the investigation and trial of youth who are in conflict with the law.

Ontario provides additional protection to youth who are in custody through the children's rights provisions of child welfare legislation, as well as part V of the *Ministry of Correctional Services Act*.[3]

Social service workers may work with youth in conflict with the law in various ways. Some offenders, instead of being charged or tried, are referred to programs designed to circumvent the court process and assist them in not reoffending. These extrajudicial measures may include community service, counselling, and writing an essay about the behaviour. Social service workers may be involved in designing, administering, or supervising these programs. Within the corrections system, social service workers may work with youth in custody or in transitional facilities. Those who work in Indigenous communities may also be involved with alternative justice initiatives such as sentencing circles.

History of Youth Justice

Our society's view of children and youth was once very different from what it is today. Most of us now understand childhood, adolescence, and adulthood to be distinct life stages, and we generally accept the idea that children and youth are more vulnerable than adults, and therefore in need of special protection. However, these views have not always seemed so self-evident. Like most other social constructs, they are the product of certain historical developments and a corresponding evolution of ideas and values.

Until the late 17th century, children as young as six or seven were expected to begin contributing to the support and prosperity of the family and the community. They worked on farms, practised trades, and participated in commerce. A child's work was not understood, as it often is today, as "doing her chores" or "helping his mom." Instead, the child was depended upon to contribute to the family's survival.

Around the beginning of the 18th century, things began to change. First, new scholarly thinking and writing about psychosocial development introduced the idea that children and adolescents were less than full grown, not only in the physical sense, but also in the emotional, intellectual, and moral senses.

The emergence of these ideas led to increased separation of children and adolescents from adult responsibilities and activities. Upper-class children were kept in school longer than ever before. Working-class children, for the first time, were denied access to certain kinds of employment. This happened for three reasons:

- The great technological leaps of the 18th century meant that many trades and types of work were becoming more complicated. Longer and longer periods of apprenticeship were required to master the new skills and absorb the new knowledge.

---

3 *Ministry of Correctional Services Act*, RSO 1990, c M.22.

- As some kinds of work, such as manufacturing, became increasingly mechanized, the number of jobs decreased. Youth jobs were often the first to be eliminated.

- A workers' rights movement emerged, raising awareness of the dangers and health risks of factory and mining work. Social reformers argued for the need to protect children from these dangers by prohibiting their employment in dangerous work and abolishing long workdays.

As a result of these changes, many working-class teenage children whose families couldn't afford schooling were shut out of the workforce. Without a clear role to play in society, little to do, and no way to earn money, some became involved in crime. With the rise of urban youth crime, the term "juvenile delinquent" was coined, and society began paying attention to the unique developmental stage that we now recognize as adolescence. People began to understand that children behaved, or misbehaved, as they did not simply because of flaws in character, but because their character and abilities were still developing.

Before these shifts in the perception of childhood, the law typically applied equally to children and adults. While a few legal rules—notably those relating to property ownership—suspended certain rights until adulthood, most statutes that were designed either to punish offenders or to protect society applied regardless of age. Thus, children of all ages were held responsible for crimes they had committed.

As the uniqueness of childhood and adolescence became recognized, the idea of **legal capacity**—the right and ability of a person to exercise legal rights—also evolved. Children, once full participants in adult society, were deemed to lack legal capacity until they had achieved the level of physical, intellectual, emotional, and moral development that marked adulthood.

A principle closely related to legal capacity is **criminal responsibility**. As the criminal law has evolved, so has the idea that not all people who commit criminal acts should be made to bear the full legal consequences normally attached to those acts. In certain special cases, some circumstance of the act or some characteristic of the person who committed it warrants different treatment under the law. For example, as most people are aware, in appropriate cases, a court may find an accused "not criminally responsible on account of mental disorder."

A much simpler and clearer measure of criminal responsibility is an age threshold, as provided for in the existing *Criminal Code*. The relevance of age as a factor in determining criminal responsibility was recognized in Canada's statutory law early in the last century, and it has helped to shape changes in our approach to the treatment of youth who are in conflict with the law, as reflected in subsequent legal reforms.

The first statute designed to address the criminal responsibility of young offenders was the *Juvenile Delinquents Act* (JDA).[4] This statute was introduced in 1908 and remained in effect, with various amendments, until 1984. The JDA had a social welfare focus, in the sense that it characterized youth criminality as an "affliction" that could

legal capacity
the right and ability of a person to exercise legal rights

criminal responsibility
the idea that not all people who commit criminal acts should be made to bear the full legal consequences normally attached to those acts

---

4 *Juvenile Delinquents Act*, RSC 1970, c J-3 [repealed].

be remedied through appropriate help and guidance. Children aged 7 to their 18th birthday (depending on the province) who were offered assistance under the JDA were often removed from the care of their parents and "parented" by the government, under a doctrine known as **parens patriae**. This doctrine emphasized the state's duty to protect vulnerable members of society and assumed a connection between poor parenting and youth criminality.

The JDA system was closely connected to social services, and recognized very few legal rights or procedural protections for the children managed under it. In the decades leading up to the mid-1980s, criticisms of the JDA began to emerge. Committing young offenders to institutions was declared to be ineffective, and even harmful from the perspective of rehabilitation, and the lack of due process in the JDA system came under fire as children's rights became more widely recognized. In 1965, the government created a committee to study legislative reform in the area of youth justice. In 1982, the *Canadian Charter of Rights and Freedoms* reinforced the rights of children and youth who were in conflict with the law.[5] These initiatives eventually led to the replacement of the JDA with the *Young Offenders Act* (YOA), which was enacted in 1984.[6]

The YOA abandoned the JDA notion that youth criminality was a "condition," but maintained the view that children and youth lack full criminal responsibility. The YOA was designed to apply to offenders who had reached their 12th birthday until their 18th birthday at the time of the offence.

The YOA rejected the institutionalization of young people who committed criminal acts and embraced the notion of diverting youth from the normal process of the criminal justice system in appropriate cases. However, it also introduced a more punitive approach to youth justice, in an attempt to reduce **recidivism** (repeat offending). At the same time, the YOA gave formal recognition to the substantial rights of young offenders in contact with the criminal justice system.

The YOA was a controversial statute. While it sought to deinstitutionalize the treatment of young offenders, it resulted in a substantial increase in custodial sentences, drawing fire from advocates of alternative solutions. More conservative critics thought that the due process rights provided in the YOA were too broad, notably in the areas of protection of identity and provision of legal representation. Other critics argued that the YOA did not place sufficient emphasis on rehabilitation. The statute had been in effect only for a few years when pressure began to mount for a new round of reforms. This pressure soon led to the drafting of the YCJA, which came into force in 2003.

Like the YOA, the YCJA applies to youth who have reached their 12th birthday until their 18th birthday at the time of the offence. When an offence is committed by a person within this age range, the outcome of the matter, whether through prosecution or through extrajudicial measures, is governed by the YCJA's comprehensive system for the management of youth in conflict with the law.

parens patriae
a doctrine that emphasized the state's duty to protect vulnerable members of society and that assumed a connection between poor parenting and youth criminality

recidivism
repeat offending

---

5 *Canadian Charter of Rights and Freedoms*, Part I of the *Constitution Act, 1982*, being Schedule B to the *Canada Act 1982* (UK), 1982, c 11.

6 *Young Offenders Act*, RSC 1985, c Y-1 [repealed].

The Youth Criminal Justice Act: An Overview

General Principles

The YCJA incorporates four general principles, expressed in section 3(1). These include and can be summarized as follows:

- the prevention of crime and protection of the public; holding young persons accountable through measures that are proportionate to the seriousness of the offence and the degree of responsibility of the young person
- a criminal justice system for young persons that is separate from the system for adults and emphasizes rehabilitation and reintegration
- a culturally sensitive response to the offence that promotes respect for societal values and reparations to victims "within the limits of fair and proportionate accountability"
- special protections including enhanced civil rights and a role for parents

The YCJA was introduced in an unsettled socio-political climate. Criminologists and sociologists were beginning to recognize that widespread incarceration has a fairly poor track record as a means of reducing youth crime. At the same time, there was a public perception that violent crime committed by youths was on the rise. The resulting principles of the YCJA acknowledge that young persons who are in conflict with the law can be separated into two categories—young persons who are involved in less serious offences and those youth who are involved in more serious offences. The much higher percentage of young persons who are involved in less serious offences are dealt with through more reintegrative approaches, including diversion programs and alternatives to custody. The lesser percentage of young persons involved in more offensive behaviours are dealt with in a more serious manner, such as harsher sentences including custody and the possibility of adult sentences.

This approach has resulted in a significant decrease in the number of young persons sentenced to custody since the implementation of the YCJA in 2003.

Structure

The YCJA is divided into numerous parts:

- *Part 1—Extrajudicial Measures:* Extrajudicial measures provide an alternative to prosecution of an offence through the court system. The use of such measures is often referred to as diversion. The measures described in part 1 include issuing a warning or a caution to the offender, referring the offender to a community program or agency, and referring the offender to a sanctions program.
- *Part 2—Organization of Youth Criminal Justice System:* Part 2 provides for special courts and judges (youth courts) with jurisdiction over young suspects. Provided that the young person has reached his or her 12th birthday up to his or her 18th birthday at the time of the offence, the young person can be tried in a youth court.

- *Part 3—Judicial Measures:* Part 3 sets out the basic rules of youth court procedure. Where an aspect of procedure is not specifically described, regular criminal court procedure (as specified in the *Criminal Code*) applies. Matters covered in part 3 include the young person's right to counsel; the requirement for notice to parents of certain steps taken against the young person, such as the laying of a charge; the rules for detention before sentencing; and the ordering and uses of medical or psychological assessments of the young person.

- *Part 4—Sentencing:* The YCJA reflects a strong bias against custodial sentences for young people. Part 4 includes the rationale for this approach, which are reflected in specific sentencing principles to be applied by the court, as well as detailed provisions describing sentencing options and procedures.

- *Part 5—Custody and Supervision:* Part 5 deals with custody and supervision.

- *Part 6—Publication, Records and Information:* Part 6 of the YCJA prohibits the publication of identifying information about young offenders in certain cases, and creates rules for the protection and management of youth criminal justice records.

Special Protections in the Youth Criminal Justice System

In recognition of the fact that youth in conflict with the law are not fully mature, the youth criminal justice system incorporates special protections for youth in addition to the protections created by the *Criminal Code* and the *Canadian Charter of Rights and Freedoms*. These protections are designed to utilize a young person's potential for rehabilitation and for overcoming criminal behaviour, so that he or she can go on to play a productive role in society.

To support the purpose of these protections, social service workers who frequently work with young persons who are in conflict with the law should be knowledgeable enough to explain these rights to their clients in a general way. Of course, if a client has been charged with an offence, or if he or she reveals involvement in criminal activity to the social service worker, the client should be immediately referred to a lawyer.

Legal Representation

As in the case of adults, any young person suspected or accused of committing an offence is entitled to representation by a lawyer. This right arises early, even where police are considering the use of extrajudicial measures instead of prosecution. In order to encourage young persons to retain counsel, the right to counsel is specifically referred to in a notice given to the youth's parents. If the young suspect cannot afford to hire a lawyer, he or she will be referred to legal aid. In cases where the young person was denied legal aid, the court will order the attorney general to appoint counsel for the youth, or can order that the youth be represented by his or her own counsel, separate from counsel retained by the youth's parents.

Notice to Parents

Except where a youth is 20 or older at the time of the first court appearance (having been charged while under 18), the police are required to give notice of the charge (and the youth's right to counsel) to a parent, or if no parent is available, to an adult relative or guardian. The purpose of this provision is to inform the parents so that they can help the youth with specific matters such as hiring a lawyer, and so that they can provide support during the legal proceedings.

Pre-Trial Detention

Sometimes a young suspect is detained in custody before trial—that is, he or she is not released on bail. The *Criminal Code* permits pre-trial detention where the suspect is considered dangerous to society or likely to escape the jurisdiction rather than attend at the trial. The YCJA imposes additional, very strict limits on the situations in which a young person can be detained before sentencing. A youth cannot be detained before trial unless, if convicted, he or she would be subject to incarceration even after considering the restrictions on custody imposed by section 39(1) of the YCJA. These restrictions forbid a custody sentence unless

- the young person has committed a violent offence;
- the young person has failed to comply with previous non-custodial sentences; or
- the young person has committed a serious offence (one that would attract a sentence of two years or more for an adult) and the young person has a criminal record.

The combination of these restrictions means, in essence, that a young person will not be detained before trial in the absence of violence, breach of probation, or the combination of a serious offence and a criminal record.

Recent amendments to the YCJA have simplified pre-trial detention rules to help ensure that, when necessary, violent and repeat young offenders are kept off the streets while awaiting trial.

Medical and Psychological Assessments

The judge in a youth trial can order that the young person undergo a medical or psychological assessment. The court can order an assessment for one of a number of purposes, including

- to determine the appropriateness of pre-trial release (bail);
- to determine whether the young person can be subject to an adult sentence;
- to support an appropriate choice of youth sentence; or
- to support the choice of appropriate conditions for conditional release (probation).

In rare cases, the court can order that the young person be detained for the purpose of a medical or psychological assessment.

Records

The YCJA protects the identity of young offenders by banning publication of their names, to discourage labelling of young persons as criminals. The avoidance of labelling is viewed by most psychologists as a way of reducing the likelihood that the young person will reoffend because he or she has a reputation for criminal behaviour to live up to. By not publishing identifying information about young offenders, the justice system seeks to protect their reputation in the community, recognizing that young persons sometimes make mistakes because they lack maturity. By protecting the privacy of young people, the courts seek to prevent a criminal charge from limiting the future opportunities of the young offender.

The publication ban imposed by the YCJA is not absolute. Under section 110, the legislation prohibits the publication of information that "would identify the young person as a young person dealt with under this Act." However, some exceptions apply with respect to violent offences.

Extrajudicial Measures

Extrajudicial measures are a form of diversion designed to deal informally with youth involved in criminal activity, as an alternative to prosecution through traditional criminal procedure. The decision about whether to use extrajudicial measures in a particular case is made by the police and the Crown attorney, and the YCJA makes it mandatory for the officer(s) involved to consider this option. Section 4 of the YCJA outlines the principles and objectives of extrajudicial measures.

extrajudicial measures a form of diversion designed to deal informally with youth involved in criminal activity, as an alternative to prosecution through traditional criminal procedure; run by the police for low-risk offenders

The typical point at which police will consider the use of extrajudicial measures is when they have enough evidence to lay a charge. For example, police may be called when a schoolyard brawl escalates and is considered an assault by school administrators. Arriving upon this kind of scene, police normally have sufficient eyewitness evidence to lay an assault charge, and are therefore required to consider extrajudicial measures before they do so (s 6(1)).

In deciding whether extrajudicial measures are appropriate, police will consider factors such as the following:

- the degree of violence used in committing the offence
- the demeanour of the youth (whether he or she is apologetic and remorseful or belligerent)
- the youth's past criminal history
- the youth's age

In general, diversion is most appropriate for first offences, younger offenders, offences that do not involve violence, and situations in which the offenders have clearly taken moral responsibility for their actions. Some studies suggest that there is a link between the use of less punitive measures for first-time young offenders and reduced recidivism. More specifically, commencing a formal criminal process against first-time young offenders is a stronger predictor of subsequent criminal behaviour on the part of the offenders, while responses such as a police warning or no specific police action are most consistent with non-recidivism.

The following extrajudicial measures may be used, where appropriate, by the police (or, in some circumstances, by Crown prosecutors) instead of prosecution:

- choosing to take no further action
- administering a warning
- administering a caution
- referring the young person to a counselling program
- imposing an extrajudicial sanction, requiring the young person to participate in a sanctions program (YCJA, s 6(1))

A warning is spoken—for example, "You are not being charged for this offence, but if you do it again, you *will* be charged"—and is usually not communicated to the youth's parents. A **caution** is formal, and the parents will be informed. There are two kinds of cautions: police cautions and Crown cautions. The procedure for police cautions depends on local police policies; however, it is generally expected that a police caution will take the form of a letter to the young offender and his or her parents, or, in some situations, a meeting between the young offender, the parents, and a senior police officer to discuss the incident. A Crown caution typically arises where a case has been referred to a Crown prosecutor. The youth may or may not have been charged, but the Crown has decided not to prosecute. A Crown caution typically takes the form of a letter to the youth and the parents.

A referral to a counselling program requires the consent of the young offender. From a practical perspective, however, it seems unlikely that a young person will withhold consent if he or she knows that the alternative is likely to be a criminal charge. Programs that may be appropriate for such referrals include recreation programs, counselling agencies, child welfare agencies, and mental health programs. Since social service workers are often involved in these programs, they may, as a result of diversion, find that their clients include youth in conflict with the law engaged in rehabilitation.

The assistance provided by these programs is supposed to help young people not to reoffend. Because the circumstances of young offenders vary widely, assistive programs will have the best chance of succeeding if they provide an individualized approach. For example, if a 13-year-old is getting into fights at school, she might benefit from participating in an anti-bullying education program. If a 17-year-old homeless youth has been caught shoplifting winter gloves, he might benefit from job search support and referral to shelter housing.

Extrajudicial sanctions are designed to address criminal behaviour more serious than the type that warrants a warning, caution, or referral. For example, the police or the Crown may refer a young offender to a sanctions program if the offence in question is not his first criminal offence, or if the offence involved a low to moderate degree of violence. Serious violence almost always results in a charge; however, a sanction may be appropriate where the circumstances of the offence include a mitigating factor.

The YCJA provides that extrajudicial sanctions can be imposed only where other extrajudicial measures would be inappropriate. This limitation is important in order to address, at least partially, the concern that the imposition of sanctions on a person

caution
a formal extrajudicial measure in which parents are informed. There are two kinds of cautions: police cautions and Crown cautions.

extrajudicial sanctions
diversion programs under the YCJA run by the crown attorney for low-risk youth; designed to address criminal behaviour more serious than the type that warrants a warning, caution, or referral

who is suspected of committing an offence and has not had the opportunity to defend himself in a court of law violates a guaranteed right under section 11(d) of the Charter: "the right … to be presumed innocent until proven guilty." However, there is no doubt that many young offenders prefer to comply with sanctions as a way to avoid criminal prosecution, and the resulting criminal record if the offender is convicted.

Before extrajudicial sanctions may be imposed, the following conditions must be met:

- There must be a sanctions program in the jurisdiction of the offence.
- The police (or Crown) must believe that the program is appropriate for the offender.
- The offender must give her informed consent.
- The offender must accept responsibility for the incident.
- The Crown must have enough evidence, if the incident were to form the basis of a charge, to prosecute that charge. (YCJA, s 10(2))

Sanctions involve the performance of activities similar to what is commonly known as community service. For example, offenders may be required to volunteer their time to a community cleanup project. If the sanction can be tied to the offence, it should be; for example, a young person who has committed an act of vandalism may be required to clean up graffiti that he or she has applied, as well as other graffiti at the same site or another site. Tying the sanction to the offence reinforces the principle of restorative justice—achieving justice by requiring the offender to make concrete amends to the victim or others in the victim's situation.

Section 10(4) of the YCJA states that "Any admission, confession or statement accepting responsibility for a given act or omission that is made by a young person as a condition of being dealt with by extrajudicial measures is inadmissible in evidence against any young person in civil or criminal proceedings."

As well, a young person's participation in previous extrajudicial programs does not preclude the use of extrajudicial measures in subsequent matters.

Social service workers who are involved in administering sanctions programs may be called upon to use their creativity in recommending and supporting sanctions that incorporate the principle of restorative justice. However, an important consideration in designing any sanction will be the need to ensure that the youth's participation in the sanction does not pose a danger to anyone, or cause discomfort or embarrassment to a victim. Some victims may want nothing to do with a young person who has wronged them, and this wish must be respected.

Sentencing

Significant improvements were made by the YCJA over the predecessor YOA relating to refinements to the provisions governing sentencing and the rights of youth in custody.

The purpose of sentencing is stated in section 38(1) of the YCJA:

… to hold a young person accountable for an offence through the imposition of just sanctions that have meaningful consequences for the young person and that promote his or her rehabilitation and reintegration into society, thereby contributing to the long-term protection of the public.

This goal is supported by a set of explicit principles, followed by highly detailed rules, to be applied by the courts in deciding on the sentence that is most appropriate in each particular case. Generally, these principles and rules reflect a strong preference for alternatives to detention in custody for convicted young persons. Consistent with the goal reproduced above, the sentencing options emphasize rehabilitation and personal accountability. For those cases in which incarceration is deemed to be necessary to protect the public, the YCJA provides rules regarding custody, including facility choices and placement review, which are designed to support the principle of applying the least restrictive measures appropriate in the circumstances.

The principles to be applied in sentencing are set out in sections 38(2) and (3) of the YCJA. Section 38(2) requires a judge to choose a sentence that

- "… must not result in a punishment that is greater than the punishment that would be appropriate for an adult who has been convicted of the same offence committed in similar circumstances";
- is consistent with other youth sentences for the same offence committed in similar circumstances;
- is "proportionate to the seriousness of the offence and the degree of responsibility of the young person for that offence";
- is considered after "all available sanctions other than custody that are reasonable in the circumstances" are considered, "with particular attention to the circumstances of aboriginal young persons";
- is the least restrictive sentence available that is capable of achieving the purpose of sentencing (in s 38(1));
- is most likely to rehabilitate and reintegrate the young person into society;
- promotes a sense of responsibility in the young person, and acknowledgment of the harm done to victims and the community;
- denounces unlawful conduct; and
- deters the young person from committing offences.

Section 38(3) also requires a judge to take into account "aggravating and mitigating circumstances," including the harm done to the victim (and whether it was intentional or foreseeable), any reparation made by the young person to the victim or the community, and any previous findings of guilt of the young person.

Also worthy of particular note, for social service workers, are sections 29(1) and 35 of the YCJA. These sections hint at the complicated interplay between the child protection system and the youth criminal justice system. Section 35 provides that a youth court may, in addition to any other order made at any stage in the criminal proceedings, refer the young person to a child welfare agency for assessment to determine whether the young person is in need of child welfare services.

This section is designed to encourage courts to view the youth criminal justice system as separate from the child protection system, and to guide them in making dispositions for the right reasons.

Section 29(1) of the YCJA makes explicit reference to the inappropriateness of using the criminal justice system for social welfare purposes:

> A youth justice court judge or a justice shall not detain a young person in custody prior to being sentenced as a substitute for appropriate child protection, mental health or other social measures.

Whether sufficient "child protection, mental health or other social measures" will be in place to take up the slack depends on complicated issues of access, accountability, and funding. This is an issue that social workers and social service workers must deal with throughout the course of their careers.

Section 39(1) of the YCJA states:

> A youth justice court shall not commit a young person to custody under section 42 (youth sentences) unless
> (a) the young person has committed a violent offence;
> (b) the young person has failed to comply with non-custodial sentences;
> (c) the young person has committed an indictable offence for which an adult would be liable to imprisonment for a term of more than two years and has a history that indicates a pattern of either extrajudicial sanctions or of findings of guilt or of both under this Act or the *Young Offenders Act*, chapter Y-1 of the Revised Statutes of Canada, 1985; or
> (d) in exceptional cases where the young person has committed an indictable offence, the aggravating circumstances of the offence are such that the imposition of a non-custodial sentence would be inconsistent with the purpose and principles set out in section 38.

Section 39(2) goes on to specify:

> If any of paragraphs (1)(a) to (c) apply, a youth justice court shall not impose a custodial sentence under section 42 (youth sentences) unless the court has considered all alternatives to custody raised at the sentencing hearing that are reasonable in the circumstances, and determined that there is not a reasonable alternative, or combination of alternatives, that is in accordance with the purpose and principles set out in section 38.

Pre-Sentence Reports (PSRs)

Section 40(1) of the YCJA states that prior to imposing a sentence, if required under the Act, the judge must consider a pre-sentence report (PSR). The PSR includes information related to the accused young person and any information that can assist the judge. Interviews with the young person, the victim(s), family members, and friends, as well as information relating to school and employment, will be included in the report. The young person's willingness to change his or her conduct and behaviour as well as any interest in participating in community programs and activities will be included in the report.

The report is prepared by the probation office and usually is in written form. Social service workers assist with providing the probation office with relevant information on behalf of the young person.

Sentencing Options

Section 42(2) of the YCJA sets out the various sentencing options available to the youth court judge. The options can include the following:

- reprimand
- absolute discharge
- conditional discharge
- fines (not exceeding $1,000)
- restitution
- personal services
- community service (not to exceed 240 hours)
- probation (not to exceed 2 years)
- intensive support and supervision program
- deferred custody and supervision order
- custody and community supervision
- intensive rehabilitative custody and supervision

If a young person is sentenced to a custody and community supervision order, the time spent in custody will compose two-thirds of the sentence with the remaining one-third of the sentence to be under community supervision. This promotes the reintegration of the young person back into the community more effectively.

The maximum sentence for a young person who is maintained in the youth sentencing provisions is ten years of custody and community supervision with the first six years in custody and the remaining four years under community supervision. This sentence is mandatory for those young persons who have been convicted of first-degree murder.

Young persons who have been convicted of second-degree murder will receive a mandatory seven-year sentence with the first four years in custody and the remaining three years under community supervision.

Any young person convicted of an offence, other than first- or second-degree murder, that carries a life sentence, results in a three-year sentence of custody and community supervision with the first two years in custody and the remaining one year under community supervision.

All other sentences have a maximum two-year term of custody and community supervision with sixteen months in custody and the remaining eight months under community supervision.

Adult Sentences for Young Persons

Since the creation of the *Juvenile Delinquents Act* in the early 1900s and through to the current legislation, Canada has always provided adult sentences to young persons. As long as the young person was 14 years old and had committed a serious offence, under the JDA and the YOA, the youth could be transferred and dealt with under the adult criminal justice system. The current *Youth Criminal Justice Act* abolished the transfer provisions that allowed young persons to be sent into the adult criminal justice system. Under the current YCJA, young persons are charged and potentially convicted within the youth courts and can be given an adult sentence by the youth court. If the young person has committed the offence after reaching his or her 14th birthday, and the offence is of a serious nature, the Crown attorney can make an application to the youth court for an adult sentence. Section 64 of the YCJA provides direction for an application for an adult sentence for young persons.

(1) The Attorney General may, before evidence is called as to sentence or, if no evidence is called, before submissions are made as to sentence, make an application to the youth justice court for an order that a young person is liable to an adult sentence if the young person is or has been found guilty of an offence for which an adult is liable to imprisonment for a term of more than two years and that was committed after the young person attained the age of 14 years.

(1.1) The Attorney General must consider whether it would be appropriate to make an application under subsection (1) if the offence is a serious violent offence and was committed after the young person attained the age of 14 years. If, in those circumstances, the Attorney General decides not to make an application, the Attorney General shall advise the youth justice court before the young person enters a plea or with leave of the court before the commencement of the trial.

The legislation gives the Crown attorney the discretion to make the application. The Crown "may" make an application for an adult sentence if the youth was 14 years old at the time of the offence and committed an offence that an adult would be liable to imprisonment for more than 2 years, and "must consider" the application if the youth committed a "serious violent" offence. A serious violent offence is defined in section 2(1) of the YCJA and includes first- or second-degree murder, attempted murder, manslaughter, or aggravated sexual assault.

Section 72(1) goes on to state:

The youth justice court shall order that an adult sentence be imposed if it is satisfied that
(a) the presumption of diminished moral blameworthiness or culpability of the young person is rebutted; and
(b) a youth sentence imposed in accordance with the purpose and principles set out in subparagraph 3(1)(b)(ii) and section 38 would not be of sufficient length to hold the young person accountable for his or her offending behaviour.

Unlike the previous legislation, the current YCJA does not transfer young persons into the adult criminal justice system. Any adult sentencing is dealt with in the youth court.

Gender Differences in Young Offenders?

Some criminologists maintain that there are important differences between young offenders based on gender. However, programs and services for young offenders may not take such differences sufficiently into account. In a paper prepared for the Youth Services Bureau of Ottawa, Mark Totten argues that because most young offenders are boys, programs for young offenders have a strong gender bias and girls are being underserved.

According to Totten, programs catering specifically to girls are needed. He suggests specific guidelines for the design of such programs, including the following:

- A theoretical perspective based upon young women's gendered trajectories into street life, the child welfare system, and the youth justice system. This perspective is founded upon the belief that most young women are *criminalized* for having been abused, for having mental health problems, and for committing *crimes of powerlessness*.

- Safe, supportive, and nurturing female-centred environment that encourages trust, bonding, and healthy relationships between staff and young women, between clients, and between co-workers.

- Risk-resiliency therapeutic models based on theories that address the physiological, psychological, and social needs of young women.

- A strengths-based approach that builds protective "pillows" against the unique risks faced by young women and develops resiliency.

- Diverse and competent *female* staff that reflect the client population in terms of gender identity, ethno-racial origin, and sexual orientation. It is not good enough to have "just any" female staff involved in this work. They must adhere to the feminist principles of a relational approach to young women's bio-psychosocial development. Male staff, no matter how competent, should *not* be introduced into the program until that point in time when young women have had time to heal from the various forms of traumatic abuse suffered at the hands of men. Failure to adhere to this basic principle of quality programs will result in young women being re-traumatized by male staff and continuing to relate to men in unhealthy ways.

- Utilization of gender-responsive assessment tools and individualized case plans that match appropriate therapy with the identified risk and protective factors of each young woman.

- Positive, gender-responsive work environment where manager–line staff relations and relations between line staff are modelled on the theoretical underpinnings of the therapeutic program. Staff should model non-traditional gender roles as much as possible.

- Therapeutic interventions and models (based upon feminist relational theories) that address healing from physical, sexual, and emotional abuse; limited gender role socialization, which results in the sexualization of feminity, the emotional care-taking of men, the deference to male authority and privilege, and the equation of love with sex; childhood disrupted attachments and traumatic losses; family relationships; substance abuse; self-mutilation; eating disorders; mental health problems that are rooted in childhood trauma (e.g., post-traumatic stress disorder, bipolar disorder, depression, borderline personality disorder); assertiveness skills; and healthy relationships.

- Opportunities to develop skills in a range of gender-fair educational and vocational areas.

- Diverse female role models and mentors that reflect the Indigenous and ethno-racial backgrounds of clients.

- An emphasis on artistic, musical, linguistic, physical, and other activities that focus on empowerment, self-respect, and self-efficacy. These activities should be based on a multiple intelligences approach and oriented towards supporting young women to identify and rely on their learning strengths.

- Education and counselling based on a harm-reduction approach to reducing risks and increasing health (e.g., drug and alcohol abuse, smoking, prostitution, cutting and other forms of self-mutilation, abuse in dating relationships, fetal alcohol spectrum disorder, pregnancy, hepatitis, HIV/AIDS, sexually transmitted infections).

- Emphasis on parenting education and training, including child development, infant care and stimulation, attachment issues, shaken baby syndrome, and non-coercive child-rearing practices.[7]

Rights of Youth in Custody

Part 5 of the YCJA is very detailed and covers a wide range of issues that can arise while a youth is in custody. These include

- the appropriateness of the level of custody (type of facility, level of security, etc.);
- reviews of, and changes to, the level of custody;
- the separation of young offenders from adults in custody;
- appeals by the young person of administrative decisions made about custody;
- "reintegration leave" either on compassionate grounds (for example, for medical treatment) or as preparation for discharge;
- "review" of the sentence;
- appropriate conditions for supervision orders; and
- consequences of breach of supervision conditions.

---

7 Mark Totten, "Gender-Responsive Young Offender Services and the Need for Female Staff" (Paper prepared for Youth Services Bureau of Ottawa, 25 June 2007), online: <http://www .tottenandassociates.ca/wp-content/uploads/2015/03/Gender-Responsive-Justice-Programming -Totten-2007.pdf>.

Part 5 of the YCJA should be read in conjunction with part V of the *Ministry of Correctional Services Act* (MCSA), part V of the *Child and Family Services Act* (CFSA),[8] and part VI of the new *Child, Youth and Family Services Act, 2017* (CYFSA),[9] which together guarantee the rights of, and provide protection for, youth in custody. The rights guaranteed under the CFSA apply to a "child in care," who may be a child in foster care, a child who is detained temporarily, or a child who is committed to custody under the YCJA. The new legislation (CYFSA) will provide regulations involving searches and limiting the use of mechanical restraints, as well as replacing the term "isolation rooms" with "de-escalation rooms."

The guaranteed rights of a young person in custody, under the provisions of the CFSA and CYFSA, are summarized in Table 12.1:

TABLE 12.1   CFSA Rights of Young Persons in Custody

The right to receive regular visits from family members (except for Crown wards, who must make special application)
The right to receive visits from a solicitor, an advocate, the Ombudsman, or a member of the provincial or federal Parliament
The right to send and receive mail that is not opened or read by others (except as limited by section 102(3) of the CFSA, which allows examination of mail, in the child's presence, for prohibited items such as weapons or drugs)
The right to reasonable privacy and to his or her own possessions
The right to receive religious instruction and participate in religious activities of his or her choosing
The right to have a plan of care provided for him or her within 30 days of entering custody
The right to participate in the development of the plan of care
The right to food that is well balanced, appropriate, and of good quality
The right to clothing that is appropriate and of good quality
The right to medical and dental care
The right to an education that meets his or her aptitudes and needs, preferably in a community setting—that is, outside the facility (though typically, youth in custody receive their schooling inside the facility)
The right to participate in recreational and athletic activities
The right to have his or her views heard on any issue that affects him or her to the extent that the young person is sufficiently mature
The right to be informed of his or her rights and how they can be enforced, the rules of the facility, and his or her responsibilities while in custody

Source: *Child and Family Services Act*, RSO 1990, c C.11; *Child, Youth and Family Services Act, 2017*, SO 2017, c 14.

---

8   *Child and Family Services Act*, RSO 1990, c C.11.

9   *Child, Youth and Family Services Act, 2017*, SO 2017, c 14.

Youth Crime Statistics in Canada

While overall crime statistics are based on the number of criminal incidents reported by police (regardless of whether or not an accused is identified), measures of police-reported youth crime are based on the number of youth, aged 12 to 17 years, accused in a criminal incident by police. The number of youth accused includes youth who were either charged, or recommended for charging, as well as those who were cleared by other means, including those diverted from the formal criminal justice system through the use of warnings, cautions, referrals to community programs, and other diversion programs.[10]

Although the media might at times suggest otherwise, statistics suggest that there is no "youth violence" crisis in Canada (see Figure 12.1):

- In 2015, about 92,000 youth were accused of a criminal offence, about 2,700 fewer than in 2014.[11]

- Of these, 45 percent were formally charged; 55 percent were dealt with by other means (e.g., warnings, cautions, referrals to community programs, other diversion programs).[12]

- Since the implementation of the YCJA, the rate of accused young persons diverted from the criminal justice system has consistently been higher than the rate of those formally charged.[13]

- The Youth Crime Severity Index (YCSI) measures both the volume and severity of crime involving youth accused (both charged and not charged). In 2015, the YCSI declined 1 percent, the ninth consecutive year of decline.[14]

- Also in 2015, the rate of youth accused by police was down 2 percent, to a rate of 3,973 youth accused per 100,000 youth population.[15]

- The rate of youth accused of crime has fallen 40 percent since 2005, largely due to a 47 percent decrease in the rate of youth accused of property crime.[16]

- The most frequent youth-accused violent crimes—common assault and uttering threats—declined in 2015 by 2 and 8 percent, respectively.[17]

- Overall, the rate of young persons accused of crime has fallen 40 percent from 2005 to 2015.[18]

---

10   Statistics Canada, "Police-Reported Crime Statistics in Canada, 2015," by Mary Allen, in *Juristat* 36:1, Catalogue No 85-002-X (Ottawa: Statistics Canada, 2016) at 25.

11   *Ibid.*

12   *Ibid.*

13   *Ibid.*

14   *Ibid.*

15   *Ibid.*

16   *Ibid* at 26.

17   *Ibid.*

18   *Ibid.*

FIGURE 12.1 Youth Accused of Crime, by Clearance Status, Canada, 1998 to 2015

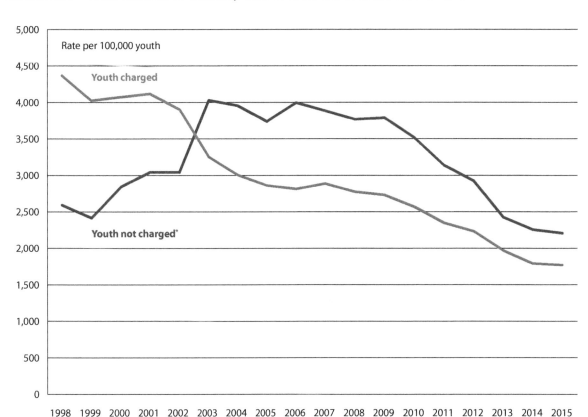

* Includes youth diverted from the formal criminal justice system through the use of extrajudicial measures, such as warnings, cautions, or referrals to community programs.

Note: Additional data are available on CANSIM (Table 252–0051). Refers to the number of youth aged 12 to 17 years who were either charged (or recommended for charging) by police or diverted from the formal criminal justice system through the use of warnings, cautions, referrals to community programs, etc. Rates are calculated on the basis of 100,000 youth population. Populations are based on July 1st estimates from Statistics Canada, Demography Division.

Source: Statistics Canada, Canadian Centre for Justice Statistics, Uniform Crime Reporting Survey.

Timothy Hartnagel, a professor of sociology at the University of Alberta, has noted that media reports substantially distort our perceptions of youth crime. While Hartnagel attributes the current 25-year low in property crime by youths in part to good economic conditions and the aging of the population, he emphasizes that violent incidents like the Taber, Alberta, shooting are usually committed by a tiny minority of seriously disturbed youth. Acknowledging the need for increased and stable funding to anti-criminogenic social programs in general, Hartnagel suggests that serious crime could be averted by targeting assistance at high-risk youth from a very young age. Among the factors he identifies as being associated with violent teenage criminality are impulsiveness, low intelligence, poor parenting, antisocial tendencies, and difficult socio-economic circumstances.[19]

All social service workers who work in youth corrections should be aware of the rights of youth in custody, and should respect them when working with young offenders. The legislation provides a complaints procedure under which children in care can seek to enforce rights that they feel are being denied.

From a social services perspective, it is important to note that part 5 of the YCJA also provides for the designation of a youth worker (who could be a social service worker) for every young person sentenced to custody. The role of the youth worker is similar to that of a parole officer in the adult system. The youth worker, with the young person, prepares and implements a reintegration plan that sets out the most effective programs for the young person.

Part VI of the CFSA and part VII of the new CYFSA deal with the commitment to secure treatment to manage the behaviour of children and youth with serious mental disorders called extraordinary measures in the CFSA and the CYFSA. This is not to be confused with extrajudicial measures under the YCJA.

Where a young offender is suffering from a mental disorder, the administration of a "secure treatment program" may be authorized to try certain measures to modify his or her behaviour. These measures can include locking up, the administration of psychotropic drugs (drugs that affect mental or emotional function), the use of mechanical restraints, the use of "aversive stimulation" techniques, or other techniques that may be prescribed to control behaviour. The CYFSA has new regulations limiting the use of mechanical restraints and replacing "isolation rooms" with "de-escalation rooms."

Because these treatments are physically intrusive and can have side effects, their use is very closely controlled. Part VI of the CFSA and part VII of the CYFSA establish a procedure for deciding whether the use of the techniques is warranted, and a procedure by which the young person (or his or her representative) can challenge the decision to use them. Where social service workers are involved in the day-to-day care of youth in custody, and particularly where a social service worker is authorized to make decisions about the use of restraints, the social service worker should undergo detailed training about the appropriate procedures that are to be followed every time extraordinary measures are used.

---

19   Timothy F Hartnagel, "The Rhetoric of Youth Justice in Canada" (2004) 4:4 Criminal Justice 355.

KEY TERMS

SUGGESTED SOURCES

Office of the Provincial Advocate for Children and Youth, <https://www.provincialadvocate.on.ca>

Justice for Children and Youth, <https://jfcy.org>

Office of the Ombudsman of Ontario, <https://ombudsman.on.ca>

Operation Springboard, <http://www.springboard services.ca>

REVIEW QUESTIONS

1. List at least three ways in which youth in conflict with the law differ from their adult counterparts.

2. What is criminal responsibility, and why is it considered not to apply to children under the age of 12?

3. What are extrajudicial measures for dealing with youth criminality?

4. List some of the sentencing options available to youth court judges when sentencing young persons under the YCJA.

5. List some of the rights of a young person in criminal custody.

Correctional Services for Adults

13

LEARNING OBJECTIVES

After reading this chapter, you should be able to:

■ Explain the difference between provincial prisons and federal penitentiaries, and what governs the choice of facility for an adult offender.

■ Describe the various types of detention facilities and detention programs at each level.

■ Understand the general rules governing prison life and the rights of inmates.

■ Explain the rules with respect to early release (parole).

■ Describe community alternatives and programs.

Introduction

Compared to the United States, Canada's prison population is small relative to the population as a whole. According to prison data as of 2013, the United States ranked first in the world with 716 prisoners per 100,000 in the general population, while Canada was near the middle with 118 per 100,000.[1]

Canada's criminal law treats prison as a last resort, although the prison population is steadily growing. Placing an offender in prison is the ultimate limit on personal freedom, and there are many critics who suggest that isolation from society—and placement within a community of other offenders—impedes, rather than assists, rehabilitation. It is also very expensive to house prisoners.

TABLE 13.1   Prison Population Rates by Country, 2013

Rank	Country	Number of Prisoners per 100,000 of National Population
1	United States of America	716
2	French Guiana	278
3	Russian Federation	475
28	South Africa	294
52	Iran	284
53	Israel	223
60	Mexico	210
106	Australia	130
113	China	121
114	Nicaragua	53
123	Canada	118
128	Italy	106
137	Germany	79
181	Pakistan	39
196	Iceland	47
214	Congo	31

Source: Roy Walmsley, "World Prison Population List (10th ed)" (21 November 2013) at 3, online: International Centre for Prison Studies <http://www.prisonstudies.org/sites/default/files/resources/downloads/wppl_10.pdf>.

While rehabilitation is a central goal of our criminal justice system, in some cases imprisonment is warranted because it supports other worthy goals, such as deterrence (discouraging other potential offenders from offending by demonstrating the consequences of conviction) and the protection of society (by keeping the offender away from potential victims).

---

1   Roy Walmsley, "World Prison Population List (10th ed)" (21 November 2013) at 3, online: International Centre for Prison Studies <http://www.prisonstudies.org/sites/default/files/resources/downloads/wppl_10.pdf>.

The corrections system is designed to provide the required level of security to protect society and those working and living in correctional facilities. At the time of admission to a facility, prisoners are classified according to the security risk they present and are assigned to a facility or unit designated as maximum security, medium security, or minimum security. However, the classification is not fixed but may change as prisoners demonstrate progress in meeting their rehabilitation goals. Offenders in a maximum-security facility or wing who comply with the rules and make a strong commitment to rehabilitation may apply for a move to a medium- or minimum-security placement, and eventually back into the community on parole. Conversely, offenders may be sentenced to a facility with a low or moderate level of security, but if they commit an act of violence while in prison, they may be moved to a medium- or maximum-security facility. This flexibility in the system exists to allow responsiveness to individual offender circumstances.

Social service workers may work with inmates and former inmates in a variety of settings and circumstances. Some work as probation officers, monitoring offenders who are sentenced to a period of probation rather than incarceration. Some work as parole officers, helping offenders released from prison on conditional release to adjust to community life while monitoring them for compliance with their release conditions.

Other social service workers may work inside prisons as part of a team. They may take social histories and help with assessing offenders in order to determine the appropriate level of security and to choose programs to meet the individual's needs. They may also help to administer such programs as addictions counselling and anger management. These programs can be offered by prisons themselves or by outside provider agencies, such as the John Howard Society or the Elizabeth Fry Society. Social service workers may work for any kind of program provider.

Finally, social service workers may work in transitional houses and in the community, helping paroled prisoners to reintegrate into the activities of normal life—for example, by obtaining employment or re-establishing a relationship with children or other relatives. Social service workers can be an invaluable information resource, referring clients to many programs and benefits provided by government and non-profit agencies.

The Prison System in Canada

Responsibility for corrections policies and programs is shared by the federal and provincial and territorial governments. The reasons for this are largely historical: When the *Constitution Act, 1867* was passed, there were already correctional facilities at both levels.[2] Section 91(28) of the constitution provides for federal jurisdiction over "the Establishment, Maintenance, and Management of Penitentiaries," and section 92(6) provides for provincial jurisdiction over "the Establishment, Maintenance, and Management of Public and Reformatory Prisons in and for the Province."

---

2   *Constitution Act, 1867* (UK), 30 & 31 Vict, c 3, reprinted in RSC 1985, Appendix II, No 5.

Both federal penitentiaries and provincial and territorial prisons house inmates who have been convicted of offences under the *Criminal Code*.[3] In general, however, offenders sentenced to two years or more serve their sentences in penitentiaries, while those sentenced to less than two years serve in provincial or territorial prisons. This is why the sentence of "two years less a day" is often ordered: It is the maximum sentence that can be served in a provincial or territorial prison.

A court that sentences a person to a penitentiary is required to provide reasons for the sentence to the Correctional Service of Canada (CSC), the federal government ministry responsible for the penitentiary system.

Inmates' Rights

Inmates of correctional facilities are entitled to respect for their rights. These include rights set out in federal and provincial and territorial human rights statutes and in the *Canadian Charter of Rights and Freedoms* (Charter).[4] For security reasons, the personal privacy rights of inmates may be curtailed; for example, all inmates must undergo a body search on admission to a correctional facility, and may be required to do so on other occasions.

Inmates also have rights and privileges under other statutes and regulations. The rights of offenders serving time in provincial facilities in Ontario are described in the *Ministry of Correctional Services Act* (MCSA)[5] and the General Regulation[6] under the Act. The rights of inmates serving time in federal penitentiaries are described in the *Corrections and Conditional Release Act* (CCRA).[7] Rights specific to young offenders are described in Ontario's *Child and Family Services Act* (CFSA);[8] the *Child, Youth and Family Services Act, 2017* (CYFSA);[9] and the federal *Youth Criminal Justice Act* (YCJA).[10]

In 2015, Parliament passed legislation creating the *Canadian Victims Bill of Rights*,[11] and amending other existing laws, including the *Criminal Code* and the CCRA.

It is important for social service workers to have a basic understanding of prisoners' rights in order to recognize a violation of a client's rights when it arises, and to participate meaningfully in policy debate and advocacy on behalf of prisoners. Those who work in correctional facilities should actively support and encourage respect for the rights and privileges of inmates, thereby reducing the likelihood of infringement and contributing to a humane living environment for individuals in

---

3 *Criminal Code*, RSC 1985, c C-46.

4 *Canadian Charter of Rights and Freedoms*, Part I of the *Constitution Act, 1982*, being Schedule B to the *Canada Act 1982* (UK), 1982, c 11

5 *Ministry of Correctional Services Act*, RSO 1990, c M.22.

6 RRO 1990, Reg 778.

7 *Corrections and Conditional Release Act*, SC 1992, c 20.

8 *Child and Family Services Act*, RSO 1990, c C.11.

9 *Child, Youth and Family Services Act, 2017*, SO 2017, c 14, Schedule 1.

10 *Youth Criminal Justice Act*, SC 2002, c 1.

11 *Canadian Victims Bill of Rights*, SC 2015, c 13, s 2.

custody. Sometimes, social service workers may be required to act as intermediaries between inmates and prison staff, communicating inmate requests, concerns, and complaints to management; other times, they may be called upon to facilitate inmate access to other helping professionals such as lawyers, counsellors, and politicians.

Social service workers may also work with or for various charitable organizations whose mission is to advocate for offenders both during their incarceration and following release. The best known are the John Howard Society, the Elizabeth Fry Society, and the St. Leonard's Society.

Table 13.2 lists some of the rights of inmates in correctional facilities (including those for young persons).

TABLE 13.2 Inmate Rights

Inmate Right
The right to be kept in the degree of custody and control that incorporates the lowest level of restrictions on freedom consistent with the protection of society
The right to be housed in a penitentiary that is accessible to the prisoner's family, community, and a compatible cultural and linguistic environment
The right to take part in programming designed to assist in rehabilitation and reintegration of the offender into the community
The right to participate in the electoral process (vote)
The right to medical care for physical or mental illness
The right not to be subject to excessive force
The right to appeal most important administrative decisions made about the inmate (for example, a decision to change the inmate's security designation, or move the inmate to a higher security wing or facility)
The right to have any property confiscated at the time of admission returned upon release
The right to have visitors
The right to send and receive correspondence, subject to some rights of review of that correspondence, in the inmate's presence, by facility staff
Limited rights to communicate with others by telephone (in some cases, subject to the monitoring of calls by prison staff)
Limited rights to assemble and associate with other inmates
The right to participate in decisions affecting inmates, except with respect to security
Limited rights to participate in religious observance and/or express belief in a religion or spirituality

Source: *Corrections and Conditional Release Act* (ss 28, 71, 73–75); *Ministry of Correctional Services Act* (s 24 and General Regulations); *Canadian Charter of Rights and Freedoms* (ss 3, 7); *Criminal Code* (s 25); *Youth Criminal Justice Act*.

Both the MCSA and the CCRA (and/or the regulations made under those statutes) create standards for the living conditions in prison. Section 70 of the CCRA codifies a commitment to a humane environment for penitentiary inmates and staff:

> The Service shall take all reasonable steps to ensure that penitentiaries, the penitentiary environment, the living and working conditions of inmates and the working conditions of staff members are safe, healthful and free of practices that undermine a person's sense of personal dignity.

Sections 68 and 69 of the CCRA provide that no inmate may be placed in restraints as a form of punishment, and that "[n]o person shall administer, instigate, consent to or acquiesce in any cruel, inhumane or degrading treatment or punishment of an offender."

The CCRA requires the corrections service to provide a range of programs designed to address offenders' needs and to support their reintegration into the community. This obligation extends to providing programs specifically tailored to the needs of female inmates.

To encourage offenders to participate in programs (and to help them earn money in preparation for reintegration), the service is permitted to offer payment for participation in these programs. Money earned by offenders is held in trust for them, and in some cases, payments may be made from earnings to an offender's dependants.

Under both the federal and Ontario legislation, offenders are entitled to access to essential health and dental care. Essential health care includes, where appropriate, treatment for mental health problems. Under the CCRA (s 86), inmates are entitled to reasonable access to non-essential health care where that care will contribute to rehabilitation and reintegration.

The General Regulation under the MCSA provides rules for the holding of inmates' money in trust for them and, in some cases, the making of payments to dependants (s 10(4)). It provides that searches must be conducted only as prescribed by the legislation, that body cavity searches be conducted by a same-sex guard or a medical professional of either sex, and that searches not be conducted in a way that tends to humiliate the inmate (ss 22–24).

The General Regulation provides that inmates can make a complaint, in writing, to the superintendent of a prison where they feel that their rights have been infringed (s 28).

To address concerns about systemic discrimination against Indigenous offenders, the CCRA requires the corrections service to provide programs designed to meet the specific needs of Indigenous offenders. The Minister of Public Safety and Emergency Preparedness has the power to contract out these services to Indigenous agencies and communities. To assist in planning programs and in determining the particular needs of Indigenous offenders, the CCRA provides for the maintenance of a National Aboriginal Advisory Committee; in addition (though this is not a specific requirement under the legislation), in Ontario a regional Aboriginal subcommittee has been constituted for each corrections region in the province. The chairs of these subcommittees serve on the national committee.

When an offender expresses a desire to be released into an Indigenous community, the CCRA requires the corrections service to give notice of the offender's plans to the relevant community leaders so that a plan can be put in place for the offender's successful reintegration.

Indigenous Offenders

Statistics consistently suggest that Canada's Indigenous population (mostly comprised of First Nations, Métis, and Inuit) is overrepresented in the prison and penitentiary communities. This means that the percentage of inmates who are of Indigenous heritage or descent is higher than would be expected, given the proportion of Indigenous people in the general population.

- First Nations, Métis, and Inuit compose 3.8 percent of the Canadian population but account for 23.2 percent of the total inmate population.
- On any given day, there are approximately 3,500 Indigenous people in federal penitentiaries.
- Between 2001–02 and 2011–12, the incarcerated Indigenous population increased 37.3 percent, while incarcerated Indigenous women have increased by 109 percent.
- Indigenous women offenders compose 33 percent of the total inmate population under federal jurisdiction.[12]

According to the Elizabeth Fry Society, a charitable agency that provides programs and advocacy for incarcerated women, Indigenous women are more markedly overrepresented in the corrections system than men. While Indigenous women represent only about 4 percent of Canada's female population, they account for approximately 35 percent of the total female prison population.[13]

Indigenous women in penitentiaries are more than five times as likely as non-Indigenous women to be designated maximum-security offenders, and are almost 50 percent as likely to serve a federal sentence in the penitentiary rather than in the community.[14]

The Elizabeth Fry Society interprets these statistics as clear evidence of systemic discrimination against all Aboriginal people in the corrections system, and against Aboriginal women in particular. While the reasons for the overrepresentation of Aboriginal people in the corrections system are undoubtedly complex, the society suggests that

> the criminal justice system is discriminatory in its treatment of Aboriginal people and Aboriginal people commit disproportionately more offences because of their marginalized status in Canadian society.[15]

---

12 "Aboriginal Issues" (14 March 2016), online: Office of the Correctional Investigator <http://www.oci-bec.gc.ca/cnt/priorities-priorites/aboriginals-autochtones-eng.aspx>.

13 "Aboriginal women now make up one-third of Canadian female prison population," *CBC News* (27 May 2015), online: <http://www.cbc.ca/news/canada/thunder-bay/aboriginal-women-now -make-up-one-third-of-canadian-female-prison-population-1.3089050>.

14 Canadian Association of Elizabeth Fry Societies, *Submission of the Canadian Association of Elizabeth Fry Societies (CAEFS) to the Canadian Human Rights Commission for the Special Report on the Discrimination on the Basis of Sex, Race and Disability Faced by Federally Sentenced Women* (Ottawa: Author, 2003).

15 *Ibid* at 17.

The society also suggests that

> [t]he marginalization of Aboriginal people is rooted in their historical exclusion from full participation in the dominant society and, more importantly, the interference with and suppression of their own culture.[16]

The justice and corrections systems have an important role to play in addressing the overrepresentation of Indigenous people in Canadian prisons. Fairness in sentencing and in post-sentencing treatment of Indigenous offenders is the first step that must be taken. The second step must be the development and delivery of programs designed in partnership with First Nations communities to address the specific needs of Indigenous offenders in a culturally sensitive fashion.

The federal Office of the Correctional Investigator has also reported on Indigenous overrepresentation in Canada's federal institutions:

> The high rate of incarceration for Aboriginal peoples has been linked to systemic discrimination and attitudes based on racial or cultural prejudice, as well as economic and social disadvantage, substance abuse and intergenerational loss, violence and trauma. These well-documented social, economic and historical factors have been recognized by the Supreme Court of Canada, originally in *R. v. Gladue* (1999) and reaffirmed in *R. v. Ipeelee* (2012): "To be clear, courts must take judicial notice of such matters as the history of colonialism, displacement, and residential schools and how that history continues to translate into lower educational attainment, lower incomes, higher unemployment, higher rates of substance abuse and suicide, and of course higher levels of incarceration for Aboriginal peoples." (Justice LeBel for the majority in *R. v. Ipeelee*, 2012)
>
> Correctional decision-makers must take into account Aboriginal social history considerations when liberty interests of an Aboriginal offender are at stake (e.g. security classification, penitentiary placement, community release, disciplinary decisions). These *Gladue* factors include:

- Effects of the residential school system
- Experience in the child welfare or adoption system
- Effects of the dislocation and dispossession of Aboriginal peoples
- Family or community history of suicide, substance abuse and/or victimization
- Loss of, or struggle with, cultural/spiritual identity
- Level or lack of formal education
- Poverty and poor living conditions
- Exposure to/membership in, Aboriginal street gangs[17]

---

16   *Ibid.*

17   "Backgrounder: Aboriginal Offenders—A Critical Situation" (16 September 2013) at "Factors Impacting Over-representation of Aboriginal People in Corrections," online: Office of the Correctional Investigator <http://www.oci-bec.gc.ca/cnt/rpt/oth-aut/oth-aut20121022info-eng.aspx>.

The Federal Corrections System

Purpose and Principles

The federal corrections system is governed primarily by the CCRA. Section 3 of the CCRA provides that the purpose of the federal corrections system is "to contribute to the maintenance of a just, peaceful and safe society" by

- carrying out sentences through the safe and humane custody and supervision of offenders; and
- assisting the rehabilitation of offenders and their reintegration into the community as law-abiding citizens through the provision of programs in penitentiaries and in the community.

These purposes are to be carried out with reference to the following principles, set out in section 4 of the legislation:

- The protection of society is paramount.
- All relevant available information shall be utilized in carrying out the sentence, including the reasons and recommendations of the court, release policies of the National Parole Board, and information from victims and offenders.
- Correctional Services shall exchange relevant information with other components of the criminal justice system in a timely manner, and communicate its policies and programs to offenders, victims, and the public.
- The least restrictive measures consistent with the protection of the public, staff members, and offenders shall be used.
- Offenders retain the rights and privileges accorded to all members of society, except as necessary as a consequence of the sentence.
- Correctional Services shall facilitate the involvement of members of the public in matters relating to corrections operations.
- Correctional decisions shall be made fairly, and the offender shall have access to an effective grievance procedure.
- Correctional policies, programs, and practices shall respect gender, ethnic, cultural, and linguistic differences, and be responsive to the special needs of women, Indigenous peoples, and other groups.
- Offenders are expected to obey penitentiary rules and conditions governing temporary absence, work release, parole, and statutory release, and to actively participate in rehabilitation and reintegration programs.

- Staff members shall be properly selected and trained and given appropriate career development opportunities, good working conditions, and opportunities to participate in the development of policies and programs.

Victims

The *Canadian Victims Bill of Rights* (CVBR) provides clear rights for victims of crime at the federal level, which include the right to information, protection, and participation, as well as the right to seek restitution. Under the CVBR, victims also have the right to make a complaint to a federal department or agency if they believe that their rights have not been respected by that entity.

The legislation introduced the following changes for the Parole Board of Canada (PBC):

- A formalized victims complaints process for victims who believe their rights under the CVBR have not been respected by the PBC.
- The definition of a victim now explicitly includes those who have experienced "property damage or economic loss."
- Registered victims now have entrenched in law the right to request and receive copies of PBC decisions from its Decision Registry.
- If a victim has provided the PBC with a statement, PBC members are required to impose any conditions on an offender with a long-term supervision order that are reasonable and necessary to protect the victim, or provide reasons why they did not do so. (Note: This provision already applies to offenders on unescorted temporary absences, day and full parole, and statutory release.)
- A victim's right to designate a representative (formerly referred to as an "agent") to receive information on the victim's behalf is now entrenched in law.
- If the PBC has imposed conditions on the offender in order to protect a victim, it is required to take reasonable steps to inform the victim and consider his or her concerns before removing or varying any of those conditions.
- Victims who do not attend a parole hearing can request to listen to an audio recording of the hearing upon request.[18]

In applying these principles, administrators of the corrections system must balance the primary goal—the protection of society—against other important objectives, including, in particular, preservation (to the extent possible) of the dignity, human rights, and personal freedoms of individuals in custody, and responsiveness to their special needs and cultural differences. The principles also place a high value on openness,

---

18 "CVBR and Changes to the Corrections and Conditional Release Act: What This Means for Victims" (19 September 2016), online: <https://www.canada.ca/en/parole-board/corporate/publications-and-forms/fact-sheets/the-canadian-victims-bill-of-rights-and-changes-to-the-corrections-and-conditional-release-act-what-this-means-for-victims-and-the-parole-board-of-canada.html>.

consultation with other participants in the criminal justice system (for example, sentencing judges, the Parole Board of Canada, victims, and offenders themselves), and opportunities for public input and involvement.

Inmate Behaviour: Controls and Privileges

Disciplinary Offences

Most penitentiaries have rules governing inmate behaviour; these rules are developed by the commissioner of corrections in accordance with section 97 of the CCRA. While the legislation expresses a preference for dealing with breaches of the rules informally, where serious or recurrent breaches occur and informal means cannot adequately address the issue, an inmate is charged with a **disciplinary offence** and a hearing is held.

An inmate who is found guilty of a disciplinary offence may be subject to a variety of sanctions, including a warning or reprimand, a loss of privileges, a fine, and/or extra duties. Disciplinary offences may also affect the inmate's security designation and opportunities for early release (parole).

The commissioner of corrections reports directly to the minister of public safety and emergency preparedness and may designate any staff person as a peace officer (section 10 of the CCRA). This designation, which is typically made for guards and administrators, gives the staff person certain law enforcement powers, such as the right to use force to suppress a riot and the right to carry out searches.

Searches

One of the most important infringements of a person's human rights that results from incarceration is being subjected to searches, including searches of belongings, frisk searches, strip searches, and body cavity searches. Subjecting prisoners to searches is a routine security measure, regardless of an individual's behaviour. In this respect, the search powers of corrections staff are very different from those of police officers in the case of a suspected offence: Police may search a suspect only when there are reasonable grounds to believe that a law has been broken. While much broader search powers exist behind prison walls, the CCRA nevertheless sets limits on the conduct of searches because they are such an infringement on personal dignity.

Inmates are subject to non-intrusive or frisk searches as a part of prison routine where such searches are reasonably necessary for security. Inmates are also subject to strip searches by a same-sex guard in certain circumstances, such as when they may have had access to contraband, such as drugs or weapons.

As you would expect, the rules for body cavity searches are narrower, because this kind of search is very intrusive. Three ways of searching body cavities are allowed, in certain circumstances: (1) the use of X-ray; (2) isolation of the inmate in a "dry cell" (that is, with no plumbing, "on the expectation that the contraband will be expelled"); and (3) where neither of the first two methods is expected to work, a body cavity search conducted by a qualified medical practitioner. In the last case, the search must be authorized by the head of the correctional institution.

disciplinary offence
an inmate offence that may be subject to a variety of sanctions, including a warning or reprimand, a loss of privileges, a fine, and/or extra duties, and that may also affect the inmate's security designation and opportunities for early release (parole)

The legislation also provides rules for demand urinalysis (used to monitor for drug use), searches of cells, and searches of prison staff members and visitors. Searches (including strip searches) of visitors are voluntary in that a visitor can choose to leave the penitentiary instead of submitting to a search.

Administrative Segregation

administrative segregation
the practice commonly known as "solitary confinement"

The practice commonly known as "solitary confinement" is described in the CCRA as **administrative segregation**. Inmates can be placed in administrative segregation by recommendation from facility staff (for example, because they are considered dangerous to others), but they can also request such segregation on their own behalf (for example, if they feel that they are at risk from other inmates). There are detailed rules for administrative segregation, both under sections 31 to 37 of the CCRA and in the regulations made under it.

The federal government has recently announced that a cap of 15 days on holding prisoners in solitary confinement will be imposed. The bill, recently introduced, stated that Correctional Service of Canada will have an 18-month transition period, during which time the cap will be set at 21 days, after it passes in to law.

> The bill is part of an overall move by the government to address issues related to inmates with mental illness, the over-representation of Indigenous people behind bars and the overuse of segregation with policy, legal reforms, and budgetary spending.
>
> • • •
>
> The bill also includes a new provision to reinstate an offender's right to an oral hearing by the Parole Board of Canada after a suspension, termination or revocation of parole or statutory release.[19]

In response to the 1994 riot at the Kingston Prison for Women, the government appointed Madam Justice Louise Arbour to conduct an investigation of the events. Her eventual report included a list of 16 recommendations, many of which have prompted changes not only to women's corrections but also to the correctional service as a whole. Examples of Madam Justice Arbour's recommendations are as follows:

1. That the position of deputy commissioner for women be created within the Correctional Service of Canada, at a rank equivalent to that of regional deputy commissioner.[20]

2. That the deputy commissioner for women be given the discretion to implement family contact programs, including financially assisted telephone calls or family visits, even if such programs are not available to incarcerated men,

---

19   Kathleen Harris, "Liberals set 15-day limit on solitary confinement of federal prisoners," *CBC News* (19 June 2017), online: <http://www.cbc.ca/news/politics/corrections-solitary-confinement-segregation-1.4167555>.

20   The Honorable Louise Arbour, *Commission of Inquiry into Certain Events at the Prison for Women in Kingston* (Ottawa: Public Works and Government Services Canada, 1996) at 251.

to recognize the different circumstances and needs of women, particularly—but not restricted to—their child-care responsibilities.[21]

3. That the sexual harassment policy of the Correctional Service of Canada be extended to apply to inmates.[22]

4. That the Correctional Service of Canada acknowledge that the following is a correct interpretation of the existing law, or that it seek modification of the existing law to accord with the following:

   a. Men may not strip search women. The only exception is where the delay in locating women to conduct the search would be dangerous to human life or safety, or might result in the loss of evidence. No man may witness the strip search of a woman, except as above.[23]

5. That inmates be given the right to counsel before expressing their consent to a body cavity search, and that inmates be advised of that right at the time their consent is sought.[24]

6. That body cavity searches only be performed in surroundings that are appropriate for consensual, non-emergency medical examination or intervention.[25]

7. That a body cavity search be performed only by a female physician, if the inmate so requests, and that the physician ensure, to her satisfaction, that the consent was not obtained as a result of inducement or coercion.[26]

8. That body cavity searches and strip searches performed in contravention of these recommendations be treated as having rendered the conditions of imprisonment harsher than that contemplated by the sentence, for the purposes of the remedies contemplated in the recommendation dealing with sanctions.[27]

9. That under the supervision of the deputy commissioner for women, all regional facilities draw on the resources of the healing lodge for the development of programs and correctional approaches relevant to the particular needs and circumstances of aboriginal women.[28]

10. That the practice of long-term confinement in administrative segregation be brought to an end.[29]

11. That the women who were the subject of the cell extractions conducted by the male IERT on April 26/27, 1994 and who were kept in prolonged

---

21   *Ibid* at 252.

22   *Ibid* at 253.

23   *Ibid* at 253–54.

24   *Ibid* at 254.

25   *Ibid.*

26   *Ibid.*

27   *Ibid.*

28   *Ibid.*

29   *Ibid* at 255.

segregation afterwards, be properly compensated by the Correctional Service of Canada for the infringement of all their legal rights as found in this report, commencing on April 22, 1994.[30]

Temporary Absences

As discussed earlier, each inmate of a penitentiary is assigned a security classification. Temporary absences are permitted for low-risk inmates in a variety of circumstances, including the following:

- for medical or dental treatment
- for reasons of community service or personal development
- for "family contact"
- to attend rehabilitation programs
- for compassionate reasons (for example, to attend the funeral of a family member)
- for "work release"—to allow the offender to work at a job outside the facility

Except for medical absences, eligibility for a temporary absence generally requires that

1. the offender be assessed as low risk to the community;
2. there is a plan for the temporary release;
3. the offender is supervised on the release; and
4. the offender is subject to having the release cut short and further temporary releases denied for breach of the release conditions.

Many inmates are eligible for unescorted absences halfway through the period preceding the full parole eligibility date, or six months after entering the facility, whichever is longer. However, this varies depending on factors such as whether the inmate is serving an indefinite sentence.

Prisoner Information

The CCRA has detailed provisions about the handling of information. Penitentiaries are expected to gather accurate information about inmates, their offences, and any other relevant information (for example, a history of violence while serving other sentences). There are rules requiring facilities to provide offenders with information about themselves and the opportunity to challenge the accuracy of the information, and there are rules for providing victims, upon request, with limited information about offenders (for example, a victim can request to be advised if the offender is permitted to be out of the prison on work release).

---

30 *Ibid* at 259.

Conditional Release and Long-Term Supervision

Conditional Release

Conditional release means any release before the last day of an offender's full sentence. Any time that an offender is released before serving the entire sentence imposed by the court, the release is conditional, which means that it can be revoked for breach of conditions. When this happens, the offender is taken back into custody and returned to the penitentiary.

Consistent with the purpose of the CCRA, decisions on the timing and conditions of release should both support the goal of maintaining a just, peaceful, and safe society, and facilitate the rehabilitation of offenders and their reintegration into the community as law-abiding citizens.

There are two types of conditional release:

- statutory release, which in most cases is available automatically after the offender has served two-thirds of the sentence
- parole, which is discretionary

Statutory Release

Offenders who are sentenced to imprisonment for life or for an indeterminate term are not eligible for statutory release because these sentences do not have a fixed termination date. However, most offenders are entitled to **statutory release** on completion of two-thirds of their sentence unless the Parole Board of Canada believes that the inmate is likely, while on statutory release,

- to cause death or serious harm to another person;
- to commit a sexual offence against a child; or
- to commit a serious drug offence.

If the board considers that the offender is likely to commit any of these offences, it may refuse to release the inmate before the full sentence is served. However, once the sentence is served, the inmate must be released even if one or more of the above conditions exist and there are serious concerns about reoffending. There is no authority to maintain supervision or monitoring of an offender who has served his or her full sentence. Therefore, while keeping high-risk offenders behind bars for the duration of their sentence temporarily protects the public, it also has a downside: It does not allow for a gradual, supervised release back to the community.

Parole

Unlike statutory release, **parole** is not automatic—it is discretionary. Parole is granted to an offender who is deemed not to pose an undue risk of reoffending within the term of his or her full sentence. It generally occurs when one-third to two-thirds of the sentence has been served, depending on the offence, the circumstances, and the offender's behaviour while in prison. Parole is not available for young offenders.

While on parole, the offender (the parolee) is monitored by a parole officer, who ensures compliance with the conditions of parole. Parole conditions may be very

conditional release
any release before the last day of an offender's full sentence; because the release is conditional, it can be revoked for breach of conditions

statutory release
in most cases available automatically after the offender has served two-thirds of the sentence

parole
discretionary release granted to an offender who is deemed not to pose an undue risk of reoffending within the term of his full sentence; generally occurs when one-third to two-thirds of the sentence has been served, depending on the offence, the circumstances, and the offender's behaviour while in prison; not available for young offenders

similar to the conditions of probation, but their purpose is to ease the parolee back into society. A parolee is required to report to the parole officer and the police department immediately after release, and must report to the parole officer regularly thereafter. If a parolee violates a parole condition, parole may be suspended and the offender returned immediately to prison.

The parole eligibility rules differ somewhat between the federal system (sentences of two years or longer), which is administered by the Parole Board of Canada, and the Ontario system (sentences of less than two years), which is administered by the Ontario Parole Board. Parole hearings are held in the institution where the offender is incarcerated, and interested parties (such as victims) may make submissions regarding the appropriateness of granting parole.

Offenders who would like to be released before their statutory release date may apply for parole, if and when they are eligible as provided by statute. In most cases, a person may apply for parole after serving seven years or one-third of the sentence, whichever is less. For example, generally a person with a 21-year or longer sentence may apply for parole after serving 7 years.

There are additional rules governing the parole eligibility date in certain circumstances. For example, offenders who have been convicted of certain crimes under the *Crimes Against Humanity and War Crimes Act* are not eligible for parole until they have served at least 25 years.[31] Also, offenders who have been sentenced "without possibility of parole" for a specified number of years are excluded from the general parole formula.

Despite the general parole rules, all but the most serious offenders may be granted parole in certain exceptional circumstances. These exceptions include

- an offender who has a terminal illness;
- an offender who is likely to suffer serious damage to his physical or mental health from continued confinement;
- an offender "for whom continued confinement would constitute an excessive hardship that was not reasonably foreseeable at the time the offender was sentenced" (section 121(1)(c) of the CCRA); or,
- in some cases, a person who is being held for extradition purposes.

day parole
normally granted as a stepping stone to full parole; offenders on day parole can go to work or attend rehabilitation/work-readiness programs in the daytime and enjoy a certain degree of daytime freedom, but must return to the penitentiary at night

If an offender sentenced to life or an indeterminate term is released on parole, he or she continues to be on parole for life. This means that the parolee is required, for example, to report on a regular basis to a parole officer and to inform authorities of any change in his or her living, employment, or financial situation.

To assist in the reintegration of offenders into society, the CCRA allows some federal inmates to be released on **day parole**. Day parole is normally granted as a stepping stone to full parole: Offenders on day parole can go to work or attend rehabilitation/work-readiness programs in the daytime and enjoy a certain degree of daytime freedom, but must return to the penitentiary at night. Day parole is granted

---

31 *Crimes Against Humanity and War Crimes Act*, SC 2000, c 24.

after a review similar to the review performed for full parole. Day parole is for a maximum six-month term, though the term can be renewed if the offender is not yet ready for full parole.

Since 2012, the government has introduced a series of laws that make it tougher for persons convicted of serious offences to be released from custody. Increased mandatory minimum sentences and tougher rules for early release have made it more difficult for those persons who are incarcerated to be released.

Long-Term Supervision

Some offenders may be subject to an additional period of community supervision of up to ten years, if the sentence is at least two years and the court determines that there is both

- a substantial risk that the offender will reoffend, and
- a reasonable possibility of eventual control of the risk in the community.

These long-term offenders serve their original sentence normally, including eligibility for all types of early release. However, once this sentence expires, they begin their additional term of long-term supervision.

Community Programs and Services

The federal and provincial and territorial correctional services agencies are responsible for offenders until the completion of their full sentence, both in prison and out on parole. The parole officer (who may be a social service worker) refers the offender to appropriate community services to assist reintegration into the community. These may include public assistance, housing, and community support groups like Alcoholics Anonymous.

RESIDENTIAL SERVICES

Some offenders may return to private homes immediately upon their release. This depends on whether there is a suitable home, supportive of the changes the offender is making to his life. Many offenders are released to transitional houses, such as community correctional centres or community residential facilities.

Community correctional centres are operated by the CSC and provide residential services to offenders on conditional release or released under a long-term supervision order who require the structure of a residential program. These centres are technically minimum-security penitentiaries; however, residents are all on release programs and are not considered incarcerated offenders.

Community residential facilities provide similar services as community correctional centres but are operated by private agencies. These facilities set their own admission criteria and, unlike community correctional centres, may reject applicants.

COMMUNITY PROGRAMS

The first few months are the most critical in the reintegration process. Many offenders struggle as they return to the environment that fostered the criminal behaviour that led to incarceration. They require the support of ongoing programs, positive relationships, and controls on their behaviour.

There are many community programs that target issues such as substance abuse, mental health, sexual violence and pedophilia, and anger management, or otherwise focus on community reintegration skills. The parole officer monitors the offender's progress in programs, as well as overall compliance with the conditions of release.

EMPLOYMENT SERVICES

CORCAN, an agency of the CSC, operates employment services in institutions and the community. Its purpose is to help offenders to obtain suitable and satisfactory employment upon their release. It assists offenders with the preparation of resumés, job searches, and training.

Ontario's Corrections System

Note that the general principles and practices discussed here for Ontario also apply to Canada's other provincial and territorial corrections systems.

Ministry Mandate

As discussed earlier, the operation of Ontario's prisons is governed by the MCSA. The responsible ministry is the Ministry of Community Safety and Correctional Services (referred to in this discussion as "the ministry"). The statute makes it clear that corrections services include more than just keeping inmates behind bars. Section 5 of the MCSA requires the ministry

- to supervise the detention and release of inmates, parolees, probationers, and young persons; and
- to create a social environment in which inmates may achieve changes in attitude by providing training, treatment, and services designed to afford them opportunities for successful personal and social adjustment in the community.

Advocates for Inmates: The John Howard Society, the Elizabeth Fry Society, and the St. Leonard's Society

Inmates of federal and provincial and territorial correctional institutions are isolated from society and often have poor social and political support networks. As a group, they have significant advocacy needs. Three important charitable organizations—the John Howard Society, the Elizabeth Fry Society, and the St. Leonard's Society—have emerged to champion the interests of incarcerated offenders. While there are other charitable organizations that also work to help individuals who have been charged with or convicted of criminal offences, these societies are the most prominent, and so their history, missions, and goals are presented here by way of introduction to advocacy on behalf of inmates.

The John Howard Society

The John Howard Society is the successor to the Prisoner's Aid Association, later called the Citizens' Service Association. A Toronto police chief, General Draper, worked to revitalize the association in 1929, because he believed that the unfavourable circumstances into which prisoners were being discharged were driving inmates to reoffend. Renamed the John Howard Society (after a famous British advocate for prison reform) in 1946, the Ontario group was joined by other groups across the country between 1931 and 1960. The national society is actually an association of independent local societies, which do most of the actual service delivery.[32]

The John Howard Society performs a range of functions; specifically, the society

- works with people who have come into conflict with the law;
- reviews, evaluates, and advocates for changes in the criminal justice process;
- engages in public education on matters relating to criminal law and its application; and
- promotes crime prevention through community and social development activities.

Local societies have small staffs but depend heavily on the involvement of volunteers to deliver programs. These programs include addictions counselling, anger management, relationships management, communication training, housing support, discharge planning, and crime prevention.

The Elizabeth Fry Society

The Elizabeth Fry Society was named after a Quaker who initiated reforms in the treatment of women and children in prisons in the early 1800s. The first Canadian Elizabeth Fry Society was established in 1939, and today, there are 25 societies across Canada.

The Canadian Association of Elizabeth Fry Societies supports the principle that all individuals are equal before the law and deserve to be treated equally, without prejudice on the basis of individual attributes, including gender. The association strives to ensure that women have equal access to advocacy (including legal counsel) and justice (including due process).

The association's goals include the provision of advocacy to draw attention to the situation of women in the corrections system, and the promotion and support of

---

32 The John Howard Society of Canada, online: <http://johnhoward.ca/about-us/history>.

programs to meet their needs.[33] Programs include, for example, the following services provided by the Elizabeth Fry Society of Ottawa:[34]

- individual counselling
- group counselling
- shoplifting prevention
- Healthy Choices (communication and relationship management program)
- Anger Solutions (anger management program)
- conflict resolution (for youth)
- Hooked-Up (for sex trade workers)
- Gateway (supper club program for sex trade workers)
- family support (peer network for parents and youth)
- housing retention and support
- J.F. Norwood House (housing)
- discharge planning
- court support and accompaniment

The St. Leonard's Society

The St. Leonard's Society began its advocacy work on behalf of people in conflict with the law with the opening of a first "halfway house" in Windsor, Ontario, in 1962. It has since grown into a national advocacy organization with the following goals:

- to prevent recidivism (reoffending) by providing educational programs, industrial workshops, community residential centres, and other supportive programs
- to prevent crime by promoting, developing, and implementing improved policies, procedures, and service delivery within the criminal justice system
- to promote acceptance of responsibility and accountability by persons in conflict with the law, in order to change behaviour that contributes to crime
- to help the community to understand its responsibility regarding the incidence of crime and the community's response to crime[35]

The MCSA allows the ministry to subcontract corrections services to municipalities or other agencies and corporations, and the ministry does in fact delegate many functions to outside agencies. Organizations like the John Howard Society, the Elizabeth Fry Society, and the St. Leonard's Society provide support and educational/rehabilitation services to inmates and parolees. In addition, non-profit corporations

---

33   Elizabeth Fry Society of Toronto, online: <http://www.efrytoronto.org/about-us/>.

34   Online: <http://efryottawa.com>.

35   St Leonard's Society of Canada, online: <http://www.stleonards.ca>.

often manage transitional housing for offenders who have been released from correctional institutions but who are not yet ready for independent living and full integration into the community.

Types of Detention Facilities

There are three types of detention facilities operated by the province:

- correction centres
- jails and detention centres
- youth custody facilities

Correction centres are used to hold offenders serving longer sentences, up to two years less a day. A court cannot sentence an offender to a specific provincial institution; the decision about placement of the offender is made by the ministry.

Jails and detention centres are used primarily to hold people who have been accused but not yet convicted of an offence, while they await trial. However, they may also house convicts who have been given short sentences. Typically, jails are smaller, older centres, often run by individual municipalities, whereas detention centres are typically larger, with a regional service base.

Youth custody facilities can be either stand-alone facilities or youth "wings" of adult prisons (provided that the population of young offenders is kept separate from the adult offenders). The administration of correctional facilities for youth is governed by the federal YCJA and Ontario's CFSA.

Correction and detention centres have different kinds of corrections programs and apply different designations for the level of security. Temporary detention centres have secure custody (strict control/restriction) and open custody (less strict/restricted) programs. Non-temporary detention facilities identify two levels of security: maximum security and medium security.

Prison Staff

As in the federal system, prison guards and other staff are designated as peace officers and therefore have law enforcement powers. For example, they can search inmates and seize contraband items such as weapons and drugs.

Volunteers working in provincial corrections are required to work under the supervision of an employee of the ministry, a contractor, or an employee of a contractor. This provides accountability for the actions of volunteers, who may not be as well trained or as knowledgeable about legal standards and procedures as paid staff.

Prison staff who act in good faith in carrying out or attempting to carry out their duties are protected from lawsuits for damages under section 12 of the MCSA. This protection extends to the acts of inmates, young people, probationers, or parolees in staff care. In practical terms, this means that prison staff cannot be held vicariously liable for the act of an inmate when that inmate commits a tort or a crime while under staff supervision. For example, consider a prison guard responsible for supervising an inmate while outside the prison doing groundskeeping for a library as community service work. If the inmate overpowered the guard, stole the riding lawn mower, and drove away, the prison guard could not be sued by the library or the municipality for the cost of the lawn mower. The guard would also be protected from liability for any harm, such as assault, inflicted on members of the public by the escaped inmate.

It is important to recognize that this protection extends to employees only where the employees are doing or attempting to do their jobs in good faith. As soon as employees do something that is outside their duties, neglect to perform their duties, or act in a way that is not in good faith, they are no longer protected from legal liability. For example, if the prison guard turned a blind eye while the prisoner escaped on the mower, the guard could be held liable for harm consequently caused to the public by the prisoner.

Absences

Inmates are sometimes allowed to leave the facility temporarily, in order to work or to participate in rehabilitation programs. In some cases, they can leave to attend academic programs; some youth in custody, for example, attend regular public schools under programs of supervision.

The MCSA contains provisions regulating inmates' absences from the facility for rehabilitation, education, and work purposes. Being absent from prison with or without supervision is a privilege that is extended only to those inmates whose history suggests that they pose no undue risk to the people with whom they will come into contact. Misbehaviour, such as violation of a release condition, will usually lead to revocation of the inmate's absence privileges.

Inmates who would not normally be eligible to be absent from prison can be granted this privilege in certain situations—for example, to receive medical or dental treatment, or for "humanitarian reasons." Not returning to the prison as scheduled, however, can lead to a new conviction with a sentence of one additional year of imprisonment.

Remission and Release

remission
a system of good-behaviour-time credits that accumulate for earned release (parole)

Inmates who obey the rules while in prison and actively participate in rehabilitation programs earn **remission**, which is a system of good-behaviour-time credits that accumulate for earned release (parole). The formula for calculating remission is provided in the (federal) *Prisons and Reformatories Act*.[36]

As in the federal corrections system, inmates must apply for parole. Provincial parole decisions are made by the Ontario Parole Board. In considering an application for parole, the board must decide whether the inmate has earned remission, and how much. The amount of remission earned determines the timing of release.

Victims may take part in parole hearings, with permission. A social service worker who works in a victim support program may accompany a victim to a parole hearing. As described earlier in this chapter, the *Canadian Victims Bill of Rights* provides victims with rights with respect to parole hearings.

---

36 *Prisons and Reformatories Act*, RSC 1985, c P-20.

Parole decisions cannot be appealed to or reviewed by any court. The only recourse for an inmate whose parole is denied is to wait until the next opportunity to request a parole review.

As in the case of federal parole, an early release is a conditional release; the parolee must comply with certain conditions. If the parolee violates any of those conditions at any time before the full sentence expires, he or she will be apprehended and returned to prison. The board also has the power to suspend the parole of a parolee who has not yet breached a condition where the board is satisfied that suspending parole is necessary to *prevent* the breach of a condition or to protect the public. When the board suspends parole and brings an offender back into custody, it must hold a hearing as soon as possible to consider whether the parole should be revoked.

Alternative Sentences

The *Criminal Code* provides the courts with a range of sentencing options, consistent with the objective of imposing imprisonment as a punishment of last resort. Two forms of conditional sentences are reviewed briefly below.

Conditional Sentence of Imprisonment

In appropriate cases, a court may order that a sentence of imprisonment is to be served in the community. Generally, this means house arrest. A conditional sentence of imprisonment cannot be ordered for a crime that carries a minimum sentence or a sentence of two years or longer (s 742.1 of the *Criminal Code*).

When a court orders a sentence to be served in the community, the offender must comply with the terms imposed by the court. Non-compliance can lead to an order that the offender serve the rest of the sentence in custody.

Cases decided under section 742.1 have established, as a matter of precedent, that community sentences are meant to serve both rehabilitative and punitive purposes; that is, they should be designed so as to incorporate elements that remind the offenders that they are serving a criminal sentence, such as restriction of freedom during off-work hours.

Recent changes have limited the number of offences that can now qualify for house arrest.

Release Subject to a Probation Order

Again in appropriate circumstances, a court may impose a suspended sentence (s 731 of the *Criminal Code*) or a conditional discharge (s 730). In both of these cases, the offender must comply with the conditions contained in a probation order. Probation may be ordered alone, or with either a fine or a prison term, but not both. Thus, a person convicted of assault could be sentenced to one year in prison and two years of probation, subject to the conditions in the probation order. Alternatively, the sentence could be a fine of $1,000 plus two years of probation, subject to the conditions in the probation order.

KEY TERMS

administrative segregation, 234
conditional release, 237
day parole, 238
disciplinary offence, 233
parole, 237
remission, 244
statutory release, 237

SUGGESTED SOURCES

Correctional Service of Canada (CSC), <http://www.csc
-scc.gc.ca>

The John Howard Society, <http://johnhoward.ca>

Canadian Association of Elizabeth Fry Societies,
<http://www.caefs.ca>

St. Leonard's Society, <http://www.stleonards.ca>

National Aboriginal Advisory Committee, <http://www
.csc-scc.gc.ca/aboriginal/002003-3004-eng.shtml>

Office of the Correctional Investigator, <http://www.oci
-bec.gc.ca>

Parole Board of Canada, <http://www.slasto.gov.on.ca/
en/opb/Pages/default.aspx>

Ontario Parole Board, <http://www.opb.gov.on.ca>

REVIEW QUESTIONS

1. List the two most important justifications for incarceration of people convicted of crimes.

2. Why does Canada's justice system view incarceration as a penalty of last resort?

3. Why is "two years less a day" a fairly common sentence for less serious crimes?

4. List three statutes that describe the rights of incarcerated people.

5. Identify the paramount principle of the *Corrections and Conditional Release Act*, and describe the other important objectives that corrections authorities must balance against that goal.

6. What are the two kinds of early release and how do they differ?

Immigration and Refugee Law

14

LEARNING OUTCOMES

After reading this chapter, you should be able to:

- Describe the central goals of Canada's immigration policy.

- List the classes under which prospective immigrants can apply for permanent resident status.

- Explain what is meant by sponsorship.

- List some of the factors supporting refugee protection.

- Understand the general admissibility rules that apply to applicants in all classes.

- Describe how social service workers can support newcomers who are seeking permanent resident status or who want to sponsor family members.

Introduction

Canada is a wealthy country with a highly developed social support system, a diverse population, and vast natural resources, making it an attractive destination for newcomers from around the world.

According to government records, more than 15 million people have immigrated to Canada since Confederation in 1867. In the last ten years, approximately 250,000 immigrants and refugees have been admitted to Canada annually. The current immigration target is 1 percent of the total population, or about 350,000 new immigrants per year. The Canadian Council for Refugees (CCR) "welcomes the fact that, at 300,000 new permanent residents, the overall immigration level for 2017 remains above the levels in recent years," although still below the target level (Figure 14.1).[1]

FIGURE 14.1   Overall Immigration Numbers

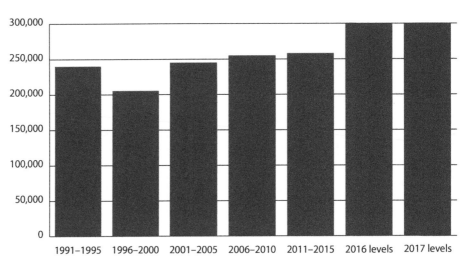

Adapted from "2017 Immigration Levels – Comments" (nd), online: Canadian Council for Refugees <http://ccrweb.ca/en/2017-immigration-levels-comments>.

The Canadian government's policy on immigration is guided by three main goals:

- to encourage the influx of skilled workers and entrepreneurs;
- to offer protection to people fleeing violence in their own country; and
- to reunite families by allowing immigrants to bring family members to Canada.

---

1   "2017 Immigration Levels—Comments" (nd), online: Canadian Council for Refugees <http://ccrweb.ca/en/2017-immigration-levels-comments>.

The implementation of Canada's immigration policy is governed by the *Immigration and Refugee Protection Act* (IRPA),[2] which was passed into law in 2001, replacing the previous *Immigration Act*.[3] The government department that administers this statute and its regulations is Citizenship and Immigration Canada (CIC). The CIC is responsible for the following general functions:

- admitting immigrants, foreign students, visitors, and temporary workers who have the potential to enhance Canada's social and economic growth
- resettling, protecting, and providing a safe haven for **refugees**
- helping newcomers to adapt to Canadian society and become Canadian citizens
- managing access to Canada to protect the security and health of Canadians and the integrity of Canadian laws

refugee
a person who has fled a nation in which he or she has suffered or was at risk of harm or unjust persecution

Because there are more applicants wanting to move to Canada than our immigration policy allows, the CIC applies formal criteria to determine which applicants will be accepted. In general, Canada is most supportive of the entry of applicants who

- have valuable skills needed by Canadian employers;
- have the means, ability, and ambition to become entrepreneurs in Canada, or to extend the operation of existing, successful business enterprises to Canada;
- have come to Canada for protection when fleeing persecution in their own countries, particularly under conditions of war; or
- are family members or dependants of immigrants in the first three groups.

The *Immigration and Refugee Protection Act* provides criteria and procedures for admission of non-Canadians. Immigrants admitted on a temporary basis include visitors, students, temporary workers, caregivers, and others on humanitarian and compassionate grounds. Immigrants admitted permanently are skilled workers (marketable skills and language skills are measured on a point system), entrepreneurs (assets, management experience and viability of business plan are examined), and sponsored relatives. To be admitted as a refugee, a claimant must have a "well-founded fear of persecution" based on race, religion, nationality, political opinion, or membership in a particular social group (IRPA, s 3(2)(d)).

In general, Canada does not support the entry of foreign nationals who

- may pose a threat to national security;
- have a history of criminality or close connections to organized crime; or
- will likely impose a heavy burden on Canada's social support systems (for example, the medical system) without contributing to the Canadian economy.

---

2   *Immigration and Refugee Protection Act*, SC 2001, c 27.

3   *Immigration Act, 1976*, SC 1976–77, c 52.

Social service workers may work with new immigrants and refugees in many different capacities. Newcomers to Canada often need help with finding housing, arranging for financial assistance, obtaining appropriate education and training, and securing employment. In addition, newcomers who are seeking formal permanent resident status or Canadian citizenship may need help with completing forms, making applications, upgrading language skills, obtaining police or medical clearances, or appealing immigration or refugee decisions.

Immigration Classes

An immigrant is any person who has come to Canada from another country with the intention of living here permanently. Many aspects of participation in Canadian life, including working and benefiting from Canada's social services, are restricted to Canadian citizens and **permanent residents**. To become a permanent resident, an immigrant must comply with Canada's immigration policy. Permanent residents may obtain citizenship if they meet additional criteria.

permanent resident
a non-citizen who has complied with Canada's immigration law and policy and has the right to stay in Canada indefinitely

In order to successfully apply for and be granted permanent resident status in Canada, a foreign national must generally obtain an entry visa before leaving his or her country of origin. Visas are available to successful permanent residency applicants who fall into one of the following three categories:

- *Family class:* A person may be a family class applicant if he or she is the spouse, common-law partner, parent, child, or "other prescribed family member" (generally a grandparent) of a Canadian citizen or permanent resident (s 12(1) of the IRPA and related regulations). Family class entrants must be sponsored by the citizen or resident.

- *Economic class:* A person is an economic class applicant if he or she has good potential to become economically established in Canada (s 12(2) of the IRPA). This typically means one of two things: Either the person has money to bring into Canada that will be used to begin a business enterprise, or the person has skills that are in demand by Canadian employers (especially if the immigrant can show proof of an offer of employment from within Canada).

- *Refugee class:* A person is a refugee class applicant if he or she meets the definition of a Convention refugee (discussed in the section on refugees below) or is "in a similar circumstance"—that is, the person does not meet the definition of a Convention refugee, but the Canadian government deems that there are valid reasons to admit the person, "taking into account Canada's humanitarian tradition with respect to the displaced and the persecuted" (s 12(3) of the IRPA).

These general classes are defined and limited by detailed selection criteria set out in the regulations to the IRPA. For example, the regulations provide, for the purpose of defining family class applicants, a definition of spouse that includes anyone who has been in a conjugal relationship with the sponsor for at least a year. They also provide that a person is not eligible as a member of the family class if the applicant and the sponsor are claiming to be spouses only for the purpose of immigration. The declaration of a spousal relationship must be bona fide—meaning genuine.

Family Class Immigrants and Sponsorship

Family members of Canadian citizens and permanent residents can be sponsored for immigration into Canada as part of the government's policy to reunite families. The following family members are eligible for sponsorship:

- spouses and common-law partners
- children, including dependent biological children, dependent adopted children, and children under 18 to be adopted in Canada
- parents
- grandparents
- other orphaned dependants who are brothers, sisters, nieces, nephews, or grandchildren of the sponsor

If the person who is seeking to immigrate is the sponsor's spouse or partner or dependent child, the sponsor and the applicant prepare a joint application package. The sponsor obtains the package from the CIC, fills out the relevant portions of the application, and asks the applicant to provide the necessary documents. The sponsor then forwards the completed package to the CIC.

If the applicant is living in Canada, the CIC will interview the applicant and conduct the necessary medical, security, and criminal record checks. If the applicant is living in a foreign country, the sponsor will need to mail the application to the Canadian visa office in that country, and that visa office will review the application and conduct the medical, security, and criminal record checks.

A conditional permanent status was introduced in 2012 in an effort to limit marriage fraud whereby, under certain conditions, the sponsored spouse must reside with his or her partner for two years upon obtaining permanent residence status.[4]

If the applicant is not a spouse or partner or dependent child, the sponsor completes only his or her portion of the application and submits it to the CIC. The applicant, after receiving an application guide from the sponsor (who will receive it from the appropriate visa office), must fill out a separate application form and submit it to the visa office, where it will be assessed.

If the application is being made on behalf of an adopted child, or a child whom the sponsor plans to adopt upon the child's arrival in Canada, the rules are somewhat more complicated and vary according to which of these circumstances applies.

The CIC will not accept a child for entry into Canada if there is reason to believe that the adoption will not create a true parent–child relationship, or that it has been done for the primary purpose of securing Canadian residency for a child. For example, if a permanent resident living in Canada does not have the financial means to sponsor her child, and so asks her neighbour to adopt and sponsor the child with the expectation that the child will actually live with the biological parent, the CIC will decline the sponsorship application.

---

4 "Conditional Permanent Residence for Sponsored Spouses: What front–line workers should know" (March 2013), online: Canadian Council for Refugees, <http://ccrweb.ca/files/cprfrontlineen.pdf>.

Also, before bringing a child into Canada after foreign adoption or for the purposes of adoption here, certain extra requirements must be met. For example, the sponsor will have to prove that the child was legally available for adoption in his home country, that a home study of the adoptive parents was performed (as is also required for domestic adoptions), that the adoption was made with the consent of the person who was originally the legal parent of the child, and that the original parental relationship was terminated by the adoption. Finally, the CIC will need to be satisfied that the adoption was not made for gain—that is, that it was not a case of child trafficking.

In order to qualify as a sponsor, a citizen or permanent resident must prove that he or she is able to financially support the sponsored family member for a period of three to ten years, depending on the age of the applicant and the familial relationship. The sponsor makes this promise in the form of an **undertaking** to the CIC. The sponsor also signs a sponsorship agreement with the applicant, promising to support him or her, in return for the applicant's promise to make efforts to become self-supporting in Canada. The sponsor must provide financial information (for example, proof of salary) as evidence of his or her ability to support the applicant, which the CIC will assess on the basis of established guidelines.

undertaking
a promise; in this context, a promise to financially support a sponsored family member for immigration

Economic Class

Business Immigrants

To promote economic growth, Canada welcomes the arrival of foreign businesspeople and skilled workers. There are three classes of business immigrants: investors, entrepreneurs, and self-employed people.

INVESTORS

A person applying to immigrate as an investor must come prepared to make a minimum $800,000 "investment" to the Receiver General for Canada, who in turn disburses the funds to the provinces and territories for use in job creation and economic development programs. This money is paid back, without interest, to the investor after five years.

Investor immigrants must also have a net worth of at least Cdn$1.6 million, and they must meet requirements specified in the regulations that indicate business acumen and managerial experience. These rules are intended to weed out those who might have the funds to "buy their way in" to Canada but lack the ability to run a successful business and contribute to the economy in the long term.

ENTREPRENEURS

The rules for people applying to immigrate as entrepreneurs are technically complex. In essence, an entrepreneur is a person who

- has gained business experience abroad;
- has a net worth of at least $300,000; and
- is demonstrably able, within three years of arriving in Canada, to acquire control and management of a minimum 33⅓ percent interest in a qualifying Canadian business, and to create a full-time job for one additional person here.

The regulations define in quite complicated terms what is meant by a qualifying Canadian business. In essence, however, a business must be a real business that earns profits and employs people, not simply a tax shelter or another business operated chiefly to generate interest, dividends, or capital gains.

SELF-EMPLOYED PEOPLE

A person applying to immigrate as a self-employed person must work in one of three areas: athletics, cultural activities, or farming.

People who work in farming must have at least two years of farm management experience in the five years preceding their immigration, and must have plans to purchase and manage a farm here in Canada.

Athletes and people who participate in cultural activities (for example, musicians) must have either competed or participated at the international level, for two out of the five years preceding their arrival, or be self-employed (and self-supporting) in athletics or cultural pursuits.

Individuals who are selected provincially or territorially can contribute to economic activities selected by the province or territory.

ADDITIONAL REQUIREMENTS FOR BUSINESS IMMIGRANTS

A business applicant who meets all of the requirements for his or her class (investor, entrepreneur, or self-employed person) must also receive a passing score when assessed under five additional selection categories:

- education
- employment experience
- age
- proficiency in English or French
- adaptability

This selection grid is designed to predict the likely success of each applicant becoming economically established in Canada. It is similar to but less stringent than the self-assessment test used for applicants in the skilled worker class.

Skilled Workers

Prospective immigrants who hopes to qualify in the skilled worker class must meet three criteria:

- They must receive a "passing" point score when assessed against CIC's skilled worker assessment grid.
- They must have at least two years' full-time qualifying work experience.
- They must have sufficient savings to be able to support themselves while they becomes settled in Canada.

The assessment grid allows CIC staff to score applicants in six categories, which include the same five categories as for business immigrants with the addition of "pre-arranged employment in Canada":

- education
- employment experience
- age
- proficiency in English or French
- pre-arranged employment in Canada
- adaptability

Prospective immigrants who would like to apply as skilled workers can get an idea of their likelihood of success by scoring themselves on CIC's online self-assessment test.

In addition to getting a passing score, the applicant must show that she has at least two years' qualifying work experience. Qualifying work is either management work or work that requires university, college, or technical training. This work is defined under the National Occupational Classification as Skill Type O or Skill Level A or B:

- Skill Type O refers to legislators or senior and middle management workers in all types of industries.
- Skill Level A occupations are those for which a person normally requires a university education (whether or not she works as a manager).
- Skill Level B occupations typically require a college education or apprenticeship training.

In 2015, the Federal Skilled Worker Program, the Federal Skilled Trades Program, the Canadian Experience Class, and a portion of the Provincial Nominee Programs were integrated into a new application management system called Express Entry.

Express Entry requires applicants to create an online profile, with top applicants receiving an invitation to apply for permanent residence from the federal government.[5]

Meeting Language Requirements

As indicated above, both the business and skilled worker categories of economic class immigrants require applicants to have some proficiency in at least one of Canada's two official languages (English or French). The CIC scoring grids rate four kinds of proficiency—speaking, listening, reading, and writing—on four proficiency levels: high, moderate, basic, and none.

Social service workers can help prospective immigrants to meet language requirements, either by working in language training centres or by referring clients to language schools or other sources of language training. Often, the best way for a newcomer to build speaking and listening skills is by practising with people who are fluent in the language and with other learners. Social service workers can help to

---

5   "Ministerial Instructions for the Express Entry Application Management System Current instructions" (6 June 2017), online: Government of Canada, Department of Citizenship and Immigration <http://www.cic.gc.ca/english/department/mi/express-entry.asp>.

develop, or can work in, recreational programs designed to provide opportunities for people to converse in English or French. Examples include book clubs, games nights, and other social clubs where conversation is encouraged.

New immigrants can also seek help in upgrading their language skills from LINC, the federal government's Language Instruction for Newcomers to Canada program. LINC offers free language training in English or French to adult newcomers. Social service workers should research the availability of LINC classes in their local area so that they have this information available to share with newcomer clients.

Refugee Class

Canada has admitted the largest number of refugees in a single year in nearly four decades, according to the Office of the United Nations High Commissioner for Refugees. The resettlement of 46,700 refugees in 2016 marks a "tremendous achievement" and a record for Canada since 1978, when the Immigration Act came into effect.[6] The government's pledge to take in 25,000 Syrian refugees in 2015—and thousands more since—has become one of Canada's largest resettlement efforts. The previous record for refugee intake in a single year was set in 1980, when Canada accepted 40,271 people during the resettlement of Indochinese refugees, the UNHCR said.[7]

According to CIC, in the last ten years, 20,000 to 45,000 people a year have sought refugee status in Canada. People who wish to settle in Canada as refugees (as opposed to applying as immigrants in the family or economic classes) are assessed, not on the basis of how they can contribute to our economy or whether they can support themselves here, but rather on the basis of their need for protection.[8]

Applying for Refugee Status

Applicants may be considered for refugee status under the IRPA as **Convention refugees** (s 96) or as persons in need of protection (s 97). A Convention refugee is a person who has a well-founded fear of persecution for reasons of race, religion, nationality, membership in a particular social group, or political opinion, and who is unable or afraid to seek protection from his or her country of nationality or residence. For example, a person who is subjected to threats and beatings because he belongs to an ethnic minority may be a refugee if his or her country does not offer protection by enacting and enforcing laws against such behaviour. This definition comes from the Geneva Convention, an international **treaty** or **convention**.

A person in need of protection is of broader scope and expands the definition of refugee beyond that of the Geneva Convention. A person in need of protection is a person in Canada whose removal to his or her country of nationality or former residence might subject him to torture, death, or cruel and unusual treatment or punishment.

Convention refugees
persons who have well-founded fear of persecution for reasons of race, religion, nationality, membership in a particular social group, or political opinion, and who are unable to seek protection from their country of nationality

treaty
a formal multiparty contract often between nations

convention
in the context of international law, an agreement between two or more nations

---

6 Sonja Puzic, "Record number of refugees admitted to Canada in 2016, highest since 1980," *CTV News* (24 April 2017), online: <http://www.ctvnews.ca/canada/record-number-of-refugees-admitted-to-canada-in-2016-highest-since-1980-1.3382444>.

7 *Ibid*.

8 "How Canada's refugee system works" (nd), online: Government of Canada, Immigration and Citizenship <http://www.cic.gc.ca/english/refugees/canada.asp>.

Applicants may claim refugee status from either inside or outside Canada. If a person seeks status as a refugee while in his own country, he or she must apply to the United Nations High Commissioner for Refugees for a referral to a Canadian visa office, or be sponsored by a private sponsor who has been pre-approved by the CIC.

If a person seeks refugee status after arriving in Canada, he or she must first report to an immigration officer. The officer then has three days to decide whether the case is suitable for hearing by the Immigration and Refugee Board (IRB) for a determination. A case may not be suitable for an IRB hearing if the person is clearly ineligible because of the country from which he or she has arrived, or because of serious criminal behaviour. Section 101 of the IRPA sets out detailed rules for determining eligibility for a hearing.

If the case is referred to the IRB for a determination, the IRB will hear the facts of the case and will decide whether the applicant meets the definition of a Convention refugee or a person in need of protection.

A person appearing before the IRB for a determination of his or her refugee status claim is not required, by law, to have legal representation; however, considering the importance of this hearing in the context of a person's life, social service workers who work with clients appearing before the IRB should do their best to assist those clients in finding legal advice. Refugee claimants can apply for legal aid, seek the help of a community legal clinic, or hire an immigration consultant. Besides having a legal adviser present, a refugee claimant may also want to be accompanied by the social service worker for moral support.

Because many refugees speak a language other than English or French, the IRB has an obligation to provide an interpreter who can speak the applicant's language to assist in the proceedings.

Sponsorship of Refugees

Refugees applying from abroad for permanent residence must be sponsored; that is, someone must undertake to provide financial support and assistance to enable the refugee to relocate in Canada. Any one of the following agencies or groups may sponsor a refugee:

- the Canadian government
- a group of five Canadian citizens or permanent residents, all over the age of 17 and living in the area in which the refugee will be resettled
- an agency that has a sponsorship agreement with the Canadian government, such as the Afghan Women's Organization and other qualifying agencies that regularly sponsor refugees in order to expedite the sponsor approval process
- an organization, an association, or a corporation that is not party to a sponsorship agreement, and that operates in the area in which a refugee will be resettled and has the funds available to support a refugee—for example, a community church whose congregation has heard of the plight of an individual or a family

Like all other immigrants, applicants for refugee status are subject to medical, criminal, and security clearance, as discussed below.

General Entry Requirements for All Prospective Immigrants

As well as meeting the criteria specified for each immigration class—family class, economic class, and refugee class—all prospective immigrants are subject to a medical examination and criminal record and security checks. These assessments are done to protect the Canadian public from individuals who might pose a risk from a public health or safety perspective.

Medical Examinations

All applicants for permanent residence in Canada must submit to a medical examination. Medical examinations may also be required for shorter-term visitors—for example, those who hold temporary work visas and work in a field in which protection of public health is essential (such as hospital care), those who expect to stay for six months or longer, and those arriving from a country with a high rate of communicable disease.

Medical examinations are conducted for two reasons: first, to determine whether the applicant has a communicable disease that could pose a risk to Canadians, and second, to determine whether the person suffers from a medical condition that would place an excessive demand on Canada's health care system. Medical examinations are conducted by a "designated medical practitioner"—a physician from a list maintained by the CIC. Examinations can include a physical examination, a mental health assessment, a review of past medical history, and "routine diagnostic tests." These tests can include urinalysis, a chest X-ray, and blood tests for syphilis and human immunodeficiency virus (HIV).

Section 38(1) of the IRPA provides that a person is ineligible for permanent resident status if his or her medical condition(s) would impose an excessive burden on the health care system. However, this does not apply to sponsored members of the family class, or to refugees or protected persons.

Criminal Background and Security Checks

All applicants must establish that they are not ineligible for permanent resident status on the basis of criminality. Criminality means that the accused

- was convicted in Canada of an indictable or hybrid offence, or of two or more offences of any kind (not arising out of the same occurrence), or
- was convicted of, or committed, an equivalent offence or offences in another country.

Where the applicant can show that he or she was pardoned, successfully appealed a conviction, or has since been rehabilitated, the applicant may be found admissible.

The simplest means of establishing the lack of a criminal record is for the applicant to obtain a police certificate and provide it to the CIC. A police certificate is an official document, signed by a police authority or government official, that indicates whether a person has a criminal record and, if so, the details of the offence(s). An applicant for permanent residence status must obtain a police certificate from every country in which he or she lived for six consecutive months or longer after reaching the age of 18. The police certificate(s) must have been issued no more than three months earlier than the date of the application for permanent resident status, and must be accompanied by a translation if written in a language other than English or French.

In some cases, a person may be inadmissible to Canada as a security risk even if he or she has no criminal record, if the CIC is satisfied that the person has links to terrorism, organized crime, or groups (including governments) with a history of attempts to overthrow elected governments, to commit genocide, or to engage in serious human rights abuses. The IRPA sets out the details of these grounds of inadmissibility, but each individual case is decided on its own facts by the Immigration and Refugee Board (IRB).

Appeals and Opposing Removal

Appeals by Family Class and Economic Class Immigrants

Where a person has applied to sponsor a foreign national as part of the family class, and the CIC has declined to issue a visa for the foreign national, the sponsor may be able to bring an appeal of the decision before the Immigration Appeal Division of the IRB. Grounds for appeal include an error of law or fact, a procedural error, and other issues where the best interests of a child are at stake.

There is no right of appeal where an applicant has been found inadmissible for reasons of

- security,
- violation of human rights,
- serious criminal behaviour, or
- involvement in organized crime.

Appeals by Refugee Status Claimants

When the IRPA was first drafted, some commentators were highly critical of the legislation's lack of provision for appeals from refugee status decisions. In response, the drafters of the IRPA laid the groundwork, in the legislation for the introduction of a Refugee Appeal Division (RAD) of the IRB; however, implementation was delayed.

Launched in 2012, the Refugee Appeal Division considers appeals of Refugee Protection Division decisions "on the merits" of the particular appeal. This means that the RAD would review decisions based on alleged errors of fact and/or law.

A refugee claimant whose claim is dismissed has the following options:

- Seek judicial review (by the Federal Court of Canada) of the IRB decision that went against him or her.
- Argue for permission to stay in Canada while a pre-removal risk assessment is conducted.
- Request to remain in Canada on compassionate and humanitarian grounds.

Pre-Removal Risk Assessment

Canada is committed to the international law principle of **non-refoulement**. This means that Canada has agreed not to send people who have arrived in Canada back to a country where they will be at risk.

When a person is denied permanent resident status, he or she must ordinarily leave Canada when his visitor's visa, study permit, or work permit, if any, runs out. (If the person is a refugee, he or she may have none of these.) To ensure that this happens, the Immigration Division of the IRB may make a removal order directing that the person must leave. However, persons who believe that they would be at risk if they had to return to their country of origin can apply for a pre-removal risk assessment (PRRA).

Some people are not eligible to have a PRRA performed on their behalf. Ineligible applicants include

- a person who has already been recognized as a Convention refugee in another country to which he or she can return;
- a person who is subject to extradition (usually, removal by agreement between Canada's government and the government of another country for the purpose of facing criminal charges in the other country);
- a person who was not given a hearing by the Refugee Protection Division because he or she had arrived from a designated "safe" third country; and
- a repeat claimant who was removed from Canada within the preceding six months.

The assessment is usually a paper-based process, not an in-person hearing. PRRAs are conducted by CIC risk assessment officers. The CIC officer considers available information about conditions in the country to which the person is supposed to return, and then makes a determination as to whether the person, if returned, would be at risk of the following:

- persecution, as defined in the Geneva Convention
- torture, as defined in the Convention Against Torture
- execution
- cruel and unusual treatment or punishment

After an application for a PRRA has been filed and while it is being considered, the person may stay in Canada. If the assessor determines that the person is not at risk, the applicant must leave Canada.

If the assessment suggests that the person is at risk, he or she is generally permitted to apply for permanent resident status *unless* he or she is ineligible for reasons of security, serious criminality/organized crime, or human/international rights violations. If the person is ineligible on these grounds, he or she will usually be permitted to stay only until conditions improve in the destination country.

non-refoulement
a principle of international law denouncing any attempt by a country to send displaced people who are at risk of serious harm or persecution back into the nation in which they are at risk

Requests to Remain on Compassionate and Humanitarian Grounds

Section 25(1) of the IRPA provides that, where an applicant is found to be ineligible for permanent resident status and requests to remain in Canada on compassionate and humanitarian grounds, the Minister of Citizenship and Immigration may grant permanent residence status on that basis.

The procedures for making a request on compassionate and humanitarian grounds are described in sections 66 to 69 of the IRP regulations. Requests can be made from either within or outside Canada, and must be submitted in writing along with an application for permanent residence status.

A person might make and be granted an application to stay on compassionate and humanitarian grounds where, for example, the person is a close relative of a Canadian citizen, but not a member of the family class, and depends on the Canadian citizen for financial support and assistance. The applicant may be the widowed sister of a Canadian citizen, with a young child whom she cannot support because she is disabled. Or perhaps the person has fled family violence in a "safe" country to come and live with a relative in Canada, and therefore does not qualify for refugee protection.

Human Trafficking and Migrant Smuggling

human trafficking
the facilitation of illegal immigration for the purpose of exploiting the immigrants in the new country

Human trafficking, in the Canadian context, involves a person or a group that brings people into Canada from another country for financial gain or exploitation. These newcomers are generally from impoverished areas or families, do not meet immigration class criteria, and do not have sponsors in Canada. The traffickers use deception to convince the migrants to come to Canada, giving them inaccurate information about employment opportunities and their chances for resettlement here. In these respects, human trafficking is not unlike **human smuggling**.

human smuggling
the facilitation of illegal immigration for the purpose of collecting payments from people who are desperate to immigrate

The main differences between trafficking and smuggling are that in the latter case, the migrants pay the smugglers to get them into the country secretly and illegally, and the connection with the smugglers usually ends when the human "cargo" is delivered at the border, or, in some cases, abandoned. In the case of human trafficking, which often involves organized criminals, the victims may initially consent to move to Canada; however, on arrival, they are forced into unpleasant, difficult, or dangerous work, and they are required to pay the trafficker a percentage of the money they earn. They are prevented from either reporting their "employer" to the police, or simply leaving the situation, under threat of prosecution and deportation by Canadian authorities.

Social service workers should be alert to the issue of human trafficking, and should not be afraid to ask questions when they encounter people in circumstances that suggest they might be victims of this crime. Among the possible indicators are

- recent arrivals without permanent resident or refugee status and without family ties in Canada;
- sex trade workers from "exotic" cultures;
- children or minors from foreign countries whose immediate family is not in Canada; and/or
- newcomers who are fearful, or unwilling to talk about their immigration status or employment arrangements.

Victims of human trafficking who are under the control of criminals may resist offers of help. When there are grounds for possible concern about a client, a logical first step for a social service worker might be to ensure that the client understands Canada's immigration laws. The person may be under the influence of threats about what will happen to her if she discloses her situation, and these threats may be based on misinformation. Arranging a confidential consultation with legal clinic staff or an immigration consultant may help to reassure the client and encourage her to take appropriate steps toward either obtaining permanent resident status or returning home.

KEY TERMS

SUGGESTED SOURCES

Canadian Council for Refugees, <http://ccrweb.ca>

Citizenship and Immigration Canada,
   <http://www.cic.gc.ca>

Immigration and Refugee Board of Canada,
   <http://www.irb-cisr.gc.ca/Eng>

LINC (Language Instruction to Newcomers to Canada),
   <https://ymcagta.org/employment-and-immigrant
   -services/immigrant-services/language-assessment
   -and-referral-services>

United Nations High Commission for Refugees,
   <http://www.unhcr.ca>

REVIEW QUESTIONS

1. Why does Citizenship and Immigration Canada (CIC) impose qualifying criteria on immigration candidates?

2. What are the four general categories of immigrants favoured by Canada's immigration policy?

3. Which characteristics, in immigrants, are most strictly screened out by Canada's immigration policy?

4. What is permanent resident status, and why do immigrants to Canada need it?

5. How is a person's claim for refugee status assessed when he or she applies for that status while outside Canada? What about after arrival in Canada?

6. What are some of the warning signs that might alert a social service worker to the possibility that a client or contact may be a victim of human trafficking?

Privacy and Access to Information and Accessing Legal Services

15

LEARNING OUTCOMES

After reading this chapter, you should be able to:

- Describe the client confidentiality principles prescribed for social service workers by the Ontario College of Social Workers and Social Service Workers.

- Identify several federal and Ontario statutes that regulate the disclosure and use of personal information.

- Describe the procedures under the federal and Ontario statutes for requesting access to information and making a complaint in the event of non-compliance with privacy law.

- Understand when legal advice and representation should be obtained.

- Explain how the legal profession is regulated.

- Explain the criteria used to establish a person's eligibility for legal aid.

- Describe how the legal aid system works, from the point of view of the lawyer and of the client.

Introduction

The nature of social service work requires social service workers to speak with clients about matters that most people consider highly personal and private: family relationships, finances, employment issues, and mental and physical health, among others. Sometimes, personal information is revealed during counselling; in many cases, it is required for the purpose of determining a client's eligibility for assistance under a range of programs and services provided by government and private agencies.

Social service workers have a legal, professional, and moral responsibility to handle clients' personal information with care and discretion. Failure to live up to that responsibility can result in legal and professional sanctions, as well as the loss of clients' confidence and trust. The *Code of Ethics and Standards of Practice Handbook* of the Ontario College of Social Workers and Social Service Workers provides detailed guidelines for the protection of confidential information, in support of the following general principle:

> College members respect the privacy of clients by holding in strict confidence all information about clients and by complying with any applicable privacy and other legislation. College members disclose such information only when required or allowed by law to do so or when clients have consented to disclosure.[1]

Protecting client privacy is also a legal requirement under a number of federal and provincial statutes. Here we will focus on four statutes:

- the *Privacy Act* (federal)[2]
- the *Personal Information Protection and Electronic Documents Act* (federal)[3]
- the *Freedom of Information and Protection of Privacy Act* (Ontario)[4]
- the *Personal Health Information Protection Act, 2004* (Ontario)[5]

The discussion that follows provides a general overview of the professional standards and statutory rules governing the collection and protection of information, and access to information from public sources.

Professional Standards

The obligation to protect client confidentiality imposed by the Ontario College of Social Workers and Social Service Workers is a strict one. According to the *Code of Ethics and Standards of Practice Handbook*, the only circumstances under which information may be divulged are

---

1 Ontario College of Social Workers and Social Service Workers, *Code of Ethics and Standards of Practice Handbook* (Toronto: OCSWSSW, 2008), at 27.

2 *Privacy Act*, RSC 1985, c P-21.

3 *Personal Information Protection and Electronic Documents Act*, SC 2000, c 5.

4 *Freedom of Information and Protection of Privacy Act*, RSO 1990, c F.31.

5 *Personal Health Information Protection Act, 2004*, SO 2004, c 3, Schedule A.

- when disclosure is required by law; or
- when the client has consented to the disclosure.[6]

Disclosure Required by Law

Disclosure required by law means required by statute or court order. For example, the duty to report the suspicion of child abuse is mandated by the *Child, Youth and Family Services Act* (s 125).[7] In other cases, a court may order the disclosure of information for use as evidence in a legal proceeding. This can pose a moral dilemma for social service workers, as well as create practical concerns.

For example, if a client raises the subject of sexual feelings toward a child and wants to talk about his struggle to control such feelings, the social service worker should immediately warn him of the duty to report suspicion that a child may be at risk of harm. Even though encouraging the client to speak freely could better enable protection of the child, until information is actually disclosed the social service worker's duty is to the client. The social service worker must warn the client of the possible consequences of disclosure, even if doing so may put a child at risk. However, if the client nevertheless discloses information, the social service worker's duty to report supersedes the duty of confidentiality.

A court may order disclosure to be used as evidence—for example, discussion of criminal acts committed by the client. Again, the social service worker has an obligation to warn the client that such information could be used against him in a court of law.

More controversial is the subject of the use of the therapeutic records of victims of crime as evidence called by the accused perpetrator in his or her defence. With respect to domestic violence and sexual offences, victims often wrongly blame themselves. Courts are sensitive to this issue, and don't wish for victims to shy away from seeking needed counselling for fear that their most private feelings will be exposed and even used against them. Nevertheless, clients should be warned that, in some cases, a court may order the disclosure of such information. When deciding how information is conveyed in their clinical notes, social service workers may wish to keep in mind how these notes might be used in court.

Disclosure by Consent

Disclosure by consent is disclosure made in conformity with privacy legislation—that is, it is allowed, rather than required, by law. Generally, privacy legislation permits the disclosure of "personal" information only with the written consent of the person. The consent limits disclosure to the purposes specifically described; it does not give blanket permission to reveal the information.

Client information of any kind may be disclosed with the consent of the client. It is important to document all client consents in writing, so that there is no

---

disclosure required by law
disclosure required by statute or court order

disclosure by consent
disclosure made in conformity with privacy legislation—that is, it is allowed, rather than required, by law

---

6 *Supra* note 1.

7 *Child, Youth and Family Services Act, 2017*, SO 2017, c 14, Schedule 1.

misunderstanding. In documenting consents, the following points should be kept in mind:

- Each new proposed disclosure requires a new consent, or a carefully drafted consent to ongoing disclosure. For example, where a social service worker is helping a client who is looking for work and the client has consented to disclose details of a disability to a particular potential employer, the social service worker should not automatically treat this consent as applying to all potential employers.

- Before the client signs a consent to disclosure, the applicable privacy laws should be explained to the client. For example, the client should be assured that any person to whom the information is provided is under an obligation to protect it from further disclosure.

- The terms of any consent should be as specific as possible. The information subject to disclosure should be precisely described, and all persons to whom the information will be disclosed should be clearly identified.

- All consents are revocable; that is, the client can suspend consent at any time. The client must be advised of his or her right to revoke a consent.

Consulting Colleagues

Social service workers often share clients or work in agencies in which a client's file is shared with co-workers. It should be made clear to the client which people within the agency are entitled to access the client's information.

In environments where colleagues may discuss their clients' cases, they should take care to ensure that these conversations are not overheard by other clients or by anyone else who is not entitled to receive confidential client information. This means being discreet about conversations in lunchrooms and staff rooms, ensuring privacy when on the telephone, and avoiding discussing clients in settings where other clients may be present, such as group therapy rooms, gymnasiums and recreational facilities, public areas of community centres, and waiting rooms.

Group Therapy

Group therapy, and certain other group programs, can pose a challenge to confidentiality, because information is shared not just with the counsellor but also with other participants. Group therapy specifically involves discussion of personal information, often of a highly sensitive nature.

Most people who are interested in group therapy are prepared to share in this way; however, all participants in this kind of program should be asked to sign consents ahead of time. It's also important that clients understand that they have been entrusted with each other's private information, and that they have an obligation of confidentiality toward each other. This means that information revealed in the group setting should not be discussed outside that context.

Meeting in the Community

Particularly in small communities, or in tight-knit ethnic communities, a social service worker may have non-professional contact with clients and former clients. This may include running into each other at the grocery store, being neighbours, being the customer of a client who works in a local business, or having friends or even relatives in common.

The parameters of the relationship should be discussed with each client. For example, the social service worker should explain that if she sees the client on the street with someone she doesn't know, she will not greet the client until the client acknowledges her. This is to protect the client from being asked, "How do you know her?" Caution is also necessary when using a client's case as an anonymous case study. In a small community, people are more easily identified.

If a social service worker inadvertently breaches a client's confidentiality, she has a moral responsibility to report the breach to the client immediately.

Suicidal Clients

What if a social service worker has reason to believe that a client may harm himself or herself? Should the social service worker disclose his or her suspicions to someone who can help? Arguably, there is an implied consent to do whatever is necessary to stop a client from committing suicide. However, a disclosure, if unexpected, can erode the client's trust.

Where a social service worker believes that a client may be suicidal, the best course of action is probably to report the suspicions to a supervisor at the first available opportunity, and to encourage the client to see a helping professional (such as a psychiatrist) who is better able to treat the client. This referral should be made without delay, and the social service worker should follow up to ensure that the client has in fact sought the help suggested.

Federal Legislation

The two key federal privacy statutes that protect personal information are the *Privacy Act* and the *Personal Information Protection and Electronic Documents Act* (PIPEDA). Both statutes are administered by the Privacy Commissioner of Canada.

Privacy Act

The *Privacy Act* was introduced in 1983. It governs the handling of personal information by a list of over 150 federal government offices and agencies, including the following:

- Department of Health
- Department of Finance
- Canada Mortgage and Housing Corporation
- Canada Post Corporation
- Canada Revenue Agency
- Canadian Human Rights Commission
- Correctional Service of Canada

The *Privacy Act* regulates the collection, retention and safe storage, disclosure, and disposal of individuals' personal information by the federal government. Personal information generally includes information relating to race, religion, age, and marital status; health, criminal, employment, and financial records; addresses; social insurance numbers; and even personal opinions.

The *Privacy Act* also mandates access by individuals to their own personal information held by the regulated agencies, and allows individuals to request that corrections be made to this information (s 12). Social service workers who work in listed federally regulated agencies need to understand their obligations under this law.

Managing Personal Information

If, as a social service worker working in a federal agency, you are unsure of your employer's privacy policies, you should speak up and request appropriate support or training with respect to how personal information is collected and managed in your office.

As a general rule, no personal information collected by a federal agency can be used for a purpose other than the purpose for which it was collected, and that purpose must be defined in specific terms and communicated to the information provider at the time the information is sought. While in the possession of the agency, the information must be securely protected to prevent unauthorized access.

Permitted Disclosure

Personal information must not be disclosed except for specified reasons or in specified circumstances, including the following:

- for the purpose for which it was collected and with the consent of the provider
- as specifically permitted by another statute
- for certain narrowly defined research purposes
- as ordered by a court
- where the public interest in disclosing the personal information clearly outweighs the invasion of privacy that would result from disclosure

Before disclosing personal information, it is important to ensure that the disclosure falls within one of these categories. In some cases, you may be permitted to disclose part of the information that you have about a client but required to keep the rest confidential.

Accessing Personal Information

Social service workers serving clients whose information was collected by a federal agency may need to assist clients in accessing their own information, and requesting corrections to it. Section 13 of the *Privacy Act* describes the process for obtaining access to one's own personal information.

The government maintains a directory (actually, a collection of four separate publications) called Info Source, which can help individuals find out which federally regulated institutions are holding their personal information. The request must be made in writing to the agency holding the information. Upon receiving the request, the agency or institution is usually required to respond within 15 days.

For example, an individual who successfully obtained a pardon of a criminal offence might want to confirm that his criminal record, held by the Parole Board of Canada (PBC), reflects his pardoned status. The PBC is on the list of agencies governed by the *Privacy Act*, and a social service worker may be asked to assist in this process.

Complaints

A client who is dissatisfied with the handling of his or her personal information or request for access may seek the help of a social service worker in making a complaint under section 29 of the *Privacy Act*. Briefly, the complaint procedure is as follows:

1. The individual makes a complaint in writing to the Privacy Commissioner of Canada (s 30).

2. The commissioner notifies the head of the institution that a complaint has been made and specifies the nature of the complaint (s 31).

3. The commissioner may choose to investigate the complaint if it is satisfied that there are reasonable grounds to do so (s 32).

4. The commissioner conducts the investigation in private (s 33(1)), calling witnesses and subpoenaing information as appropriate (s 34(1)(a)); however, both parties are given the chance to make representations (s 33(2)).

5. The commissioner communicates the findings to the parties. Depending on the nature of the complaint, the commissioner determines whether or not the individual should be given access to the information requested, or makes another kind of recommendation (for example, that the institution change its procedures to avoid inappropriate disclosures in the future) (s 35).

Personal Information Protection and Electronic Documents Act

When PIPEDA came into force on January 1, 2004, it brought sweeping changes to Canadian privacy law, extending the regulation of the collection, handling, disclosure, and disposal of personal information to organizations in the private sector. The purpose of PIPEDA is set out in section 3:

> … to establish, in an era in which technology increasingly facilitates the circulation and exchange of information, rules to govern the collection, use and disclosure of personal information in a manner that recognizes the right of privacy of individuals with respect to their personal information and the need of organizations to collect, use or disclose personal information for purposes that a reasonable person would consider appropriate in the circumstances.

PIPEDA is designed primarily to govern the collection, use, and disclosure of personal information for commercial activities, or for the management of federal employees. Organizations subject to the *Privacy Act* are exempt from the operation of PIPEDA, because the scheme of both acts is substantially similar. Since Ontario's *Personal Health Information Protection Act, 2004* (PHIPA) is also substantially similar to PIPEDA, the PHIPA governs privacy in the health sector in Ontario, to the extent of its application.[8]

---

8 *Personal Health Information Protection Act, 2004*, SO 2004, c 3, Schedule A.

Managing Personal Information and Permitted Disclosure

The Privacy Commissioner of Canada (<http://www.priv.gc.ca>) provides the following plain-language summary of PIPEDA:

> If your business wants to collect, use or disclose personal information about people, you need their consent, except in a few specific and limited circumstances.
>
> You can use or disclose people's personal information only for the purpose for which they gave consent.
>
> Even with consent, you have to limit collection, use and disclosure to purposes that a reasonable person would consider appropriate under the circumstances.
>
> Individuals have a right to see the personal information that your business holds about them, and to correct any inaccuracies.
>
> There is oversight, through the Privacy Commissioner of Canada, to ensure that the law is respected, and redress if people's rights are violated.

Organizations should take the following steps to comply with PIPEDA:

1. Identify the purposes for which the business needs to collect personal information, and narrow the scope of such collection to fit those purposes.

2. Develop a procedure for obtaining and renewing consents to use or disclose information, and develop a privacy policy that is available for review by customers.

3. Develop internal policies for the use of information.

4. Establish procedures and physical facilities for the secure storage of information files and electronic data.

5. Establish guidelines for the retention and eventual secure destruction of personal information.

6. Appoint a privacy officer or committee to monitor compliance with privacy laws.

Complaints

Social service workers may encounter clients who have complaints about the invasion of their privacy in violation of PIPEDA. Requests for access or corrections to information and complaints about inappropriate disclosures are handled by the Privacy Commissioner of Canada. The complaint procedure is very similar to that for complaints under the *Privacy Act*, and it commences with the submission by the complainant of a written complaint to the privacy commissioner.

To minimize the submission of complaints on issues that have been addressed previously, and to assist organizations in avoiding compliance pitfalls, the Privacy Commissioner of Canada publishes summaries of its decisions on complaints that have been resolved.

Ontario Legislation

Ontario has two key privacy statutes, the *Freedom of Information and Protection of Privacy Act* (FIPPA)[9] and the *Personal Health Information Protection Act, 2004* (PHIPA). FIPPA applies to provincial government organizations. A similar statute, the *Municipal Freedom of Information and Protection of Privacy Act*, applies to municipal governments and agencies in Ontario.[10] It is not discussed separately here.

All three statutes are administered by the Information and Privacy Commissioner of Ontario. The commissioner is appointed by the legislature, but is independent of the ruling government. The commissioner investigates complaints about the mishandling of individuals' personal information by public-sector information gatherers, and manages requests for access to information. Complaints about mishandling of personal information by private sector information gatherers fall under the federal PIPEDA, discussed above.

Freedom of Information and Protection of Privacy Act

The *Freedom of Information and Protection of Privacy Act* is intended to provide a right of access to information, based on the principle that information should be available to the public. The statute provides for an independent body to make decisions about the disclosure of government information, and it also offers privacy protection to individuals who may be affected by the disclosure.

Examples of kinds of information that a social service worker or his or her client might wish to access include the following:

- the government's reasons for denying a benefit that the client has applied for
- the government's criteria for making a decision with respect to social benefits
- the government's reasons for declining to provide requested funding or grants to a not-for-profit corporation or other charitable project
- a list of corporations or projects that have received government funding

Like the federal *Privacy Act*, the Ontario FIPPA provides a mechanism for individuals to inquire about the information that government holds about them, and to request corrections to that information. If an individual believes that the information is incorrect, and the government disagrees and refuses to make the requested correction, the individual has a right to request that a "statement of disagreement" be attached to the information, and that this statement be provided to all government holders and users of the information to which FIPPA applies. These include all Ontario government ministries, agencies, and boards; most provincial commissions; community colleges; and district health councils.

Like the *Privacy Act*, FIPPA provides rules for the government's handling of personal information. The legislation and the regulations made under it govern the collection, use, disclosure, storage, and disposal of personal information.

---

9   *Freedom of Information and Protection of Privacy Act*, RSO 1990, c F.31.

10   *Municipal Freedom of Information and Protection of Privacy Act*, RSO 1990, c M.56.

Accessing Information

The first step for an individual seeking access to information is to direct the request to the agency that holds the information. Only if the agency refuses the request, or fails to provide access, should an individual seek recourse from the IP commissioner.

Besides creating a mechanism for allowing individuals access to their own information, FIPPA allows individuals to request access to "general" government information. This is information that is not about the requesting individual or other third parties, but rather about the government and its dealings.

The government is not required to disclose all information. It shall not disclose information that would infringe on the privacy interests of a third party (another individual, for example), and it is also not allowed to disclose Cabinet records. Other kinds of information are subject to government discretion, that is, the government can decide whether or not to disclose it. These categories of information are

- information about intergovernmental relations, if the information was received in confidence;
- advice or recommendations within the organization;
- law enforcement;
- defence;
- information that could prejudice the financial or other specified interests of the organization;
- solicitor–client privilege;
- information that could endanger the health or safety of an individual; and
- information already available to the public or soon to be published.

Complaints

FIPPA sets out the procedure for pursuing disclosure where the agency that holds information denies a request for access. Requests are to be made in writing and generally must be responded to by the agency within 30 days. Efforts are made to resolve complaints informally. If informal negotiations are unsuccessful, the Information and Privacy Commissioner may conduct a formal review, which may result in an order to disclose the information. In most cases, the agency is required to change its procedures to ensure that similar violations of individual privacy will not occur in the future. Applicants whose requests are denied by the agency and are not made subject to disclosure by the commissioner have a right of appeal to the courts.

Like the federal privacy commissioner, the Information and Privacy Commissioner publishes reports of some of the cases that it has resolved as a reference for individuals and information gatherers.

Personal Health Information Protection Act, 2004

In Ontario, the PHIPA applies in lieu of the health information provisions of PIPEDA, because the PHIPA has been declared "substantially similar" to PIPEDA in respect of those provisions. In health care settings regulated by the provincial government, either the PHIPA or FIPPA (but generally not both) applies: FIPPA applies to district health councils; the PHIPA applies to all other "custodians" of personal health information. As noted above, the PHIPA is administered by the Information and Privacy Commissioner.

Accessing Legal Services

The clients of social service workers often require lawyers to advise them on a variety of legal issues and to represent them in court or before administrative tribunals. It is important that social service workers be able to identify legal issues that require the attention of lawyers, so that they can help their clients to find a lawyer when appropriate. It bears repeating that while social service workers may provide clients with basic legal information, such as that included in this text, they must be very careful not to advise clients about what to do.

Qualifications and Professional Regulation

While the law is publicly accessible—anyone can look up cases and statutes in a library or online—a person with legal training is often needed to decipher it. The amount of legal training needed depends on the complexity of the issue. For example, some legal transactions, such as entering into a lease with a landlord, may be simple enough for non-lawyers to accomplish on their own. In fact, the legislature and the courts have made efforts to make the handling of some of the simpler and more common issues, such as defending against a parking ticket or even taking a case to Small Claims Court, accessible to people who cannot afford, or choose not to engage, a legal representative.

Whether a person seeks legal representation generally depends on the complexity of the matter and on how much is at stake. For example, it may be sensible to defend a $30 parking ticket on your own, but it is unwise to defend a charge of impaired driving without a lawyer, because the consequences of losing at trial include possible loss of your driver's licence and even imprisonment. A lawyer who has experience in criminal law will be better able to protect your rights and present a persuasive case in court.

Lawyers qualified to practise in Ontario have a three-year law degree from a Canadian university, or the foreign equivalent, and have undergone an apprenticeship period, known as *articling*. They have also passed examinations for admission to the Law Society of Upper Canada, the regulatory body of the legal profession in Ontario. Members of the Law Society are expected to conform to a code of conduct, and they are required to carry professional liability insurance. Anyone who questions the credentials of a person who claims to be a qualified lawyer, or who wants to know whether a particular lawyer has ever been disciplined for professional misconduct, can ask the Law Society to provide this information. The Law Society also offers a referral service to assist people seeking legal advice.

In Ontario, **paralegals** are permitted to represent clients on relatively simple matters, such as civil claims tried in Small Claims Court, minor traffic offences, and issues adjudicated by administrative tribunals. Paralegals have some training in matters of law and legal procedure but have not passed the exams for qualification as a lawyer. Regulation of paralegals, establishing minimum standards of professional practice, was introduced in 2006. Paralegals are required to meet specific educational

paralegals
permitted to represent clients on relatively simple matters, such as civil claims tried in Small Claims Court, minor traffic offences, and issues adjudicated by administrative tribunals; they have some training in matters of law and legal procedure but have not passed the exams for qualification as a lawyer

standards, pass a licensing examination, and carry professional liability insurance. A separate governing body has been created to regulate paralegal practice, including the investigation of complaints and the imposition of disciplinary sanctions if necessary.

Finding Legal Representation

There are many ways to choose a lawyer in Ontario. You might ask a friend or colleague to recommend a lawyer; you might choose a lawyer whose office you pass every day on your way to work; or you might look in the local telephone directory. You can also make use of lawyer referral services provided by the Law Society of Upper Canada and the Canadian Bar Association. The Law Society charges a very small fee to use the service, and all lawyers who accept referrals under the system offer a free 30-minute consultation to potential clients. The service is neutral: It simply lists lawyers by name, not according to any kind of rating system, so that all participating lawyers have an equal chance of being referred.

People who have limited financial resources to pay for a lawyer's services, and who are eligible for subsidized legal assistance, may find a lawyer by applying to a legal aid office or a community legal clinic.

Legal Fees and Other Costs

Lawyers calculate their charges for legal services in three main ways:

- *Hourly rate:* The most common type of billing is by the hour. Most lawyers charge an hourly rate that reflects the lawyer's level of experience. Often, in more complex cases, a senior lawyer will work on the more difficult aspects of the case, and others in the firm—junior lawyers or articling students—will handle the more routine details. In such cases, the senior lawyer's time is charged at a higher hourly rate and the work done by other staff is charged at a lower rate. Some lawyers charge different rates for different kinds of work, such as a higher hourly fee for court time.

- *Transaction-based flat fee:* Some lawyers charge a flat fee for routine transactions—for example, handling the sale of a residential property or an uncontested divorce. These fees generally apply only to transactions that follow the usual pattern. Flat fees can also apply to stages in a proceeding; for example, a lawyer could charge a flat fee to file a statement of claim or defence, a separate flat fee to conduct discoveries and attempt settlement out of court, and an hourly rate thereafter if the matter goes to trial.

- *Contingency fees:* In a case involving a claim for monetary compensation, the lawyer and the client may agree to a **contingency fee** arrangement, whereby the lawyer's fee is calculated as a percentage of any amount recovered in the action. If the client loses the case, the lawyer loses too. The advantage of this arrangement is that clients with a strong case but little money are able to afford representation. There are strict rules governing contingency fee arrangements, including maximum contingency payment rates, and a contingency fee may not be appropriate in some cases. Understandably, lawyers prefer to

contingency fee
an arrangement whereby the lawyer's fee is calculated as a percentage of any amount recovered in the action

accept contingency fees only in cases with a reasonable likelihood of success. For example, if a client has a strong case in a damages claim for, say, $200,000, she may agree to pay the lawyer 18 percent of the money recovered from the defendant. If the client is awarded $200,000, she will pay the lawyer $36,000. If she is awarded $180,000, the lawyer will get $32,400. However, if the claim fails, the lawyer will get nothing.

In addition to legal fees, clients must pay for the lawyer's disbursements. **Disbursements** are out-of-pocket expenses incurred in the course of representing the client; they include photocopying costs, courier costs, court filing fees, and fees to obtain experts' reports.

Some lawyers occasionally take on a worthwhile legal cause on a **pro bono** basis. The full term, *pro bono publico*, means "for the public good"; the short form, *pro bono*, is widely used to refer to legal work undertaken without charge. In general, a lawyer will accept a pro bono case where legal aid funding is not available but the litigant's claim is worthy of support for ethical or moral reasons. One example would be a case where a person has been convicted of a criminal offence and has gone to jail, but maintains his innocence in circumstances that strongly suggest wrongful conviction. A criminal defence lawyer might take on an appeal on a pro bono basis in the interests of justice, and for his or her own personal or professional reasons. Anyone who has a case that is unusually significant to the broader community, and/or likely to attract the interest of the media, and who lacks the resources to pay legal fees, should consider consulting a lawyer who is known for doing pro bono work.

disbursements
out-of-pocket expenses incurred in the course of representing the client, including photocopying costs, courier costs, court filing fees, and fees to obtain experts' reports

pro bono
the full term, *pro bono publico*, means "for the public good"; the short form, *pro bono*, is widely used to refer to legal work undertaken without charge

Subsidized Legal Services

Sources of Legal Assistance

Legal Aid Ontario

In Ontario, the principal source of subsidized legal assistance is a publicly funded but independent agency called Legal Aid Ontario (LAO). LAO delivers legal assistance in accordance with the *Legal Aid Services Act*. One mandate of LAO is

> to promote access to justice throughout Ontario for low-income individuals by means of providing consistently high quality legal aid services in a cost-effective and efficient manner.[11]

To qualify for legal aid, a candidate must meet specified criteria, discussed in more detail below. In general, the candidate must have a low income, and the legal assistance requested must meet a basic need—for example, the need to defend oneself against a serious criminal charge. Individuals seeking legal aid must submit an application to LAO. If successful, the candidate is granted a legal aid certificate that he can use to obtain legal assistance, either from a lawyer in private practice or from an LAO staff lawyer.

---

11 "About Legal Aid Ontario" (nd), online: Legal Aid Ontario <http://www.legalaid.on.ca/en/about>.

Lawyers who agree to provide services pursuant to a legal aid certificate are reimbursed by LAO for their services, but the amount they can charge must be within a specified range (referred to as "the legal aid tariff"). The amount that may be charged depends on the lawyer's experience and the legal matter involved.

Community Legal Aid Clinics

Legal assistance is also available from community legal clinics. These clinics are funded by LAO, and their availability and the diversity of their legal practice varies from region to region. Community legal clinics often have a small complement of staff lawyers who supervise students, paralegals, and/or other lawyers, some of whom may serve on a volunteer basis. According to LAO, community legal aid clinics can do other work besides simply assisting clients directly and individually: "clinics also can engage in test cases, public legal education, community organizing, and other law reform initiatives."[12]

Duty Counsel

duty counsel
lawyers who are available in the criminal and family courts to provide "emergency" legal representation to unrepresented individuals

If a person is required to appear in court and he or she has not yet secured legal assistance or representation, he or she may request the services of duty counsel. **Duty counsel** are lawyers who are available in the criminal and family courts to provide "emergency" legal representation to unrepresented individuals. Duty counsel can also attend at mental health facilities to assist patients in exercising their rights under mental health law.

The role of duty counsel used to be restricted to the client's first appearance in court, but it has expanded somewhat, in recognition of the fact that duty counsel not only assist the client but also help to make the court system as a whole function more efficiently.

Qualifying for Legal Aid

Legal aid is available to low-income individuals who need help with any of the following legal matters:

1. Family law disputes that involve
   a. seeking custody of a child;
   b. seeking access to a child;
   c. child protection proceedings;
   d. gaining access to spousal or child support;
   e. preventing a spouse from selling or destroying family property; and
   f. negotiating rights to assets that could provide the client with income, such as registered retirement savings plans or pensions.

---

12 "Clinic Funding Q & As" (24 March, 2009), online, Legal Aid Ontario <http://www.legalaid .on.ca/en/news/newsarchive/0903-24_lettertoclinics_2.asp>.

2. Immigration and refugee matters that involve

   a. refugee hearings (attempts to gain refugee status);

   b. sponsorship and deportation appeals; and

   c. detention reviews.

3. Mental health hearings and appeals.

4. Litigation to gain access to

   a. workplace safety and insurance benefits (sometimes referred to as workers' compensation);

   b. social benefits (for example, Ontario Works benefits or disability benefits); and

   c. employment insurance appeals.

5. Criminal law matters in which there is a probability of incarceration if the client is convicted.

Legal aid is not available to assist a client with

- wrongful dismissal;
- change of name;
- personal bankruptcy;
- power of attorney;
- money lent to others or money owed to others;
- sponsorship of relatives for immigration;
- commercial litigation;
- libel, defamation, and slander; or
- real estate matters.

To determine eligibility for legal aid, LAO scrutinizes the financial position of the applicant, the spouse and/or partner, and any dependent children. The first step of the legal aid financial test is a review of assets. The assets scrutinized most closely are cash and investments, such as RRSPs. LAO does not typically require a person to sell a house to pay for legal fees, but he or she may be required to seek a loan by way of a mortgage against the house before he or she can be eligible for legal aid.

The next step is an assessment of income. LAO sets a series of income thresholds below which applicants (other than those who have assets) are generally considered eligible for legal aid. These thresholds are related to family size and correspond, more or less, to the income brackets for social assistance

If an applicant's income is above the threshold, LAO will conduct a detailed financial assessment. This assessment compares an applicant's income against his or her expenses to determine financial means. The assessment applies ceilings for housing expenses; for example, if a person has a low income but very high mortgage costs, only a portion of these costs will be counted as an expense in calculating the applicant's financial means. However, necessary expenses, such as medical expenses for a chronic condition, are taken into account in determining eligibility.

In some cases, an applicant will be required to pay a share of the legal costs while LAO pays the remainder, or the applicant may be asked to agree to repay the legal costs in the future. A promise to repay may be secured—for example, by a lien placed on the applicant's house. When a person recovers money in the course of litigation paid for by legal aid, legal aid costs must be at least partially repaid from the amount awarded.

Other Avenues for Advocacy

advocacy
the making of
representations or
arguments on behalf of
another party or parties
in an effort to help them

Lawyers advocate for their clients on particular legal matters, such as the defence of a drug trafficking charge, a claim for child support, or the appeal of a Social Benefits Tribunal decision. Social service workers are often involved in social **advocacy** on a broader scale. They represent their client's needs and interests on a personal level, but also work to effect political and social change. This may involve lobbying for funding, petitioning for changes to laws, and attempting to change attitudes and behaviours in society. Clients also may play an active role in social advocacy.

Social service workers can assist their clients in getting in touch with the appropriate advocacy organizations. In this way, clients can work toward improving their own situation and that of others like them.

KEY TERMS

advocacy, 278

contingency fee, 274

disbursements, 275

disclosure by consent, 265

disclosure required by law, 265

duty counsel, 276

paralegals, 273

pro bono, 275

SUGGESTED SOURCES

InfoSource, <http://infosource.gc.ca>

Law Society of Upper Canada, <http://www.lsuc.on.ca>

Legal Aid Ontario, <http://www.legalaid.on.ca>

Privacy Commissioner of Canada, <https://www.priv
.gc.ca>

The Canadian Bar Association, <https://www.cba.org>

REVIEW QUESTIONS

1. In what circumstances is it acceptable to divulge client information, according to the *Code of Ethics and Standards of Practice Handbook* of the Ontario College of Social Workers and Social Service Workers?

2. If a social service worker thinks that a client may disclose information to her that she would be required by law to disclose, what should she do?

3. If a social service worker believes that a client may be suicidal, what steps should he take?

4. Identify two privacy statutes that apply to social service agencies and employees within the federal government.

5. Why should a social service worker be able to identify common legal issues on behalf of her client?

6. What are the two main factors that are considered in deciding whether a client is eligible for legal aid?

Glossary

absolute discharge a sentencing order that imposes no penalty on an accused—a finding of guilt but is deemed not to have been convicted

abuse of process an improper action or a series of actions on the part of the police or prosecution that undermines the fairness of the criminal proceedings

access generally refers to the arrangement by which the parent who does not have custody is permitted to spend time with the child

actus reus the physical act or omission that, when combined with the required intent, constitutes an offence

administrative law the body of law that governs how government administrators and employees exercise the decision-making powers granted to them under statute

administrative segregation the practice commonly known as "solitary confinement"

advance directives instructions regarding a person's wishes for care should that person at some point be incapable of consenting

adverse-effect discrimination discrimination that is indirect and often unintentional

advocacy the making of representations or arguments on behalf of another party or parties in an effort to help them

affidavit a sworn written statement by a witness that replaces testimony

agency applies to actions of an employee taken in the line of duty—that is, actions taken on the employer's time that are within the employee's job description

alternative dispute resolution (ADR) a term used to describe a range of recognized strategies—for example, assisted negotiation, mediation, and arbitration—that are designed to help resolve disputes without recourse to the traditional court system

applicant a person who has initiated a legal process

arbitration the most formal of ADR processes, and the closest to litigation in style; parties attend before a neutral person

attorney a representative who is formally appointed by a person to make decisions on his or her behalf

balance of probabilities the party making a claim (or counterclaim) against another party must prove that the basis for the claim is more likely than not to be valid

beyond a reasonable doubt the sum of all the facts pointing to guilt must be so convincing that no reasonable person would question that conclusion

bona fide job qualifications specific skills or training that an employee must have to be able to perform a job

by-laws rules created by a municipality, county, or other level of government smaller than a province or territory

capacity the ability to understand the information required for making a decision regarding treatment or admission to a facility, and to understand the consequences of the decision

case management procedures that have been established in cities with busy courts, with the objective of alleviating bottlenecks in the justice system

caution a formal extrajudicial measure in which parents are informed. There are two kinds of cautions: police cautions and Crown cautions.

child support the requirement of both parents, under the *Divorce Act*, to contribute to the support of a "child of the marriage," including the biological children of the two partners, adopted children, stepchildren to whom one of the partners has stood *in loco parentis* (in place of a parent), and children born outside the marriage union; paid by one parent to the other, and is an issue separate from custody and access

Children's Lawyer a court-ordered or government-funded lawyer for children, who represents children in a range of cases, such as contested wills and personal injury lawsuits; in custody and access cases, the Office of the Children's Lawyer may appoint a lawyer to represent the child

civil law all non-criminal law; differs from judge-made common law

code of ethics a system of moral principles designed to guide the conduct of a person or profession

cohabitation agreement type of domestic contract made by a couple who are cohabiting or who intend to cohabit

common law a body of legal principles established through the decisions made in court cases

conditional discharge a sentencing order that includes no penalty other than probation

conditional release any release before the last day of an offender's full sentence; because the release is conditional, it can be revoked for breach of conditions

consecutive order interim society care followed by supervision

consensual something that is agreed to and/or permitted by the party to whom it is done or who participates in it

consent order an agreed plan for a child's care, developed with input from the parents and/or the child, and consented to by them

Constitution the statute that establishes the political structure of a nation and sets out its fundamental law

contingency fee an arrangement whereby the lawyer's fee is calculated as a percentage of any amount recovered in the action

convention in the context of international law, an agreement between two or more nations

Convention refugees persons who have well-founded fear of persecution for reasons of race, religion, nationality, membership in a particular social group, or political opinion, and who are unable to seek protection from their country of nationality

criminal responsibility the idea that not all people who commit criminal acts should be made to bear the full legal consequences normally attached to those acts

cross-examination the opportunity for opposing counsel to ask a witness questions

custody generally refers to the legal arrangement for the day-to-day care of and decision-making with respect to a child

cyberbullying harassment or abuse of other students or teachers via electronic media such as emails, text messages, or posting comments or pictures on the Internet

day parole normally granted as a stepping stone to full parole; offenders on day parole can go to work or attend rehabilitation/work-readiness programs in the daytime and enjoy a certain degree of daytime freedom, but must return to the penitentiary at night

defence in criminal or civil law, the accused or the party who is responding to a lawsuit; the arguments put forward by an accused or a defendant

defendant in a criminal matter, the person accused of a charge, usually used with respect to summary conviction offences; in a civil matter, the person opposing a plaintiff's claim

direct discrimination discrimination that is blatant and obvious

disbursements out-of-pocket expenses incurred in the course of representing the client, including photocopying costs, courier costs, court filing fees, and fees to obtain experts' reports

disciplinary offence an inmate offence that may be subject to a variety of sanctions, including a warning or reprimand, a loss of privileges, a fine, and/or extra duties, and that may also affect the inmate's security designation and opportunities for early release (parole)

disclosure by consent disclosure made in conformity with privacy legislation—that is, it is allowed, rather than required, by law

disclosure required by law disclosure required by statute or court order

diversion a program designed to divert individuals away from the formal criminal justice system

domestic contract a valid contract that provides for different rights on separation than those that are described in legislation; the contract may take precedence over the legislation

duty counsel lawyers who are available in the criminal and family courts to provide "emergency" legal representation to unrepresented individuals

entitlement a right to receive a benefit based on objective criteria

equalization payment in a separation agreement, equal to one-half of the difference between the net family property of each spouse

euthanasia a deliberate act undertaken with the intention of ending the life of another person to relieve the suffering of that person

express consent consent that can be obtained in writing or orally

extended society care an order in which the court determines that it is unlikely that the parents or guardian will ever be able to care for the child adequately

extrajudicial measures a form of diversion designed to deal informally with youth involved in criminal activity as an alternative to prosecution through traditional criminal procedure; run by the police for low-risk offenders.

extrajudicial sanctions diversion programs under the YCJA run by the crown attorney for low-risk youth; designed to address criminal behaviour more serious than the type that warrants a warning, caution, or referral

harassment engaging in a course of vexatious comment or conduct that is known or ought reasonably to be known to be unwelcome

home-schooling exemption to the *Education Act* that allows absence from school for children who are receiving satisfactory instruction at home or elsewhere; must comply with basic curriculum standards set by the province or territory

homemaker a person who works in the home of a vulnerable child in an effort either to support a struggling parent or to care for the child during the parent's temporary absence

homestudy the assessment of a family or individual who is considering an adoption

human smuggling the facilitation of illegal immigration for the purpose of collecting payments from people who are desperate to immigrate

human trafficking the facilitation of illegal immigration for the purpose of exploiting the immigrants in the new country

hybrid/dual offence an offence that can be charged either as a summary conviction offence or as an indictable offence according to the Crown's election

identification, placement, and review committee (IPRC) committee established within the Ministry of Education to assist in determining which students require and are eligible for special services

implied consent consent that can be given by a person's actions or inactions

"in camera" hearing a court hearing conducted privately with no public access

indictable offence a serious offence that attracts a significant penalty and that is tried through a more complex criminal procedure

indictment a type of charging process or document that is used to begin a prosecution, usually of an indictable offence

information a type of charging process or document that is used to begin a prosecution of a summary conviction offence

intentional torts a category of tort that involves causing harm on purpose rather than through negligence

interim society care an order that provides for a child's placement in residential custody for a maximum of 12 months

internal review the review of an administrative decision by a different decision-maker within the institution

judicial interim release also called bail; release from custody pending first court appearance

judicial review a legal challenge to a tribunal decision on procedural grounds

kinship care placement of an at-risk child (or children) in the care of grandparents, aunts, uncles, other close relatives, or even non-relatives, such as godparents, with whom the child has a kinship bond

legal capacity the right and ability of a person to exercise legal rights

legal information general information about the law without specific reference to an individual's particular circumstance

liability the legal responsibility to fulfill an obligation

malpractice failure of a professional to perform in compliance with one's professional duty

marriage contract type of domestic contract made by a couple who are married or who intend to marry

matrimonial home property that the spouses ordinarily occupied as their family residence at the time of separation

mediation a form of alternative dispute resolution in which a trained, neutral professional supports the parties in working out their issues and achieving an acceptable agreement

mens rea the mental element of a crime; the intent required to satisfy the description of an offence

needs- and means-tested assessing someone's situation on the basis of his or her needs (i.e., rent, food, and medical necessities)

negligence implies a lack of action in circumstances where action is warranted

negotiation the act of "working things out"

non-profit housing providers encourage the building of affordable housing units and offer these units to people who cannot afford to pay market rents

non-refoulement a principle of international law denouncing any attempt by a country to send displaced people who are at risk of serious harm or persecution back into the nation in which they are at risk

notes documentation primarily designed as memory aids for the social service worker or to provide information to colleagues

paralegals permitted to represent clients on relatively simple matters, such as civil claims tried in Small Claims Court, minor traffic offences, and issues adjudicated by administrative tribunals; they have some training in matters of law and legal procedure but have not passed the exams for qualification as a lawyer

parens patriae a doctrine that emphasized the state's duty to protect vulnerable members of society and that assumed a connection between poor parenting and youth criminality

parole discretionary release granted to an offender who is deemed not to pose an undue risk of reoffending within the term of his full sentence; generally occurs when one-third to two-thirds of the sentence has been served, depending on the offence, the circumstances, and the offender's behaviour while in prison; not available for young offenders

permanent resident a non-citizen who has complied with Canada's immigration law and policy and has the right to stay in Canada indefinitely

plaintiff the party in a civil lawsuit who initiated the lawsuit

plea bargain a negotiation between the prosecutor and an accused that results in a guilty plea

power of attorney the legal act that appoints someone as another person's attorney for property or attorney for personal care

precedent the principle that requires courts to follow the legal rulings made by superior courts in decisions based on similar facts

private adoptions adoptions handled by private agencies or individuals licensed by the government

pro bono the full term, *pro bono publico*, means "for the public good"; the short form, *pro bono*, is widely used to refer to legal work undertaken without charge

probation a sentence that includes the imposition of terms that if breached may result in a more severe penalty

professional standards benchmarks against which a professional is expected to measure performance

prohibited grounds grounds upon which discrimination is forbidden, which typically include race, nationality, religion, sex, disability, family status, criminal record, and age

prosecution the process of presenting the case for convicting and sentencing a person accused of an offence, undertaken by the Crown attorney

prosecutor the Crown attorney prosecuting a case

public adoptions adoptions involving children who are in extended society care (formerly known as Crown wards); individuals who are interested in public adoptions must work with a children's aid society

quiet enjoyment the right to occupy and use rented premises free from unexpected intrusions by the landlord

recidivism repeat offending

records material prepared and organized to provide a means to understanding the client and planning the social work and social service work intervention

refugee a person who has fled a nation in which he or she has suffered or was at risk of harm or unjust persecution

regulations rules made by authority provided in a statute, which help guide the application of the statute

remission a system of good-behaviour-time credits that accumulate for earned release (parole)

rent control legislated restrictions on rent increases on rental properties under certain circumstances

reparation a payment made to compensate for harm

reports documents written by persons who have direct knowledge of or experience with a client, an event, or a set of circumstances that are designed to be read by a third party

reprisals actions or statements intended to punish, threaten, intimidate, or discriminate against a complainant

respondent the person opposing an applicant in a legal process

restorative justice an approach to justice that places an emphasis not on punishing the offender but on taking responsibility for actions, compensating for harm done to victims, repairing relationships, and restoring harmony in the community; focuses equally on the offender, the victim, and the community

rights adviser a person who is available to speak with patients about their legal rights

sanctions officially imposed consequences that follow misconduct or the failure to meet compulsory standards of performance; can include fines, suspension of licence, or loss of privileges

sentencing circle alternative sentencing procedure in which the penalty for a crime is decided through a consultative process involving the offender, the victim, and the community

separation agreement type of domestic contract made between a couple who are married or cohabiting with the intention of separating or who are already separated

sexual harassment harassment of a sexual nature that may include threats, stalking, sexual touching, and assault, among other actions

spousal support a spouse can claim support under the *Divorce Act* provided that the couple was legally married; in Ontario, a common law partner can claim support under the *Family Law Act*

statutes laws that are passed by either the federal Parliament or a provincial/territorial legislature

statutory release in most cases available automatically after the offender has served two-thirds of the sentence

stay of proceedings a court order that stops proceedings against an accused

student action plan (SAP) developed for every expelled student; the principal, in cooperation with staff, the student, and his or her parent(s), must set out a series of goals, measures of success, and strategies and types of support for the student

sublet to lease a property from the first tenant to a new tenant, who is called the subtenant

subpoena a legal document that compels a witness's appearance by force of law

subsistence needs a person's very basic living requirements, such as food and shelter

substitute decision maker a person who makes decisions about legal, financial, or health matters on behalf of a person who is incapable of making these decisions

summary conviction offence usually a less serious offence that is tried by means of a simplified procedure and that attracts less serious penalties

supervised access by a parent to his or her children at a special access and exchange centre

supervision order a directive that allows a child to remain in the care of the parents or guardian under the supervision of a children's aid society for a period of 3 to 12 months

survivor benefit a benefit paid to the dependants of the benefit recipient after his or her death

suspended sentence the release of an offender into society, subject to certain conditions set out in a probation order that if breached may result in serving a sentence

systemic discrimination discrimination that permeates or is incorporated into policies and practice

temporary care agreement where a parent recognizes that he or she is unable to cope and that an order that the child be removed to a place of safety will likely be ordered by a court, the parent may agree to place the child in the care of a children's aid society and reserve the right to active participation

treaty a formal multiparty contract often between nations

truancy the act of missing school regularly, usually without reason; students between 12 and 15 years old who miss school regularly can be charged with truancy, penalties for which can include a fine or the possibility of a probation order

undertaking a promise; in this context, a promise to financially support a sponsored family member for immigration

vicarious liability when employers are held accountable for actions that fall outside the scope of the employee's work

zero tolerance mandated immediate suspension or expulsion for prohibited behaviours, especially acts of violence

Index

Credits

Chapter 1

Table 1.1. "Code of Ethics," *Code of Ethics and Standards of Practice Handbook, Second Edition—2008*. Ontario College of Social Workers and Social Service Workers, (Toronto: Author, 2008), p. ii, online: <http://www.ocswssw.org/wp-content/uploads/2017/03/Code-of-Ethics-and-Standards-of-Practice-March-2017.pdf>.

Table 1.2. "Code of Ethics," Code of Ethics and Standards of Practice Handbook, Second Edition—2008. Ontario College of Social Workers and Social Service Workers, (Toronto: Author, 2008), p. iii, online: <http://www.ocswssw.org/wp-content/uploads/2017/03/Code-of-Ethics-and-Standards-of-Practice-March-2017.pdf>.

Chapter 2

Figure 2.1. "The Judicial Structure," Government of Canada, Department of Justice, online: <http://www.justice.gc.ca/eng/csj-sjc/just/07.html>. Used with permission.

Chapter 5

Table 5.2. J.N. Beaudette, J. Power, & L.A. Stewart, (2015). *National Prevalence of Mental Disorders among Incoming Federally-Sentenced Men Offenders* (Research Report, R-357). Ottawa, ON: Correctional Service Canada. Used with permission.

Chapter 9

Table 9.1 and **Table 9.2**. "Ontario Works (OW) Rate Chart," Toronto Employment & Social Services (1 November 2015). Retrieved from <https://www1.toronto.ca/City%20Of%20Toronto/Employment%20and%20Social%20Services/Files/pdf/P/ratetable-community%20Nov%202015%20FINAL-s.pdf>.

Chapter 13

Table 13.1. Roy Walmsley, "World Prison Population List (10th edition)," International Centre for Prison Studies, (21 November 2013), online: <http://www.prisonstudies.org/sites/default/files/resources/downloads/wppl_10.pdf>. Used with permission.